Church, Chapel and the Unitarian Conspiracy

Also by Donald Davie from Carcanet

POETRY

Collected Poems 1970-1983

Selected Poems

To Scorch or Freeze

Collected Poems

CRITICISM

Under Briggflatts: a history of poetry in Great Britain 1960-1985

Slavic Excursions: essays on Polish and Russian literature

Studies in Ezra Pound

Older Masters: essays and reflections on English and American literature

AUTOBIOGRAPHY

These the Companions

ESSAYS IN DISSENT

Church, Chapel, and the Unitarian Conspiracy

DONALD DAVIE

CARCANET

This edition published in Great Britain in 1995 by
Carcanet Press Limited
402-406 Corn Exchange Buildings
Manchester M4 3BY

A CIP catalogue record for this book
is available from the British Library.
ISBN 1 85754 123 5

The publisher acknowledges financial assistance
from the Arts Council of England.

Funded by THE ARTS COUNCIL OF ENGLAND

Set in 10pt Bembo by XL Publishing Services, Nairn
Printed and bound in England by SRP Ltd, Exeter

Contents

Foreword

Of the three pieces here brought together for the first time, the first two I suppose explain themselves. Each is a series of lectures addressed to a learned, but not exclusively learned, institution. Each, as read in cold print, embarrasses me a little by seeming ingratiating; I was, as any lecturer must be, anxious to establish common ground with my audience (British in the first case, American in the second), and my efforts to that end are not always dignified. The third section is different: in essays addressed to academic specialists, it is at pains to observe certain proprieties expected by such an audience. Moreover it addresses historians, not just literary historians, still less (what I had hopes of in my Lectures) the common reader.

Specialists and common readers alike will tend to think that I have addressed myself to a marginal concern. Who cares nowadays, or needs to care, about the sentiments and political initiatives since 1700 of those whom the British, when they think of them at all, describe as *Nonconformists*? My first lecture in Cambridge explains the personal reasons why this largely unregarded matter is important to me. But my later studies, which led to 'Disaffection of the Dissenters under George III', have persuaded me that the so-called 'liberalism' which emasculates the witness of the churches at the present day, derives from just this historical background – from jostling among the nonconformist sects, though inside the Established Church also, between roughly 1760 and 1820. If I am right, perhaps I'll be credited with revising the accepted historical account of that period in England. If so, I'll be gratified, but it isn't what I mostly aimed at. Why at the present day are the Churches' directives on social conditions in Britain, on personal morality and political action, so largely ineffective? We commonly look for the answer anywhere but in theology. But quite possibly it is theological muddle, and mistakenly charitable tolerance of heretical doctrines, that we must convict of having, two hundred years ago, precipitated the mish-mash of humanitarian options that now constitutes effectively the teaching of the Church. That is the possibility that this volume – obliquely to be sure – tries to explore.

DONALD DAVIE

Exeter, 1995

A Gathered Church

The Literature of the English Dissenting Interest, 1700-1980

The Clark Lectures for 1976

There are so few people now who want to have any intimate spiritual association with the eighteenth and nineteenth centuries:... who bothers at all now about the work and achievement of our grandfathers, and how much of what they knew we have already forgotten?
DIETRICH BONHOEFFER, *Letters and Papers from Prison*

It is certain, that the latitudinarian and the fanatic mutually prepare proselytes for each other... The repeated admonitions that have been given to parents, to avoid making their children bigots, or teaching them mysteries before their reason ripened, has caused young people to be trained up in such ignorance of the faith which they profess, as would have astonished every age since the Reformation. To this, I am persuaded, we must ascribe the recent progress of Calvinism...
MRS WEST, *Letters to a Young Lady*

It was not politics that produced Nonconformity, and it is not politics that can perfect it. If an Established Church were the clear will of Christ, any sense of political injustice would have to be educated into submission. The question is a religious one, and must be settled on religious principles.
P.T. FORSYTH, *The Charter of the Church*

1 The Nonconformist Contribution to English Culture

If anyone thinks that the title of this series of lectures seems demure, the presumptuous title of this first one ought to disabuse him. And I should like to explain... Thirty-six years ago, when I came up to this university [Cambridge] as a freshman from the West Riding, I was happy to join the Robert Hall Society, which I am glad to know still flourishes (or at any rate persists) as the association for Baptists in the university. At the same time I was – and not reluctantly either, but with enthusiasm – studying for the English Tripos. How did those two allegiances come together, to define the sort of Englishman that I was, or wanted to be? This wasn't a question which at that time agitated me much, chiefly because my Baptist allegiance was already by then lukewarm. Over the years, however, the question has interested me a good deal, and in these lectures I want to sketch the answer that I have found to it. It is not a straightforward answer, but nuanced and elusive; so much so, that I've decided the only practical way of conveying it is by sketching the fortunes of English Dissent over the last 280 years.

And 'sketch' of course is the best it can be; yet, sketchy or not, I hope it will give me opportunities for clearing the English dissenting tradition of various libels that circulate about it. Accordingly it is not too soon for me to make it plain that I speak no longer as a Baptist, nor indeed from within the ranks of Dissent at all. To that extent I can claim to be impartial. Moreover, since what we are concerned with is English *culture*, our history cannot be a history of ideas, nor a history of events, nor yet a narrowly *literary* history, but a history of people and the styles in which they lived – a history, therefore, which, whenever I can manage it, shall incorporate thumbnail biographies.

We may begin by taking note of Sir Ernest Barker declaring, in his *Britain and the British People* (1942): 'Apart from any question of their relative numerical strength, it may be said that the general relations, the general balance, and the general interaction of Anglicanism and Nonconformity have been a cardinal factor in English life and development for over three centuries.' And we may set beside that G.M. Trevelyan deciding, in *An Autobiography* (1949): 'from the Restoration to the later years of the Nineteenth Century, the continuity of the two parties in English politics was very largely due to the two-party system in religious observance, popularly known as Church and Chapel.' It will hardly be contested that among literary historians of the last three centuries in England we look in vain for anything that parallels these assertions by distinguished social and political historians like Barker and Trevelyan. 'Chapel' as against 'Church' isn't a distinction that our literary historians have found much use for, though their colleagues in social history and political history have found it indispensable. How can this be?

In an introductory lecture some painting in bold strokes may be permitted. And in this spirit we may venture a broad and facile reply to the question just raised: 'Chapel', it may be said, fails to figure in literary history as crucially as in social and political history, precisely because literature, and the creative and performing arts in general, are just what 'Chapel' distrusts, if indeed it does not positively condemn them. This is a commonly received notion; for what is the dissenter ('the nonconformist') if not the heir of those Cromwellian Roundheads who defaced the icons of our cathedrals and parish churches? The chapel-goer is the iconoclast, by origin and by definition; the literary *ikon,* no less than the painted or the carved ('graven images'), is what he is committed to destroying, or to tolerating only on unacceptably restrictive and emasculating terms – and in this way the 'Chapel' interest does indeed play a crucial and momentous part in the literary history of England, as 'the enemy', as precisely that which, in each generation, English artists must do battle with, and circumvent as best they can. On this showing, you perceive, that my situation all those years ago – as a young Baptist in love with English poetry, and determined to write poems himself – was quite simply anomalous, self-contradictory.

But that view of the matter does not square with my experience, nor is it borne out by the historical record. In particular it does not square with our records of England in the early eighteenth century. Ian Watt showed this twenty years ago, in relation to one dissenter of that period, Daniel Defoe. In my next lecture I shall argue a similar case, in relation to one of Defoe's contemporaries, a rather different sort of dissenter, the poet Isaac Watts (1674–1748). When I began studying Watts closely some years ago, I found (if I may quote myself) that:

> the curiously ambiguous status of Watts as poet – his figuring modestly in all respectable anthologies and a great deal more largely in our oral tradition, yet never remembered as one in the succession of our illustrious poets – reflects, one cannot help but think, a similar ambiguity in the official or received version of English culture when it comes to assessing the contribution to that culture of puritanism in general and of nonconformists in particular.

And I observed in print, with some indignation: 'One looks in vain for any general recognition that the artistic culture of the nation, so far from being repudiated by nonconformists as the product of a ruling class or an alien caste, has been embraced by the best of them in every generation, and enriched (though also at times valuably purged) by their efforts.' I now think this was excessive. Distinguished individuals from the ranks of Dissent have indeed enriched our culture in every generation since 1700, but Dissent as such, as a corporate force in our society, can at a certain point be shown to have ceased to do so. And in so far as I shall have to show this, the story I have to tell is a sad one.

Two misunderstandings can be cleared up, or at any rate indicated, here and now, for they arise from two words in what I have just quoted from myself – the words 'puritanism' and 'culture'. First, 'culture'... It should be clear that I am using this word in a restricted sense, which is nowadays old-fashioned. I am supposing that at or very near the centre of what we take 'culture' to mean, there is the practice and appreciation of the traditionally fine arts, of certain performing arts, and certain crafts; also the practice and appreciation of free speculation, philosophical in the full sense, including that *natural* philosophy which we call 'science'. Everyone knows that there is current a quite different usage, by which 'culture' is defined and diagnosed far more as a matter of social and political organization, and of patterns of social and political behaviour. In this second sense of the word, the culture of English Dissent has been studied exhaustively and respectfully, though also at times tendentiously; to the names of Ernest Barker and G.M. Trevelyan we may add the names of (among a multitude of others) Elie Halévy, Eric Hobsbawm, E.P. Thompson. It's precisely because Dissent has been looked at from this point of view so often, that I have thought it may be interesting and useful to look at it through a more old-fashioned pair of spectacles. However, it would be foolish to think that these two meanings for 'culture' are mutually exclusive; on the contrary we may be sure that these two meanings overlap and slide into each other – the arts and speculations of a culture (or of a subculture, such as we may take English Dissent to be) are intimately related to the patterns of social behaviour in that subculture. On the other hand we too seldom acknowledge that these interrelations, though they certainly exist, are still, as they always have been, too subtle and intricate for our historical scholarship to draw them out with any confidence. And in my third lecture, when I'll be concerned with the very special sort of Dissent which we call Wesleyanism, I shall take note of what I take to be an illegitimate transition, from Wesleyanism considered as a pattern of social and political behaviour to the body of literary art which Wesleyanism produced – that is to say, the hymns of Charles Wesley.

Moreover, religious belief and religious observance are themselves cultural phenomena, and from yet a third point of view may be seen as more central to 'culture' than either the aesthetic tastes and achievements which chiefly interest me, or the social behaviour-patterns which interest, for instance, E. P. Thompson. Charles Wesley, if he returned to earth, would presumably be not much less bored and impatient with my interest in examining his hymns as poems, than with Thompson's examining them to see if they helped or hindered the social consciousness of the English working class. Either interest, he would feel, was an evasion of what was for him the central concern – Salvation. The last literary man to try to grapple with this awkward fact – that religious experience is a momentous and determining feature of culture – was T.S. Eliot, in books like *After Strange Gods* and *Notes Towards the Definition of Culture* and *The Idea of a Christian Society*. I go along with the consensus of opinion, in thinking that these are among Eliot's least satisfactory works; but I'm inclined to think that they are unsatisfactory because of the intractability of the issues to which Eliot addressed himself, at least as much as because of any slackness or self-indulgence in Eliot himself. I have tried to avoid this intractable territory as carefully as, from his different point of view, E.P. Thompson has. But neither of us has been wholly successful. And we all need to acknowledge, and remind ourselves, that the thorny issue exists. To be specific: when in April 1796 the Baptist minister in Norwich, Mark Wilks, preached two 'Jacobin Collection Sermons' to defray the expenses of the legal defence of John Horne Tooke and John Thelwall, Professor Thompson takes it for granted that this was a culturally enlightened and enlightening thing to do. My own verdict on it would have to await an examination whether, given the occasion and the circumstances, Mark Wilks's use of English testified to lively and flexible responsiveness in him and in his milieu. But to Charles Wesley or T.S. Eliot – both of them, as it happens, High Tories – the question might well be whether Mark Wilks did not fail in his pastoral duties by impeding the devotions of those of his flock who happened to hold strong sentiments in favour of the king and the *status quo*. According as we hold by the first or the second or the third understanding of 'culture', our judgment of a cultural phenomenon like Mark Wilks's two sermons will differ.

As for the second of our problematic words, 'puritanism', it must be clear that this is by no means synonymous with either 'nonconformity' or 'Dissent' – two words that for the moment may be treated as interchangeable, though there are circumstances in which they are not so. 'Puritanism' is not a phenomenon that is encountered only among the dissenting sects. Since 1700, as before that also, a remarkable number of the most devoted Puritans and iconoclasts have been in fact members of the Established Church. Augustus Toplady may serve as one example out of many: author of 'Rock of Ages', bitterly Calvinist opponent of John Wesley's Arminianism, yet himself a priest of the Church of England. As was John Wesley himself! If Wesleyanism was a Puritan movement, as in some sense it surely was, it took its rise and ran its course, so long as the Wesley brothers were alive, inside the Church of England. The same is true, after the Wesleys were dead, of the Evangelical Movement, recognizably the source of most of the allegedly 'life-denying' Puritanism that we see our Victorian writers contending with. Though there *were* dissenting Evangelicals, the justly famous or notorious Clapham Sect – the powerhouse of Evangelicalism – was Anglican. Henry Thornton, William Wilberforce, Charles Grant, Lord Teignmouth, Zachary Macaulay, James Stephen all were members of the Established Church. And it is these, the notabilities of the Clapham Sect, whose Puritanism engenders by reaction, two generations later, the calculated libertinism and deviance of their brilliant progeny whom we may agree to describe as 'Bloomsbury'; a positively theatrical reversal, of which the poetic justice has been delineated here in Cambridge – quite properly, since Cambridge was the forcing house in which English Puritanism flowered into such a prodigious blossom as Lytton Strachey. But this – the at once genetic and cultural logic by which Virginia Woolf and Vanessa Bell spring from the loins of James Stephen, and E.M. Forster comes of the stock of Marianne Thornton – though it is certainly a lurid and instructive chapter in the history of English Puritanism, has nothing immediately to do with the history (literary, social, political, or whatever) of nonconformity, of the English 'dissenting interest'. Evangelicalism is one thing. Puritanism is something else. What we are concerned with is *Dissent*. In my last lecture indeed I shall suggest that when D.H. Lawrence in this century challenges and assails 'Bloomsbury', we see the heir to the dissenting conscience at odds with the heirs to the Evangelical conscience – but with this melancholy qualification, that by the time of this showdown the one ethos is as far gone in decrepitude as the other. Since both parties to this dispute had suffered the evaporation of that which originally fuelled both of them – that is to say, Christian belief – neither of them offers a coherent or self-consistent ideology; and hence, it may well seem, the conflict between them hardly deserves the pother that it has provoked, and continues to provoke, among us.

There is of course one literary masterpiece of English Dissent which cannot escape the attention of even the idlest undergraduate reading for the English Tripos: *The Pilgrim's Progress*! Certainly I knew Bunyan's great book, and knew that it was 'a classic', long before I came up to St Catharine's – knew it not from my schoolmasters either, but from the exiguous library of my grandfather, Baptist deacon and lay-preacher. Alas, it was long after the Tripos had come and gone that I applied myself to the atrociously printed edition of *The Pilgrim's Progress* that came to me off his shelves, and there discovered – because the edition was designed and annotated as a book of devotion for the pious, not as an ornament of

'English Literature' – that over and above Bunyan's humanity and his raciness and his humour and everything that makes him a proto-novelist, there was a rigorously consistent intellectual armature to the whole of his narrative, the intricately and impressively logical structure of the Calvinist scheme of salvation. Things change, not always for the worse; and so I'm prepared to believe that it's now impossible to study Bunyan's book in the university without studying Calvinist theology also. But I put it on record that it was abundantly possible, thirty-six years ago.

In any case, what happened, once Bunyan was dead, to the England that John Bunyan stood for? Did that Calvinist England achieve cultural respectability just once, once and for all, in *The Pilgrim's Progress* and *Grace Abounding*? Was the story, from then on, all downhill? Was it indeed worse than that? Did the Englishman that John Bunyan stood for and spoke for become thereafter a grotesque, a comical though also sinister bogey-man, a bigot and an obscurantist, whose role in the arts and the speculative thought of England was thereafter as 'the enemy' ? Here in another form is that same question which I was too harried or too timid to confront all those years ago, to which I address myself now.

Whichever way one comes at it, one has to contend with one's own ignorance. Certainly this is true if one's education has been literary, as mine was. One does not have to read very far to discover how disabled we are, as literary historians, by our customary ignorance of theology and church history. One egregious error, for instance, I slipped into my last paragraph, when I spoke of Bunyan's England as 'that Calvinist England', quite as if Calvinism were a monopoly of the dissenting churches. Yet in 1773 in the House of Lords, the elder Pitt, Earl of Chatham, replied to Drummond, Archbishop of York:

> The Dissenting Ministers are represented as men of close ambition; they are so, my Lords; and their ambition is to keep close to the college of fishermen, not of cardinals; and to the doctrines of inspired apostles, not to the decrees of interested and aspiring bishops. They contend for a scriptural and spiritual worship; we have a Calvinistic Creed, a Popish Liturgy and Arminian Clergy.

Here 'we' means 'we Anglicans', and so Pitt is saying that the Creed in *The Book of Common Prayer* either is a Calvinist document or at all events is capable of being given a strictly Calvinist interpretation. And of course this is manifestly true: the Calvinist doctrine of election and (its fearsome corollary, which is the real sticking-point) the doctrine of *reprobation* could be, and were, preached from Anglican pulpits as often as in dissenting chapels. Toplady was one who preached thus, and George Whitefield was another. On the other hand, many dissenting ministers were affronted by the doctrine of reprobation, and did their best to alleviate it or to get round it. Even before Bunyan, the great Richard Baxter attempted this, and evolved what the strict Calvinists through the next century, in Church and Chapel alike, condemned as heretical 'Baxterianism'. Again, in his *Help to Zion's Travellers* (1781), Robert Hall the elder, a Baptist minister like his more famous son who ministered and is commemorated here in Cambridge, argued – with a linguistic nicety that must appeal to the literary man – that 'reprobation' is in Scripture opposed not to 'election' but to *approbation* (as of course propriety of usage would seem to require). Or again (most poignantly) there is the Anglican but rigorously Calvinist William Cowper. Which is the more characteristically Calvinist response – Cowper's seeing the solitude of Alexander Selkirk as the worst of all possible privations, or Defoe's Crusoe exulting in it, as the condition of his autonomy? In short, it is not on doctrinal issues that 'Chapel' divides off from 'Church', nor for the most part one dissenting sect from another. In nearly every communion including the Established Church could be found, at any given date, the full range of theological positions from the strictest Calvinism to Arminianism and indeed beyond; and the Wesleyan movement itself was from the start cleft down the middle, between the Arminianism of the Wesley brothers and the Calvinism of George Whitefield. Perhaps the most startling example of how little it was doctrine that held a communion together is the evolution in the eighteenth century of English Presbyterianism which, lacking the Establishment status that held Scottish Presbyterianism together, had by 1800 dissolved almost completely into Unitarianism – that is to say, from one point of view had removed itself outside the field of revealed religion altogether, and certainly to a point as far as possible from John Knox! The significance of this development is very great, and yet nowadays almost invariably overlooked; we shall need to return to it.

However, there is more to be said about John Bunyan... The seventeenth century is the heroic age of English Dissent. Nothing is more common than to find it applauded thus, alike within and without the dissenting communions, indeed by infidels like Leslie Stephen as by believers. But in this there is a species of sentimentalism that is discreditable. To be plain about it, the scheme of salvation that Bunyan advances in *The Pilgrim's Progress* is, in its ferocious rigour, such as few Christians today – not to speak of unbelievers – can stomach; and is there not accordingly an unpleasant duplicity about applauding Bunyan for the humane feeling that he managed to express inside a framework inimical to it, without at least acknowledging the inhumanity of that frame? More certainly, there is an unpleasantness about extolling the heroically uncompromising consistency of the old Puritans when they maintained their doctrines in all their primitive ferocity, and then going on to speak sneeringly of temporizers and compromisers when one finds later dissenters who, sharing our sense of affront, attempt to modify doctrine so as to remove those stumbling blocks. This is how Leslie Stephen – himself safely outside the Christian fold, and watching from the sidelines – treats of the Baxterian compromise that Isaac

Watts was trying for in the generation after Bunyan. Certainly the Puritanism of Bunyan and John Knox was 'grand'; it was also bigoted, ferocious and uncharitable. Perhaps the issue is at its clearest when Leslie Stephen writes of Burns:

> A hundred years before, Burns might have been a Covenanter and have met the shock of Claverhouse's troopers at Drumclog. But the old Covenanting spirit had become a thing of shreds and patches – an effete idol no longer capable of rallying true men to its side. And therefore Burns puts his whole heart into such tremendous satires as 'Holy Willie's Prayer'.

In its context, this carries the unmistakable implication that for Burns to have been a Covenanter would have been something very splendid and stirring. Had Walter Scott written *Old Mortality* in vain, that Stephen should thus warm to an image of Burns made over into the image of Balfour of Burleigh? There is a sort of *machismo* at work here – one notes the invocation of 'true men' ('capable of rallying true men to its side') – which is by no means dead among historians of Dissent at the present day, and which makes it certain that the enlightening and civilizing work for Dissent of such as Watts and Philip Doddridge and Job Orton, or of either of the two Robert Halls, will continue to be scouted as somehow effeminate and emasculating, and that commentators will be proud to admit to 'a sneaking respect' for such a seventeenth-century survivor into Watts's day as Thomas Bradbury, his redoubtable opponent in the quarrels of early eighteenth-century Congregationalism. All one asks is that when people confess to a 'sneaking respect', they give some weight to the epithet; few of us would like to live with the Calvinist tenets of election and reprobation in their primitive seventeenth-century ferocity, and it is certainly 'sneaking' to think we can take over the masculine force of that ideology without paying the price in private terror and despair.

In 1710, it seemed to many that these bogeys had been laid to rest once and for all, for Daniel Whitby, a Salisbury rector, in his *Discourse* published that year, seemed to have dealt a death-blow to the concept of predestination on which both doctrines rest; and this was as welcome to enlightened dissenters as to middle-of-the-road Anglicans. But fortunately or unfortunately there was a seven-year-old boy then growing up on the frontier of the settlements in North America, who would turn out to be a theologian and logician of genius who could and did rebut Whitby and prove that predestination and free will are compatible. This was the great Jonathan Edwards, whose vindication of strict Calvinist dogma was not to be published until 1754, as his *Careful and Strict Enquiry into the Modern Prevailing Notions of Freedom of Will*. But Edwards's thoughts had matured long before that, and they may have been brought back to England as soon as George Whitefield returned from his first evangelizing swing through the American colonies in 1738, having preached in Edwards's church in Northampton, Massachusetts. In any case, by the end of the century Edwards's restatement of Calvinism in all its uncompromising rigour had so carried the day that his son could point contemptuously to English Calvinists like Watts and Doddridge as having been compelled to 'bow in the house of Rimmon'.

To regret the emergence of this rejuvenated Calvinism may look like the merest sentimentality, for after all if Edwards's Calvinism was thought through and simply *true*, as Watts's wasn't, should we not rejoice that the truth prevailed? It would need a theologian to deal with that question. Edwards's doctrine, as far as I can see, has never been controverted, and perhaps it is incontrovertible, but in the last hundred years it has for the most part been tacitly laid aside, as experimentally unacceptable to the worshipper in the act of private devotion or public worship. The strict Calvinist doctrinal system was never overthrown; and yet it has been very largely abandoned as offensive to *sensibility*. Is the same not true of other systems of ideas, in other fields – such as Robert Filmer's theory of a patriarchal monarchy? A question for historians of ideas! What seems certain is that this later history of strict Calvinism removes from Doddridge and Watts the reproach of being weakly genteel temporizers and compromisers; they apprehended the revulsion of sensibility, doubtless indeed they shared it, and they attempted to save Calvinism none the less by accepting Baxterian and other modifications. Perhaps unfortunately, Edwards's revitalizing of the logical rigour of the pure doctrine gave a new lease of life to it, through such as Whitefield and Toplady, and Evangelicalism generally after the deaths of the Wesleys.

I return to my point that an enthusiasm for *The Pilgrim's Progress*, and for seventeenth-century Puritanism in general, is likely to disqualify us from valuing eighteenth-century Dissent at the rate that it deserves. Bunyan's masterpiece is likely to arouse expectations; expectations of 'the heroic', such as later dissenting literature can only disappoint. And the same is true of that other, very different masterpiece of seventeenth-century Puritanism, *Paradise Lost*. In particular our sentimentalizing of the old Puritans takes a special turn when we call up an image of the ragged and humble congregations that Bunyan addressed in the fields of Bedfordshire. When we turn from that picture to the sleekly sober and wealthy congregation that Isaac Watts ministered to in London only a generation later, the shock is a severe one. And we are likely to jump to the conclusion that Dissent has 'sold out', that it has abandoned its natural and original constituency among those whom E.P. Thompson calls 'Christ's poor', and has settled hypocritically for the flesh-pots of the mercantile *bourgeoisie*. And yet most of us are familiar, if only sketchily, with the reasons why that explanation needn't be, and probably isn't, the correct one. I have in mind the argument associated with the names of Max Weber and R.H. Tawney, which proceeds by showing how many of the social practices applauded and adopted by Puritanism – regularity, sobriety, frugality, and so on – are practices which, other things being equal, lead to success in the counting-house. One need go no further to explain how often worldly and financial success came to those whose hopes were set – so they would have said, and no doubt sincerely – on another world altogether. To be sure, this argument is suspiciously neat and schematic; and an exhaustive demographic survey of eighteenth-century dissenting congregations – something which I believe has never yet been attempted, and may indeed be impossible – would doubtless blur the outlines very greatly. It seems certain, for instance, that one must make a sharp distinction between congregations in London and other centres of commercial enterprise such as Bristol or King's Lynn, and congregations in the countryside. There is evidence that through to the end of the century Dissent was drawing much of its strength from artisans and mechanics in the towns, and from farm labourers in the country. As late as 1830, if we may believe Mark Rutherford in *The Revolution in Tanner's Lane,* there were to be found in country towns congregations like the Baptist one he describes, whose minister was ignored by the Independent (i.e. Congregational) minister, by the Wesleyan minister, and of course by the rector – 'not because of any heresy or difference of doctrine, but because he was a poor man and poor persons sat under him'.

In any case, dissenters suffered under legal disabilities throughout the eighteenth-century. And their political disabilities may well have helped their economic well-being, such as it was, for their energies, arbitrarily shut out from government service and from many of the professions, flowed the more strongly into the channels of trade and finance. Nevertheless, all concessions and dubieties allowed for, the contrast between Dissent in Bunyan's lifetime and in Isaac Watts's remains stark. What had intervened was the Revolutionary Settlement, which ensured the Protestant succession; a constitutional guarantee which for the more restive and suspicious dissenters was perfected only when, at the death of the last Stuart, Anne, the Hanoverian succession was assured. Thereafter, at least until the trouble with the American colonies, the house of Brunswick had no more loyal and zealous subjects than the dissenters, and the Whig hegemony no more reliable supporters. Politically disabled they might be, and would growl and protest about it, but mostly it seems they tolerated it readily enough as a price to be paid for getting protection from Papists, Jacobites and high-flying Tories. Thus, whereas the dissenters remained in tension with the national society both religiously and politically, that tension had been let down so notably since Bunyan's day, that 'accommodation' – that very unheroic process – may justly enough be seen as the characteristic endeavour and achievement of Dissent in the generations of Defoe and Watts and Doddridge. Accordingly, no one can be much further from the truth than was Helen Corke, D.H. Lawrence's friend, when she was commenting on a passage from Lawrence's *Apocalypse*. Lawrence had written: 'Every citizen is a unit of worldly power. A man may wish to be a pure Christian and a pure individual. But since he *must* be a member of some political State or nation, he is forced to be a unit of worldly power.' And Helen Corke comments: 'Ignorance of this plain fact was the prime error of early Nonconformity, and *The Pilgrim's Progress* was its most vocal expression. Eighteenth and nineteenth century Nonconformity walled itself round with a crude individual arrogance uglier than the walls of its ugly chapels.' On the contrary, there could be no clearer example of 'giving unto Caesar that which is Caesar's, and unto God that which is God's' than the unswerving devotion of the eighteenth-century dissenters to the Hanoverian dynasty, even though that dynasty continued to load them with civic disabilities. And as it happens eighteenth-century chapels were not uniformly, nor usually, 'ugly'. Such ignorance by twentieth-century dissenters of their own dissenting heritage is, I'm afraid, rather the rule than an exception.

What the dissenters accommodated to was 'bourgeois'? Well, to be sure! If we make any sense at all when we put 'bourgeois' along with 'culture' (and Raymond Williams for one has doubted if we do), who has ever questioned that the culture of eighteenth-century England was a bourgeois culture? Isaac Watts was bourgeois as Dr Johnson was, or Edward Gibbon, or even John Wilkes. The term is descriptive, not pejorative; and in that sense it may be doubted whether 'bourgeois' is not the word for the culture that we have, which we study and presumably try to preserve, from all the years between 1700 and the present day. As I have explained, the dissenters' contribution to that common culture is precisely what we are concerned with.

What needs to be said is that the romanticizing of seventeenth-century Puritanism, which we have seen in Leslie Stephen, is not a peculiarly Victorian vice, but is rife among us today. In fact, through many decades now, it has taken a new turn, fuelled by new motives and given a new polemical purpose. Our Left-wing historians and opinion-makers have an obvious interest in extolling the Cromwellian republic and the intransigent or radical Dissent which brought that republic into being and sustained it, as also in censuring the Dissent which, once the Cromwellian interregnum was over, sought an accommodation with the restored monarchy, Stuart in the first place and Hanoverian later. And accordingly we find the Master of Balliol, in one of his more popularizing works (*Reformation to Industrial Revolution: A Social and Economic History of Britain, 1530-1780*), declaring of Dissent in the early eighteenth century: 'The cosmic battles which Milton and Bunyan depicted were succeeded by sterile controversies over deism and unitarianism.' But of course, sterile is as sterile does; a controversy will seem fruitless when the fruit that it bears is such as you don't want and can't digest. If the fruit that Christopher Hill had been looking for had been a more exact grasp of doctrinal truth, and greater sincerity in religious worship, then eighteenth-century controversies about deism and unitarianism might seem even today to bear fruit that is wholesome enough. For the moment we are not looking for that fruit any more than Christopher Hill is; we are looking for something else – for literature, and in particular, devotional poetry. And the point to be made is simply that such poetry cannot get an unprejudiced scrutiny so long as the whole sub-culture from which it springs is closed off from us by such a blanket condemnation as the one just quoted.

Nor does Christopher Hill leave it there; in the less than six pages which he devotes to 'Religion and Intellectual Life' in the eighteenth century, he finds room to declare (p. 231): 'The years of Walpole's rule, so peaceful, so prosperous, seem also to have been years of spiritual desolation as men contemplated the barren mechanical universe of Newton, and the new dismal science of economics which Mandeville took to its logical conclusion.' Who am I to demur when economics is called a 'dismal science'? Nor do I pretend that all these emphases can be laid at the door of Christopher Hill's Marxism; on the contrary, 'the barren mechanical universe of Newton' is a locution that I remember in my undergraduate years hearing from mouths that were impeccably High Church and Tory. Indeed, there is a curious unanimity on these matters which produces strange bedfellows. We may set beside Christopher Hill's 'years of spiritual desolation', Father Ronald Knox, of all people, advising us in 1950: 'We need not doubt that the Evangelical movement had a powerful effect in waking up eighteenth-century England from its religious apathy, or that eighteenth-century England needed it.' But with all due deference to Christopher Hill and Ronald Knox alike, that is precisely what we *do* need to doubt! To give Leslie Stephen his due, he made this point very firmly (*History of English Thought in the Eighteenth Century*):

> It has become a common practice to denounce the frigidity and formality of the eighteenth century... But I do not feel certain that we could mention in the first half of the nineteenth century three bishops whose characters make upon us a greater impression of purity and devotion than those of Berkeley, Butler, and Wilson; I doubt whether among those of less dignity we should find men more honest and manly than Clarke, or with a finer glow of devotional sentiment than William Law; and if the dissenters, freed from persecution, could no longer boast of Baxters and Bunyans, it is impossible to think without sincere respect of the honourable and laborious lives of such men as Watts, Doddridge, and Lardner, by whom the chances of preferment were voluntarily rejected for conscientious reasons.

I suggest that Leslie Stephen in 1876 was not only more charitable than Christopher Hill in 1967, but also more trustworthy. And in a later lecture we shall see that at least one dissenter whom Stephen named had earned from Dr Johnson not just respect but positive veneration.

I have reached a point where I seem to be defending, not just dissenting Christianity in the early eighteenth century, but eighteenth-century Christianity in general. And I would not go so far as Professor Donald Greene, whose exasperation with this hoary *canard* of the eighteenth century's supposed religious torpor led him a few years ago to suggest in all seriousness that instead of calling this age 'Augustan' we start calling it 'Augustinian'. But we do need to keep open minds, or rather we need to prise open minds (our own) which propaganda over many generations has contrived to close – to close to the possibility that Christian devotion and Christian worship played just as large a part in English life between 1700 and 1740 as in any other forty years of our history. In due course we shall find that nearly all the propaganda to the contrary, whether from the Right or the Left, can be traced to one source in one poet – to William Blake, whose specially perverse and complicated relation to English Dissent I shall touch upon, too sketchily, in a later lecture.

Since I have more than once already struck into a vein of autobiographical reminiscence, I should not like to end this introductory lecture without indulging myself in one further flight, or rather without discharging two further obligations that I am conscious of. In the first place, all the time I was here as an undergraduate there was in the university, had I only known it, one man who could have answered most of my questions, perhaps all of them: Bernard Lord Manning of Jesus College (1892-1941), author of *Essays in Orthodox Dissent* and *The Hymns of Wesley and Watts*. Elegant and searching books, both of them; though, once again, I discovered them only years after I had gone down, and indeed when I was out of England. The right time for me to have discovered them was when I returned from the war with both parts of the Tripos still before me, and by a private arrangement enjoyed through one long summer the hospitality of Cheshunt College, lineal heir of a dissenting academy, renewed as a foundation of the famous evangelical lady, Selina, Countess of Huntingdon. Remembering that Homerton College was also originally a dissenting academy, I cannot help but think that Cambridge – traditionally the Puritan and Cromwellian university – is, for the investigation I propose, not just an appropriate place, but the one right place. And accordingly I am very grateful to Trinity College – not the most Cromwellian nor the most puritanical of houses – for the chance to give these lectures in the place where they may get the most sympathetic, if not the most indulgent, hearing.

2 Old Dissent, 1700-1740

I want to begin by reading a poem. And since I shall rather seldom in these lectures be able to do this, let us enjoy together while we may the *presence* of poetry, as distinct from more or less impertinent prattle about it. The poem is called 'Man frail, and God eternal', and it will be familiar to most of you, though probably not under that title.

I

O God, our help in ages past,
   Our hope for years to come,
Our shelter from the stormy blast,
   And our eternal home.

II

Under the shadow of thy throne
   Thy saints have dwelt secure;
Sufficient is thine arm alone,
   And our defence is sure.

III

Before the hills in order stood,
   Or earth receiv'd her frame,
From everlasting thou art God,
   To endless years the same.

IV

Thy word commands our flesh to dust,
   'Return, ye sons of men':
All nations rose from earth at first,
   And turn to earth again.

V

A thousand ages in thy sight
   Are like an evening gone;
Short as the watch that ends the night
   Before the rising sun.

VI

The busy tribes of flesh and blood,
With all their lives and cares,
Are carry'd downwards by thy flood,
And lost in following years.

VII

Time like an ever-rolling stream
Bears all its sons away;
They fly forgotten as a dream
Dies at the opening day.

VIII

Like flowering fields the nations stand
Pleas'd with the morning light;
The flowers beneath the mower's hand
Lie withering ere 'tis night.

IX

Our God, our help in ages past,
Our hope for years to come,
Be thou our guard while troubles last,
And our eternal home.

Those to whom this poem is not wholly unfamiliar will remember it as sung rather than spoken; and in the second place will remember it in parts and not as a whole. And this establishes two things about it: first, that it is a *lyric* poem, in the strictest pristine sense of 'lyric', and second, that in so far as it has been transmitted to us, the transmission has been oral, not through print. For it is characteristic of orally transmitted poetry that some parts of poems 'drop out', and in fact some of the stanzas I have just read are so habitually 'dropped out' that they may well be said no longer to belong in the poem – in the poem, that is, as it has been smoothed and moulded in the course of oral transmission through one English generation after another. And it is *that* poem – the poem as it has 'come down' to us, not the poem as originally composed and printed – that I am chiefly concerned with. It is wholly to the point to remark that the poem is for most intents and purposes anonymous, in the sense that not one in a hundred of those who partly remember the poem will be able to name its author.

What I am describing is a very ancient kind of poem, perhaps the most ancient kind known to us – from other cultures as well as our own. What we have here, it seems, is a lay, *'le chant de la tribu'*, a kind of poem that pre-dates not just the age of print but the age of script, a kind of poem from before writing was invented.

The existence of this kind of poem has been known for a long time, but it is only quite lately that our knowledge of it has come to be – for many of us – a worry and a reproach. Most of us who study literature have lately come to be uneasy, from time to time, about the extent to which the literature we study is the product not of 'the tribe' but of a self-enclosed *élite* or priestly caste within the tribe. We have become ever more frequently agitated by our awareness that most of what we study and value as 'literature' is just not known, and never has been known, to the mass of the English nation, or English-speakers across the world. Our discomfort about this, in extreme cases our feelings of guilt about it, can be allayed by attending to poems like 'O God, our help in ages past' – a poem that is known to English-speakers far outside the ranks of any highly educated minority as well as outside any Christian church; a poem, indeed, that has attained the ultimate classic status of being known to, and sometimes quoted by, people who know not what it is, nor who it is, that they quote. Poetry like this, which has sunk down so far into the common anonymous stock of our linguistic inheritance, can best allay whatever populist misgivings we have – and most of us have some – about devoting ourselves, so much of the time, to products of 'high' or 'minority' culture. Accordingly we need not be surprised if poems like this one are happily seized upon, and attentively studied, amongst us.

In such a case, I say, we need not be surprised. But what *must* be our surprise when we discover that the case is quite otherwise? That even as we bend our energies more than ever before to the ramifying traditions of the Child ballads, to the recovery and printing of anonymous broadsides and street-ballads, of threshers' songs and weavers' songs and children's songs to the skipping rope (not to speak of barrow-boy poets and Merseyside poets and country-rock poets *à la* Bob Dylan), the attention we pay to a poem like 'O God, our help in ages past' is precisely what it was fifty years ago – which is to say, no attention at all, unless we happen to be either hymnologists or else (less probably) historians of the Nonconformist churches! The reasons we may find for this – mere bad faith, mere sloth, incurious inertia – are true so far as they go; but there are other more specific, historically conditioned, reasons – and these may emerge in due course. For the moment it seems we must say that if 'O God, our help in ages past' represents a very ancient kind of poem, that kind is a great deal too ancient for our self-applaudingly 'modern' criticism to be able to deal with it.

We think of this poem as a hymn. And that sounds right, for 'hymn' is indeed the traditionally appropriate title for one sub-category of the sort of tribal lyric that we seem to have to do with. More precisely, however, our poem is not a hymn but a *psalm*. In fact it is specifically and deliberately a version of one of the Psalms of David, or rather of the first six verses of that psalm, Ps. 90, of which the first six verses in the King James Bible are as follows:

> Lord, thou hast been our dwelling place in all generations.
>
> Before the mountains were brought forth, or ever thou hadst formed the earth and the world, even from everlasting to everlasting, thou art God.
>
> Thou turnest man to destruction; and sayest, Return, ye children of men.
>
> For a thousand years in thy sight are but as yesterday when it is past, and as a watch in the night.
>
> Thou carriest them away as with a flood; they are as a sleep: in the morning they are like grass which groweth up.
>
> In the morning it flourisheth, and groweth up; in the evening it is cut down, and withereth.

Need it be said that just such dependence on a sacred or canonical text, and in consequence just such total disregard for 'originality' or 'self-expression', is entirely typical of the poet of the tribal lay? Nevertheless it is clear that our poet has intended more than a metrical translation of the verses of Scripture, such as had been effected for the Psalms by John Calvin himself, by Clément Marot at Calvin's insistence, and in England by Sternhold and Hopkins as well as (memorably) by Philip Sidney and his sister in their collaboration on the Sidney Psalter. Our poet is working in that Calvinist tradition but at the same time transforming it, administering to it a shock which in fact provoked many guardians of that tradition to rise up in arms against him. What he gives us is a psalm, not translated, but paraphrased and modernized, and yet in no sense 'freely adapted', but modernized according to a very strict method. He said himself of these compositions of his that they were 'The Psalms of David Imitated in the Language of the New Testament'. And what this means in effect, schematically, is that every time the ancient Hebrew poet looks back ('Lord, thou hast been our dwelling place in all generations'), our English poet looks back with him, but then immediately looks forward; thus, 'O God, our help in ages past', but then, immediately, 'Our hope for years to come'. Original, he had no wish to be; but independent, a radical innovator, he certainly was. As one of his few modern admirers remarks: 'He worked alone. No pope, bishop, college or committee asked him to undertake his task.' His achievement, she says, is 'a shocking example of Protestant individualism'.

Yet, all this is of no account at all if, when we hear or read or sing 'O God, our help in ages past', it strikes us as merely *dull*. And this may well be the case; for we've already found reasons why current critical precepts, and the reading habits they inculcate, should be ill-adapted to seeing anything responsible or sensitive or distinguished in verses like:

A thousand ages in thy sight
Are like an evening gone;
Short as the watch that ends the night
Before the rising sun.

or:

Time like an ever-rolling stream
Bears all its sons away;
They fly forgotten as a dream
Dies at the opening day.

About such matters there can be no argument – at least in this sense, that no one should allow himself to be browbeaten into pretending that what he registers as 'dull' somehow isn't. All that a lecturer can do is to avow quite sincerely that 'dull' isn't how such verses register for him now, though it's true that once they did; to quote from his author to show that dullness was one risk the author foresaw yet decided to take; and finally to offer what he has found for his own part to be an instructive comparison. This I now proceed to...

In the first place Isaac Watts (for he, of course, is the poet we are dealing with), speaking of such compositions as this one, declared:

> In many of these composures, I have just permitted my verse to rise above a flat and indolent style; yet I hope it is everywhere supported above the just contempt of the critics: though I am sensible that I have often subdued it below their esteem; because I would neither indulge any bold metaphors, nor admit of hard words, nor tempt the ignorant worshipper to sing without his understanding.

and in 'A Short Essay toward the Improvement of Psalmody', he made the same point more vehemently: 'It was hard to restrain my verse always within the bounds of my design; it was hard to sink every line to the level of a whole congregation, and yet to keep it above contempt.' This was a poet who, if he practised what Pope and the Scriblerus Club called 'the art of sinking', did so deliberately, after counting the cost, his eyes open to the risk he was running. His endeavour may be thought to be perverse; it was not at all events mere blundering (and if the question be put whether he was capable of any style more elevated, more exuberant and audacious – well yes, there are poems of his that prove that he was).

As for the comparison, it shall be with a poet of genius, Christopher Smart, whose paraphrases of the Psalms, on precisely the same principles, came almost exactly half a century after Watts's. Smart's version of Psalm 90 as a whole should be examined. His stanzas which correspond to the two quatrains lately quoted are these:

For years thy creatures, as they flee,
Are all responsible to thee,
The present as the past;
Ev'n thousands in thy perfect sight
Are as the watch of yester-night
When their account is cast.

Thou bidst them off into the deep
Of vast eternity to sleep
And in their peace remain;
While others like the grass succeed,
For their determin'd goal to speed,
Nor e'er revolve again.

Does Smart turn to profit the elbow-room that he gets from two extra lines in each stanza? It seems to me quite evident that he does not, that the extra lines, and rhymes, betray him into laxity and vapidity.

Well, but (it may be said) we ask of a poetic style – of a style in any art, and indeed of a style of life – that it possess more than negative virtues. It is a weighty point, and one indeed that takes us at once to the heart of the Calvinist aesthetic. For that is what we are now concerned with. And in the first place a Calvinist aesthetic exists: 'In nothing perhaps has Calvin been more misjudged than in the view that he lacked an aesthetic sense...' It was after all John Calvin who clothed Protestant worship with the sensuous grace, and necessarily the aesthetic ambiguity, of song; and who that has attended worship in a French Calvinist church can deny that – over and above whatever religious experience he may or may not have had – he has had an aesthetic experience, and of a peculiarly intense kind? From the architecture, from church furnishings, from the congregational music, from the Geneva gown of the pastor himself, everything breathes *simplicity, sobriety,* and *measure* – which are precisely the qualities that Calvinist aesthetics demands of the art-object. Just here, in fact, is where negative virtues become positive ones. And this is true not just of Calvinist art but of all art, not just of Calvinist ethics but of all ethics. The aesthetic *and* the moral perceptions have, built into them and near to the heart of them, the perception of licence, of abandonment, of superfluity, foreseen, even invited, and yet in the end denied, fended off. Art is measure, *is* exclusion; is therefore simplicity (hard-earned), is sobriety, tense with all the extravagances that it has been tempted by and has denied itself. I appeal to you, and to your experience, whether in making art or in responding to it: Isn't this the way it is? And so, even if we admit for the sake of argument that Calvinism denies sensuous pleasure, we encounter time and again the question, when faced with a Calvinistic occasion: Do we have here a denial of sensuous pleasure, or do we not rather have sensuous pleasure deployed with an unusually frugal, and therefore exquisite, fastidiousness? It is peculiarly of the nature of Puritan art to pose just this question, though that is by no means the account of it that is usually given.

The French critic Brunetière had in mind something different, though related, when he maintained that Calvin's *Institutes* constitute the first book in French of which one might say that it is 'classic': 'It is equally so', he says, 'by reason of the dignity of the plan, and the manner in which the conception of the whole determines the nature and choice of details.' It is important here to take the particular and precise force of the term *classique* in French usage; and Brunetière gives a succinct definition of it in the passage just quoted. In this sense of 'classic' or 'classical' – the subordination of detail to 'the conception of the whole' – Pope is not often classical, and is not so to just the extent that he is, as Dr Leavis showed us, in 'the line of wit'. But classical in this sense is just what, for good or ill, we can call the poet who protested: 'It was hard to restrain my verse always within the bounds of my design…' 'O God, our help in ages past' is in this sharp, Calvinist, non-English sense, 'classical', as are very few poems by Pope, and also incidentally few hymns by Charles Wesley. In fact I suggest that, just as there is a necessary and compelling and often noted connection between Methodistical Evangelicalism and Romanticism, so between Calvinism and 'classicism' there is a connection no less binding. 'Simplicity, sobriety, and measure' – do the words not speak for themselves?

If this should seem paradoxical, the paradox is not of my making. And I should be very sorry to have it thought that this is special pleading. I suggest in all earnestness that the common cause which the English dissenters felt with the Huguenots gave some of them a more direct access to the culture which produced *Athalie,* than Pope could or did get from reading Boileau or Voiture; for after all the Roman Church produces its own puritans, and Racine's *Athalie,* so far as it is Jansenist, is itself puritan art. Unless we disabuse ourselves of certain stereotyped oppositions in our thinking, we shall lose track of the dissenting thread in our culture, even at this early stage. The first such slack assumption that we need to be rid of looks like a ghost of Matthew Arnold's distinction between the Hellenic and the Hebraic emphases in our inheritance. It is the assumption that the more 'classical' a culture is or aspires to be, the less sympathy it will feel with the Hebrew Scriptures, and vice versa. We need to remember that Racine wrote *Athalie* as well as *Phèdre;* that Dryden wrote *The Hind and the Panther* as well as *Macflecknoe;* and that Isaac Watts is as authentic a voice of Augustan England as is Alexander Pope. A second false assumption is likely to be even more obstructive, if only because it is particularly rife at the present day, and is promoted by the false friends of Dissent rather than by its enemies. It can be symbolized by the latest and now current biography of Cromwell, which has the (as I find it) embarrassing title, *God's Englishman*. There is abroad among us an unformulated assumption that Dissent is in some special ways more 'English' than the Church of England is – and this in contexts where 'English' means, more or less defiantly, 'insular'. However it may be in the twentieth century, or may have been in the seventeenth, English Dissent in the eighteenth century was not insular in the least. The full cultural consequences of the influx of Huguenots into England, after the revocation of the Edict of Nantes, has I think never been assessed, nor indeed much studied. But in any case a strong and sturdy 'French connection' can be traced among dissenting leaders from before the seventeenth century is out. More surprisingly, the connection is not only with French Protestantism, still less with the lunatic fringe of that Protestantism, the Camisard 'French prophets' who irrupted upon England in 1709-10 and ultimately spawned, by way of the English prophetess Anne Lee, the Shaker communities in America. Watts and Wesley and Cowper, even the Evangelical poet Henry Kirke White, were respectfully and eagerly aware of 'surprising conversions' within French Roman Catholicism. And Isaac Watts drew upon the Counter Reformation more generally, notably upon the Latin poems of 'the Christian Horace', the Polish Jesuit, Matthew Casimire Sarbiewski (1595-1640). In short, English Dissent does not offer an insular alternative to European culture, a way of 'keeping out', but rather a way of 'going in' on special, and specially rewarding, terms.

In any case, the notion of a Calvinist classicism gives us a vantage-point from which there open up, and stretch away, vistas which may be dizzying but are also (to speak for myself) exciting and very tempting. I must resist the temptation to explore any of them except one. Can I be serious when I offer Isaac Watts as a poet of the tribal lay, a true analogue in Augustan England of David, the bard and warrior king of ancient Israel? Calling Watts to mind, undersized and sickly, demure and grave and domesticated in Hanoverian London, the notion seems ludicrous. And yet I do suggest it. The dissenters for whom he wrote conceived themselves to be, very exactly, 'a tribe', a chosen people just as ancient Israelites were chosen, in tension with their neighbours just as ancient Israel was. Watts shared their conviction, and articulated it for them once and for all, magnificently:

The Church the Garden of Christ

We are a Garden wall'd around,
Chosen and made peculiar Ground;
A little Spot inclos'd by Grace
Out of the World's wide Wilderness.

Like Trees of Myrrh and Spice we stand,
Planted by God the Father's Hand;
And all his Springs in Sion flow,
To make the young Plantation grow.

Awake, O heavenly Wind, and come,
Blow on this garden of Perfume;
Spirit Divine, descend and breathe
A gracious Gale on Plants beneath.

Make our best Spices flow abroad
To entertain our Saviour-God:
And faith, and Love, and Joy appear,
And every Grace be active here.

Let my Beloved come, and taste
His pleasant Fruits at his own Feast.
I come, my Spouse, I come, he crys,
With Love and Pleasure in his eyes

Our Lord into his Garden comes,
Well pleas'd to smell our poor Perfumes,
And calls us to a Feast divine,
Sweeter than Honey, Milk, or Wine.

Eat of the Tree of Life, my Friends,
The Blessings that my Father sends;
Your Taste shall all my Dainties prove,
And drink abundance of my Love.

Jesus, we will frequent thy Board,
And sing the Bounties of our Lord:
But the rich Food on which we live
Demands more Praise than Tongues can give.

There are good examples here of what Watts meant by 'sinking' his style. 'The young Plantation' for instance has little to do with afforestation, but a lot to do with Plymouth Plantation or the Plantation of Ulster – a pungently topical allusion, historically resonant, which might have been elaborated into something ingenious and striking, which instead is subdued to the tenor of the rest. And another example is the way in which 'spirit' and 'gale' in adjacent lines vivify each other by evoking their common element, 'breath'. But it is more important to recognize the strategy and structure of the whole occasion: how the ancient icon and figure of the *hortus conclusus,* the garden enclosed, is startlingly renovated by being applied to religious Dissent. For the 'We' of the first line – 'We are a Garden wall'd around' – is not mankind as a whole, not the whole body of Christians, not even Protestant mankind, but specifically *dissenting* mankind. For what sense would it make to describe the Church of England as 'A little Spot... Out of the World's wide Wilderness'? How could this be said of a Church whose head is the reigning monarch, whose bishops sit as Lords Spiritual in Parliament? The Established

Church is the *national* Church; that is what 'establishment' means – it is by maintaining the strenuous fiction that the Church and the nation are coterminous that Anglicans claim and attempt to sanctify or spiritualize the entire secular order. But 'tribe' implies something more intense and intimate than that, a community much more immediately in tension with its potentially hostile neighbours. And Watts's poem articulates that tribal sentiment, just as the royal psalmist articulated it for Israel. Moreover, hymns like this, and perhaps this very hymn, were composed and sung *from manuscript,* week by week through 1694 and 1695, in the dissenting chapel at Southampton to which the youthful Watts had returned from his dissenting academy in the much more sumptuous though still sober milieu of Stoke Newington. (Hence arises the charming tradition that one of the loveliest of them – 'There is a Land of pure Delight' – was prompted by the view of the Isle of Wight across Southampton Water.) Watts was there in the congregation, hearing his hymns sung at sight by his neighbours, most of whom, no doubt, he knew and could name. Can we conceive of a more tribal situation, or of a relation more immediate and intimate between a poet and his public? And this happened at the very height of what we are taught to call 'the age of print', that sad interregnum in the history of poetry from which – we are asked to believe – a Yevtushenko or an Allen Ginsberg or Leonard Cohen has come to save us, by reading his poems through massed microphones and thus (if you please!) reviving poetry as an oral art.

This poem is a hymn, not a psalm. But it is related as closely as the psalm was, to a passage of Scripture – to verses from the Song of Solomon:

> A garden inclosed is my sister, my spouse; a spring shut up, a fountain sealed...
>
> Spikenard and saffron; calamus and cinnamon, with all trees of frankincense; myrrh and aloes, with all the chief spices;
>
> A fountain of gardens, a well of living waters, and streams from Lebanon...
>
> I am come into my garden, my sister, my spouse: I have gathered my myrrh with my spice: I have eaten my honeycomb with my honey: I have drunk my wine with my milk: eat, O friends; drink yea, drink abundantly, O beloved.

And the Song of Songs or (more properly, since it is not one song but many) the Book of Canticles is, we all know, the most erotic item in the Scriptures and one of the most intensely and unashamedly erotic pieces of literature that we know of. How comical, we snigger, that our Puritan forebears should not have noticed that! But *of course* they noticed it, and relished it. If they allegorized it into a nuptial mysticism which made Christ the bridegroom and the Church his bride, they knew perfectly well that allegory can work only if the literal sense is coherent and compelling on its own account. Listen to one of them:

> The doctrine of *union* between Christ and his church is of a nature so *copious,* that no one metaphor can *properly* represent it; therefore in the scriptures we meet with *various* similitudes, tending to illustrate the important subject. Christ is frequently compared to a *foundation,* on which his people are built; but that conveying only the idea of support, therefore he is compared to a *root,* by which the idea of *influence* is likewise illustrated. But though *branches* are influenced, and rendered fruitful, in consequence of conveyed nourishment, yet Christian *activity is* not thereby properly represented: to supply this defect, Christ and his people are farther illustrated by the union subsisting between *head* and *members.* But though the idea of *activity is* thereby conveyed, there is still a material defect, *for* the relation between these is quite *involuntary.* Had it been otherwise, the *head* might possibly have chosen better feet, or better *hands;* and had *they* been the subject *of* distinct volition, they would probably have chosen to have been in union with a better *head:* therefore to supply the deficiency of the above simile, and to include the idea of *mutual choice* and *social endearments,* Christ and his church are compared to *husband* and *wife.* If then we are in such near and close connection with the blessed Jesus, as the Scriptures assert, and, by so many significant similitudes, illustrate his own people to be, let us frequently think of, and bless God for, that *sovereign* and *inseparable* love which constituted the relation. It is all of God, as is acknowledged by that sweet singer in our British Israel, the late Dr. Watts who of the Father's love and choice thus speaks:
>
> Christ be my first elect, he said,
> Then chose our souls in Christ our Head;
> Nor shall our souls be thence remov'd,
> Till he forgets his first belov'd.

This passage, from Robert Hall the elder's *Help to Zion's Travellers* (1781), is an invaluable example of how carefully, with how much sophistication (literary as well as theological), devout Christians of the eighteenth century read Watts's poetry.

Alas, it couldn't last. Haven't Puritans always had a hang-up about sex? (Vague and vulgar language; but these are vague and vulgar notions.) Well, no, it appears that they haven't. But already by 1736 Watts was printing an apology: 'Solomon's Song was much more in use amongst preachers and writers of divinity when these poems were written than it is now.' His friend and follower Doddridge took the hint, and among Doddridge's 363 scriptural hymns, published in the 1750s, not one is derived from the Song of Songs. The emergence of the hang-up, it seems, can be dated quite precisely; and sure enough, *NED* gives 1746 for the first appearance of both 'pruriency' and 'prurient' in their modern senses. After that everyone gets more and more flustered whenever erotic and devotional experience are found close together. John Wesley in a sermon asked about Watts's hymns: 'Are they not too full of expressions which strongly savour of "knowing Christ after the flesh"? Yea, and in a more gross manner, than anything which was ever before published in the English tongue? What pity is it, that those coarse expressions should appear in many truly spiritual hymns!' And Robert Southey in 1837 is close to panic:

> Pure as was the mind of Dr Watts – and its purity was equal to the lucid clearness of his style – he has in many of these pieces made so bold a use of the sensible imagery proper to amatory verse, that while the unspiritual reader is apt to linger, if not finally to rest, in the mere external sense, there is no small danger, at least in these times, lest the more pious and refined should experience a feeling bordering on disgust.

Whose minds were the more prurient and agitated: Watts's and the Baptist Hall's, or Wesley's and Southey's, both of them High Church Anglicans? 'Puritanical', it seems, may or may not be right for describing repressed sexuality – it rather looks as if it isn't right – but certainly it is something that crops up in Church at least as often as in Chapel.

While we are about it, we may as well look at some things that have been said about Watts up to our own day. Here is Leslie Stephen in 1876:

> The name of Watts, associated with certain hymns still dear to infancy, has contracted a faint flavour of the ludicrous, though other poems of greater pretensions are still preserved in the lower strata of literature. The hymns, indeed, of Watts, Doddridge, and the Wesleys, whatever their literary merit, have been popular enough to show that they are not inadequate expressions of a strong religious sentiment. It is said that for many years 50,000 copies of Watts' 'Psalms and Hymns' were annually printed: and if there be any truth in the commonplace about songs and laws, Watts' influence must have been greater than that of many legislators, and, indeed, many more distinguished writers. But such an influence is too intangible in its nature to be easily measured.

And that is all we hear from Stephen about Watts's hymns, or Watts's poetry generally! In one who, as Noel Annan says, pioneered, if not 'the sociology of literature', at least the consistent relating of literary to social history, that 'influence... too intangible... to be easily measured' is surely a very cavalier way of dismissing the phenomenon of Watts's popularity through nearly two hundred years – with English-speakers, moreover, many of whom knew no other English poetry at all. However, we are in no position to jeer at Stephen; for we, too, a century after him, have no way of dealing with such phenomena, no method by which to translate the quantitative facts of so many copies sold and printed year after year, into the qualitative consideration of how they conditioned the sensibility of the English-speaking peoples. What we can and should do, however, is to confess and insist – as Leslie Stephen does not – just what a vast lacuna this reveals in our pretensions to chart cultural history, and diagnose cultural health, on the evidence of printed literature. There is quite clearly *prima facie* quantitative evidence for supposing that Watts's *Hymns and Psalms* ('Watts Entire', as it came to be called) has been more influential than any of the works of its century that we think of as most popular – more than Johnson's *Dictionary*, more than *Robinson Crusoe* or *Gulliver's Travels*, more even than *The Seasons* or 'Ossian'; and so far are we from taking this into account, that the work in question gets either no notice at all or only marginal notice in histories of our literature!

I am not prepared nor competent to rectify this state of affairs; my concern is to probe a little behind Stephen's lordly or flurried parenthesis: 'Whatever their literary merit'. I am trying to show that their literary merit is very great, and hence that, whatever the extent of their influence, it may well have been an influence for the good, a *civilizing* influence. (And if I had time, incidentally, I would have liked to show this for Philip Doddridge, though Watts was a genius whereas Doddridge was only an exceptionally intelligent and honourable and civilized man.)

What Stephen said of Watts – that his name 'has contracted a faint flavour of the ludicrous' because of its association with 'certain hymns still dear to infancy' – is still true today. At least I can find no other explanation when, as late as 1960, a historian of Dissent declares: 'the greatest imaginative literature of Puritanism is to be found in Watts's hymns', but then goes on – inexcusably, I think – to say that this treasure can be found only 'with perseverance in thrusting through the doggerel and bathos'. This image of Watts is potent among us because Watts's name has become attached to just one of his books: his *Divine and Moral Songs for Children* (1720). And Lewis Carroll's lethal because good-humoured and hilarious parodies have conditioned us so that we cannot read with a straight face such rhymes as 'Let dogs delight to bark and bite', or 'How doth the little busy bee Improve each shining hour', or "'Tis the voice of the Sluggard: I heard him complain, "You have waked me too soon! I must slumber again!"' Not all of these poems by Watts are indefensible. But a defence of them would have to start by placing them in a tradition that runs from Bunyan's *A Book for Boys and Girls: or Country Rhymes for Children* (1686), and takes in the Wesleys' *Hymns and Prayers for Children* (1746), Christopher Smart's *Hymns for the Amusement of Children* (1770), and Mrs Barbauld's *Hymns in Prose for Children* (1782), to culminate in Blake's *Songs of Innocence* (1790). The development is, as Professor

Holloway has shown, from songs *to* or *about* innocence to songs *of* innocence. And in this department of poetry Blake so consummately crowns and transcends all his predecessors, that only by a very strenuous exertion of the historical imagination can we get sympathetic access to the climate of feeling about children which Blake's beautiful poems rule out of court. Such an exertion is possible but I do not attempt nor invite it here; and so the case that I want to make for Watts does not rest in any way on the poems he wrote for children. It should be said, however, that William Blake and Lewis Carroll are redoubtable assailants for any poetic reputation to have to contend with; and what should give us pause is that both Blake and Dodgson thought Watts worth spending their ammunition on, as did Emily Dickinson also.

Between the last two authorities that I have cited came A.E. Housman, in *The Name and Nature of Poetry* (1933), quoting four lines of Watts and declaring: 'That simple verse, bad rhyme and all, is poetry beyond Pope.' As I have declared upon another occasion, this is a great deal worse than useless. Pope is one of the greatest poets in our language, and incomparably the greatest poet of England during Watts's lifetime. Because earlier I have suggested that in one crucial and valid sense Watts's poetry is more classical than Pope's – for in how many poems by Pope do we register the whole as greater than the sum of its parts? – I must make it plain that in no way do I contend for Watts's poetry as superior to Pope's (which would be absurd), nor yet as representing an alternative tradition to his. That would be sectarian indeed! (And it's a trap that sectarian commentators have fallen into.) No! Housman is *exactly* wrong: so far from Watts representing an artless tradition rivalling the artfulness of Pope, what we must see in him is a similar artfulness, though less magisterial, in the service of a quite different artistic end.

And who was the man who wrote these poems that I ask you to admire? Was he *all* poet, or all poet-plus-preacher? By no means! But to establish what Watts stood for, what he signifies and represents, over and above whatever one thinks of his poetry – for this we go to another authority, whose testimony redeems the otherwise shabby story of how the memory of Watts has been preserved amongst us. We go – and I think we might have guessed it – to that most magnanimous of Anglicans, Samuel Johnson. Johnson's estimate of Watts is one of the things I shall take up in my next lecture.

3 Dissent and the Wesleyans, 1740-1800

As we have seen, it is hard to find anyone with a good word to say for the dissenters of the early eighteenth century. Even their fellow-sectaries, in the nineteenth and twentieth centuries, customarily appeal over their heads to their seventeenth-century predecessors. A curious instance of this is the blue-stocking historian Lucy Aikin in 1828, writing across the Atlantic to her fellow-Unitarian, William Ellery Channing:

> As for... the Calvinistic dissenters, they had the misfortune of living in one of those middle states between direct persecution and perfect religious liberty, which sours the temper by continual petty vexations, without affording scope for great efforts or great sacrifices – which drives men to find a perverse pleasure in hating and being hated, and to seek indemnification for the contempt of the world in a double portion of spiritual pride and self-importance. 'We can prove ourselves saints', 'being Christ's little flock everywhere spoken against', is the plea put into the mouth of this set by Green, a poet, who was born and bred among them.

Surprisingly, after this contemptuous dismissal of the eighteenth-century dissenters, Lucy Aikin in her very next paragraph pays tribute to the dissenting leader Doddridge, recording how 'my kindred the Jennings, the Belshams, my excellent grandfather Aikin, and his friend and tutor Doddridge, had began to break forth out of the chains and darkness of Calvinism, and their manners softened with their system'. But more immediately to our purpose is her specifying, as the spokesman of 'this set', 'Green, a poet'. This is Mr Matthew Green of the Customs House, whose most sustained performance, *The Spleen, is* one of those delightful but not very consequential poems that are continually being re-discovered, but never by enough readers to save them permanently from obscurity. For my generation the rediscovery was effected by F.R. Leavis in some well-considered and valuable pages of his *Revaluation*. That was in 1936, and over the years since, unless I am mistaken, oblivion has claimed Matthew Green once again. But as Lucy Aikin may remind us, Green *stands for* something; his poem articulates a particular moment in the spiritual and intellectual history of one kind of Englishman – a moment which otherwise in our poetry goes unrecorded. It's on these grounds – which were not Leavis's – that we may pluck him back from oblivion once more, and for as long as anyone is interested.

To say that Green was a dissenter is true, but misleading. He seems to have been in fact a lapsed Quaker – which is a very special kind of dissenter, special at any time but particularly so in 1737, the year of Green's death, when *The Spleen* was published; for George Fox, the farouche and irreconcilable founder of the Society of Friends, had died as recently as 1691, and the process by which, over no more than two generations, the English Quaker transformed himself from that stereotype into becoming the banker and iron-master of the Industrial Revolution, represents an adaptation so extreme and so precipitate that it must give pause even to someone who believes that 'accommodation' (as I have ventured to call it) was the historically necessary and in itself not ignoble duty of Dissent in this period. Accommodation, yes; but at this rate ? And on this scale ? One thinks the better of those like Matthew Green who could not change so far so fast.

Horace Walpole said of *The Spleen:* 'It has the wit of Butler with the ease of Prior without imitating either.' And the judgment is less facile than it may seem: Butler's *Hudibras,* pillorying once and for all the Old Dissenters and their pretence to 'the inner light', is consistently the presence behind Green's poem, not just as a formal and stylistic mark that Green must steer by, but as an ideological pressure that he must acknowledge and give way before. Hence, for instance, the dissenters of his time, or else of his childhood, unmistakably and excellently pinned down:

> Nor they so pure and so precise,
> Immaculate as their white of eyes,
> Who for the spirit hug the spleen,
> Phylactered throughout their mien;
> Who their ill-tasted home-brewed prayer
> To the state's mellow forms prefer;
> Who doctrines, as infectious, fear,
> Which are not steeped in vinegar,
> And samples of heart-chested grace
> Expose in show-glass of the face...

The neat, terse gibes strike home; and yet they are predictable, out of common stock. The figure being assailed is after all a stereotype, a cardboard cut-out. Such knowledgeable and spiteful apostasies from Dissent were common in Matthew Green's lifetime; Samuel Wesley the elder is another example out of many. It is permissible to feel that an attempt like Watts's, to change Dissent from inside, was a more honourable and forthright endeavour.

Certainly, we may infer, it seemed so to Dr Johnson, who said of Watts: 'Such he was as every Christian Church would rejoice to have adopted'; who specified Watts's *cultural* achievement by saying:

> He was one of the first authors that taught the dissenters to court attention by the graces of language. Whatever they had among them before, whether of learning or acuteness, was commonly obscured and blunted by coarseness and inelegance of style. He shewed them, that zeal and purity might be expressed and enforced by polished diction.

Johnson it was, moreover, who apologized for a long quotation from Gibbons's memoir of Watts, by saying: 'If this quotation has appeared long, let it be considered that it comprises an account of six-and-thirty years, and those the years of Dr. Watts.' Johnson it was who concluded his account of Watts by saying: 'happy will be that reader whose mind is disposed by his verses or his prose, to imitate him in all but his nonconformity, to copy his benevolence to man, and his reverence to God'. And it was Johnson who, when the name of Matthew Green was missing from the list of poets whom he was to introduce, made no demur; but who, when Watts's name was missing, insisted that it be included – as he is careful to tell us himself, at the start of his 'Life of Watts'. Johnson's 'Life of Watts' is nearer to hagiography than any other of his *Lives of the English Poets;* and if the significance of thus honouring a dissenter is lost upon us, it impressed and puzzled readers nearer to Johnson's time, as we see for instance from Hazlitt's *Conversations with Northcote*.

As regards poetic style, to compare Green with Watts means questioning whether 'conceited' *wit,* however submerged and subdued – as we can find it in Green but not, except in his apprenticeship, in Watts – can be taken in respect of the eighteenth century, as by and large it can be taken when we deal with the seventeenth, as the measure of imaginative seriousness. *The Spleen* itself supplies evidence that, for good or ill, wit-writing was by 1737 restricted to those parts of a composition that were relatively capricious and irresponsible; for at line 717 Green prepares for his exordium by re-addressing his addressee, Cuthbert Jackson, in the person of 'Memmius'. This signals a shift to a graver tone than the inventive banter which has preceded it; and the diction henceforth is nearer to the plain style of Watts than to Marvell:

> In one, no object of our sight,
> Immutable and infinite,
> Who can't be cruel or unjust,
> Calm and resigned, I fix my trust;
> To him my past and present state
> I owe, and must my future fate.
> A stranger into life I'm come,

Dying may be our going home,
Transported here by angry Fate,
The convicts of a prior state;
Hence I no curious thoughts bestow
On matters I can never know.

This passage, which some readers will think the most moving and the most seriously intended in the poem, is almost entirely free of wit. On the other hand it is a profession of faith so hedged about with saving clauses – consider only that 'Dying *may be* our going home' – that it can hardly be called 'Christian' at all. Indeed, could it not be subscribed to by any number of nineteenth or twentieth-century agnostics? And isn't this the reason why, when – rarely, as by Leavis – we are directed to *The Spleen*, we are able to respond to it so warmly? In any case it is all very well to say (what is true) that in Green's more vivacious passages we see the urbanity and ease of Andrew Marvell's octosyllabic couplets persisting into the eighteenth century; but we need to count the cost – that in order to reproduce this alert suavity Green permits himself a flippant or weary impudence about the tenets of Christian belief such as Marvell eighty years before neither could nor would have allowed himself.

Nevertheless *The Spleen is* invaluable, indeed irreplaceable, for giving a lively and highly intelligent account of the state of mind and feelings in which a dissenter of the 1730s might either conform to the Establishment or slide out of Christian belief altogether. There is no denying that in the 1720s and 1730s such defections and apostasies were very common. The numbers of the faithful were falling precipitately; and historians for whom as it were the box-office returns are the ultimate test have no difficulty showing that dissenting leaders like Watts and Doddridge quite manifestly in their generation *failed*. This was the reasoning of Elie Halévy when in 1906 he addressed himself to 'The Birth of Methodism in England'. Of the Methodist evangelists Wesley and Whitefield, Halévy says that 'they reanimated, as a side effect of their influence, the other Dissenting sects, which were seemingly dying of old age'. More sweepingly Halévy asserts: 'after fifty years (1688-1738) of professing religious skepticism England had her Puritan revival, and the date can be established firmly; it was in 1739 that the crisis occurred.' One does not lightly disagree with an authority like Halévy, and yet on this point he seems to be quite simply *wrong*. Moreover he backs it up with special pleading. Thus, when Doddridge in his *Free Thoughts* asked that the minister be 'an evangelical, an experimental, a plain & an affectionate preacher', he was not, as Halévy supposes, an exception that proves some quite opposite rule. Nor do the dissenting sermons of the time bear out Halévy when he declares: 'The Dissenting ministers should have been able to assume the leadership of the Protestant opinion; they were its chosen chiefs. But betraying the confidence of their followers, they preached a doctrine more and more like that of Aristotle or Cicero, instead of Christianity according to Saint Paul.' How is it possible to recognize in this description the most famous and influential dissenting minister of the time, the Isaac Watts who wrote that hell-fire sermon in plunging sapphics, 'The Day of Judgment'?

> Hopeless immortals! how they scream and shiver
> While devils push them to the pit wide-yawning
> Hideous and gloomy, to receive them headlong
> Down to the centre!

Is *that* the doctrine of Aristotle or Cicero? We are likely to find it very unaccommodating indeed! And it requires a considerable exertion of the historical imagination to recognize, in the face of such a document, that 'accommodation' (to secular enlightenment and civility) was nevertheless Watts's and Doddridge's steady endeavour – as Johnson realized.

Halévy is not the first to be so dazzled by the massive and heroic figure of John Wesley as not to realize how there could be, and was, resistance to his evangelizing on scrupulous and considered grounds. 'When the Methodists started to preach', he assures us too confidently, 'they were well received by the great majority of Dissenters':

> Was not the religion they preached a revival of Puritanism ? But they ran up against the distrust and hatred of the ministers, too enlightened and reasonable to enjoy the doctrine and method of the Awakening. And that is why those ministers were not themselves capable of bringing forth an Awakening; and why the Awakening could not come from the Dissenting Churches.

Even if all this were true, might we not conclude that the congregation failed their ministers, rather than the other way round? That by and large the ministers were too far ahead of their flocks, pursuing a cultural 'accommodation' that their congregations were not ready for? This would avoid having to use 'enlightened' and 'reasonable' as words of opprobrium, when applied to such men as Doddridge or Watts or Edmund Calamy; and it would be in the spirit of Johnson's tribute to Watts.

How some dissenting ministers responded to the Wesleyan challenge may appear from a piece of admirably vigorous mid-century prose:

> I will take this occasion with great freedom to tell you my opinion of those people who are called Methodists. I have carefully inquired after them; was willing to think well of them; loth to censure them or hear others do so. And I think still there are serious people deluded by them. But after a candid attention to them, their proceedings appear not to be wise and good. Their devotion is unseasonable, irregular and

> injudicious. Their sermons are low and loose and not at all like what they seem to assume. Their spirits appear to me to be turbulent, unruly and censorious. They practise upon weak men and poor people. They call them up to pray and sing when they should be in their business or their beds. They disturb the peace and order of families. What they pretend above their neighbours, appears to me mere enthusiasm. Their people are rather slothful, mopish and dejected or pragmatical, than sober, considerate, judicious, exemplary and regular Christians. And I have no expectation but that Methodism, like other enthusiasm, will promote infidelity and turn out to the damage of religion and the souls of men. Though I judge not their hearts, views and motives, which are secret things that belong to God, yet I thought it needful very lately to warn my hearers of these people's errors and advise them to avoid them.

This is one of the remonstrances that Philip Doddridge endured in 1743 when he had allowed George Whitefield to preach from his pulpit. Others came from Watts, from John Guyse, and from a trustee of the Coward Trust thinly veiling a threat to withhold Trust funds from Doddridge's Academy; and if this makes it seem that Doddridge was more 'liberal' than his fellow ministers, the point is that on this flank he could afford to be – his distrust of 'enthusiasm' was well established, and it was on his other flank that he was vulnerable, where he joined hands with the more or less Arian circles that we have seen Lucy Aikin connect him with. He represented firm and consistent opposition to Methodism from within Dissent – an attitude that we can find for instance in his friend and editor Job Orton up to the latter's death in 1783. And indeed, though it could be said in 1806 that 'the Independents have gone over in a body to the Methodists', there was, as we shall see, opposition from Old Dissent to the Methodist New Dissent until far into the succeeding century.

To return to Elie Halévy... His theories about the *birth* of Methodism have been overshadowed by his much more startling and influential argument as to its consequences: an argument advanced in his classic work of 1912, *England in 1815*, though in fact it was already firmly formulated by 1906. The argument is that 'England was spared the revolution toward which the contradictions in her polity and economy might otherwise have led her, through the stabilizing influence of evangelical religion, particularly of Methodism'; in other words, that the potentially revolutionary energies of the unprivileged English were syphoned off by the Wesleys and Whitefield into activities not political at all, but religious. This hypothesis in fact did not originate with Halévy; on the contrary, the bare bones of it are to be found not just in several British and French nineteenth-century historians but in Robert Southey in the first decade of the nineteenth century and indeed in the Methodists themselves as they defended themselves against the punitive measures against them proposed in 1811 by Sidmouth, the Home Secretary. Moreover, 'Halévy, like Weber, was suspicious of all efforts to understand history as the product of a single cause, and he saw religion as capable of altering what appeared to be the otherwise almost "inevitable" tendency of the internal contradictions (as both Ricardo and Marx understood them) of the new industrialism to produce Revolution'. Marxist historians are thus uncomfortable about Halévy's hypothesis, with a discomfort that is compounded by the fact that the hypothesis is rather plainly the product of a speculative and indeed literary intelligence in Halévy, rather than of 'scientific' research. In these circumstances it is remarkable that the hypothesis still stands, and that claims, by Marxists and others, to have overthrown it turn out on examination to be quibbles and qualifications not affecting the central contention, which is that the revolution which ought to have been 'inevitable' was in fact evaded. Accordingly, when a Marxist historian takes over Halévy's thesis, he does so with a specially bitter feeling of mortification.

This is compounded by the historically incontrovertible fact that Wesleyan Methodism springs out of the Moravian movement of Count Zinzendorf, which itself is plainly related to the egalitarian and enthusiastic 'Ranters' of Cromwell's time – a body, or an obscure congeries of bodies, long enshrined in English Marxist mythology as heroic pioneers and precursors. How with equanimity concede that this tradition which should have been, and once was, proto-revolutionary should, in the Wesleys' lifetime and for long after, have produced a movement that was consistently, and at times splenetically, High Tory? Certainly, in the nineteenth century, radicals and trade-union organizers were often Methodists; and in our time some Methodist historians have made much of this. But it is incontestable that radicals like Hazlitt and Leigh Hunt and Cobbett saw Methodism in their day, with reason, as on the contrary a bulwark of the *status quo*.

There is a yet further complication, in the fact that when John Wesley finally broke with the Moravians it was because of the insistent yet devious and grotesque eroticism which characterized their hymns certainly, and perhaps other aspects of their worship also. No one who has looked at the Moravian hymn book of the 1740s will want to deny that Wesley acted with good taste and good judgment in deciding that this would never do. Yet this circumstance is awkward for the Marxist historian when he wants to establish that in Wesleyan hymns 'Love' is private and airless, whereas it ought to be 'social'. Our historian levels the charge none the less:

> the cult of 'Love' was brought to a point of poise between affirmations of a 'social religion' and the pathological aberrations of frustrated social

> and sexual impulses. On the one hand, genuine compassion for 'harlots, and publicans, and thieves': on the other hand, morbid preoccupations with sin and with the sinner's confessional. On one hand, real remorse for real wrong-doing: on the other, luxuriating refinements of introspective guilt. On one hand, the genuine fellowship of some early Methodist societies: on the other, social energies denied outlet in public life which were released in sanctified emotional onanism...
>
> ... Here was a cult of 'Love' which feared love's effective expression, either as sexual love or in any social form which might irritate relations with Authority. Its authentic language of devotion was that of sexual sublimation streaked through with masochism: the 'bleeding love', the wounded side, the blood of the Lamb...

We notice how far this twentieth-century authority agrees with the eighteenth-century dissenter, in finding the Methodists 'slothful, mopish and dejected'. But he has in his sights something quite specific, a body of achieved literature, Charles Wesley's hymns. And this being so, the disciplines of the social historian will serve no longer. All sorts of further considerations now arise – notably the tradition in devotional literature of images of the Lamb and Bleeding Heart, at least from the counterreformation on; and the traditional use of the erotic analogy over the same period. For instance, is Watts's Calvinism of 1710 to be allotted the same socio-historical significance as the Wesley's Arminianism of the 1750s, because of Watts's unabashed use of the eroticism of the Song of Songs?

And not only sexual organs like the lips are to be ruled out, but liver and lights also; for we are told:

> after the Wesleys broke with the Moravian brethren, the language of their hymns... had become a public scandal. In the hymns of John and Charles Wesley overt sexual imagery was consciously repressed, and gave way to imagery of the womb and the bowels:
>
> Come, O my guilty brethren, come,
> Groaning beneath your load of sin!
> His bleeding heart shall make you room,
> His open side shall take you in...

Not all readers will be sure that they find in these indifferent verses either bowels or womb. But if we do find them, what follows? Are all bodily functions and organs too gross to serve as analogies and imagery in poetry, or in devotional poetry? Whoever is being 'puritanical' in this confrontation, it seems not to be Charles Wesley.

However, what our historian can't stand the sight of is blood. And there is blood all over the place in the Wesleyan hymns 'as if the underground traditions of Mithraic blood-sacrifice which troubled the early Christian Church suddenly gushed up in the language of 18th century Methodist hymnody'. 'The union with Christ's love', Edward Thompson decides (for he it is that I am quoting), 'unites the feelings of self-mortification, the yearning for the oblivion of the womb, and tormented sexual desire', for 'sacrificial, masochistic, and erotic language all find a common nexus in the same blood-symbolism'. And so to the indignant peroration:

> It is difficult to conceive of a more essential disorganisation of human life, a pollution of the sources of spontaneity bound to reflect itself in every aspect of personality. Since joy was associated with sin and guilt, and pain (Christ's wounds) with goodness and love, so every impulse became twisted into the reverse, and it became natural to suppose that man or child only found grace in God's eyes when performing painful, laborious or self-denying tasks. To labour and to sorrow was to find pleasure, and masochism was 'Love'. It is inconceivable that men could actually *live* like this; but many Methodists did their best.

But this is beyond a joke. A very strenuous protest is surely called for – not on behalf of Methodism, nor on behalf of Christianity (though it is Christianity as such, not just Methodism, that is the target of this sort of rant), but on behalf of poetry; for if poets are to be judged in this way, by scraps of verses torn from their context in poems and their larger contexts in iconographic and literary tradition, with a flurry of words like 'masochistic' that have no place in either literary or social history, which of all our poets will 'scape whipping ?

Yet the fault lies with our literary historians, for what I remarked of the hymns and psalms of Watts – that we look in vain through our literary scholarship for any considered assessment of their intrinsic virtues and their historical significance – is hardly less scandalously true of the more than 6,000 hymns composed by Charles Wesley. Where the literary historians have so shamefully failed to do their duty, one can hardly blame the social historian for rushing in. I would not be misunderstood. The text of the Wesley hymns has been reliably established, and this was no light undertaking in respect of such a bulky corpus; there has been valuable examination of Wesley's metres; and a great deal has been done by way of identifying sources and analogues and allusions. The *editorial* challenge has been met. In particular, like every one else who has poked his nose into this field, I must pay tribute to Henry Bett's admirable *The Hymns of Methodism*. But it is precisely the 'field' that must be questioned; Charles Wesley's poetry is thought to be a very special field indeed, something *sui generis* or at most to be compared with a few hymns by other hands. One looks for a long time before finding any attempt to place Charles Wesley, or Isaac Watts either, in relation to the more secular poetry of their times – in relation to Pope, or Thomson, or Gray or Goldsmith. One consequence is that the eighteenth century is thought to have produced little *lyric* poetry, whereas the eighteenth-century lyric is to be found in the hymn books just as surely as seventeenth-century lyric is in George Herbert's *Temple.* The dependence of line after line of Wesley on the precedent of Matthew Prior has been duly noted, but no one has explored the significance, stylistically and historically, of this surprising connection with the suave and frequently improper author of 'Henry and Emma'. Methodism is a sub-culture as Old Dissent is a sub-culture; and the tribal warmth of such a subculture, of what Edmund Burke called 'our own little platoon', is so comforting and agreeable that there is no more incentive from within its ranks to relate the sub-culture to the national culture, than there is on the part of the Establishment to acknowledge what manoeuvres the little platoons have been engaged in.

Yet John Wesley, in striking contrast to his fellow evangelist Whitefield, was at great pains not to let his followers cut themselves off from the culture of the national society as a whole, particularly not from the *literary* culture. He used his *Arminian Magazine* for many purposes; but among them was keeping in currency George Herbert and Prior and other writers he valued. He printed there, to the scandal of some of his readers, Prior's 'Henry and Emma', which Johnson the High Churchman found improper. In his late *Thoughts on the Character and Writings of Mr. Prior,* as in such a stray document as a letter of 1764 to the Reverend Mr Furley, Wesley was a master of very acute and unprejudiced practical criticism. Moreover his successful battle through his lifetime to keep Methodism within the Established Church is something that tells the same story: Wesley did not want to found a sect, and he distrusted the tribal, the sectarian temper in culture. On this point his brother the poet was even more determined: Charles jeered and mocked when John began ordaining his own preachers. For the brothers were very different, though they co-operated loyally. It was Charles, the poet, for instance, who governed his sex life better, who made a successful marriage and reared a happy family; and it was Charles's household that rang night and morning with music, some of it highly sophisticated.

One literary scholar has lately broken through the sectarian ring that otherwise still walls off Charles Wesley's poetry from English poetry generally. This is Martha Winburn England, in a volume on which ten years ago she collaborated with John Sparrow for the New York Public Library. To this book, entitled *Hymns Unbidden,* Miss England contributes a series of exceptionally erudite and perceptive papers comparing Wesley with his contemporary William Blake. Blake certainly knew Wesley's work: his autograph, dated 1790, appears in a copy of Wesley's *Hymns for the Nation, in 1782.* Written by Charles Wesley when the defeat of British forces by the American colonists was clearly inevitable, *Hymns for the Nation* sees 'America as Sodom, her leaders as murderers and fanatics, the Continental Congress as like Lucifer in its rage for power and its blind fury of insurrection', and the American Loyalists as 'martyrs, persecuted by usurpers and betrayed by weak leadership'. Blake, of course, saw Washington and his colleagues quite differently, 'not as Albion's enemies but as allies of that visionary spirit of liberated energy as it existed in Britain'. But what matters is not that Wesley and Blake drew opposite conclusions, but that they addressed themselves to the same problem, and in the same spirit; for, as Ms England puts it: 'What *Hymns for the Nation* has in common with Blake is belligerence, exuberance, excess.' And this is, throughout their careers, the common ground between these two poets: 'Wesley and Blake are comparable in their arrogance, vulgarity, and excess. These traits of enthusiasm entered into all their poetic successes and can be seen with greatest clarity in their poetic failures.' But they shared also a common intention: 'Their poetry is prophetic and evangelical, the messages are intensely personal and aimed at reformation of the social order. They meant to bring about an inner change, in the heart, the imagination, and hoped that social changes would come about as a result.'

It is against this background, of the temperamental affinity between the two men and their common dedication to a prophetic role, that the differences between them stand out most sharply. And their political differences are among the least important. In the first place, 'Wesley looked upon himself as transmitting a received dogma', whereas Blake 'claimed no connection with any existing orthodoxy'. If Blake can be called Christian at all (which may well be doubted) 'his Christianity has no institutional aspect at all. All his life, he neglected those "means of grace" to which the Wesleys refer most often'. He seems never to have taken communion nor to have attended any services other than his own christening and wedding. Second, 'the authority of academic standards of excellence had no part in Blake's aesthetic. He thanked God he was never sent to school.' Wesley on the other hand was associated with scholarship all his life. Hence, third, 'Blake professed antagonism to empirical philosophy, experimental science, and the lower and higher criticism of the Bible that were an important product of the Enlightenment', whereas Wesley accepted these ideas early in his life, and wrote his hymns in the light of them. Then again, in Ms England's words:

> An obvious difference is Wesley's acknowledged obligation to clarity. He wrote in three traditions that demanded it. The Augustan aesthetic demanded it, and he added to that demand his own emphasis on the didactic nature of his writings and the nature of the audience he addressed... None of these pressures operated directly upon Blake. He would not accede to demands for a certain sort of 'clarity', for it involved the writer in those generalizations which seemed to him a blurring of true clarity.

But over and above all these differences, there is one that goes deeper: where Wesley believes in paradox, Blake believes in dialectic. And anyone who attends with proper seriousness to the matters which preoccupied these two nobly dedicated men must, on this crucial issue, side with one of them against the other. R.H. Tawney, who was no worse a theologian and no worse a Christian for being also a historian and a Socialist, remarked:

> There is a distinctively Christian way of life... This way of life is not, as appears often to be supposed, identical with what is called 'goodness'; for... Christianity is a religion for sinners. It rests on a peculiar – and superficially, at any rate, a highly improbable – view of the nature of the universe. It implies the acceptance of a scale of spiritual values which no rationalisation can make appear other than extremely paradoxical.

'Extremely paradoxical' – just so:

> What though my shrinking flesh complain,
> And murmur to contend so long,
> I rise superior to my pain,
> When I am weak then I am strong,
> And when my all of strength shall fail,
> I shall with the God-Man prevail.
>
> My strength is gone, my nature dies,
> I sink beneath thy weighty hand,
> Faint to revive, and fall to rise;
> I fall, and yet by faith I stand,
> I stand, and will not let thee go,
> Till I thy name, thy nature, know.

In these lines, where our social historian would no doubt discover 'masochism', the central paradox of a god who is also man breeds other paradoxes, as that weakness is strength, and falling is rising – as it was for the God-Man who triumphed by being crucified. Such paradoxes are at the heart of Wesley's writing, as of any writing in the centrally Christian tradition; and time and again the laborious clarity of Wesley's verse takes on rhetorical splendour and intensity when paradox is concentrated into its appropriate rhetorical figure, oxymoron. Blake is not so much incapable of this, as profoundly averse to it. This emerges, for instance, when Martha Winburn England compares him with Charles Wesley as regards another of the central Christian paradoxes – that Law is Love: 'Wesley believed law and love were one, paradoxically related in time, but eternally one. Blake... saw no sweetness in commandment or statute, no love in any discipline imposed from without'. Paradox is what Blake cannot readily live with, though his 'Tyger' is certainly a splendid exception. His famously *dialectical* way of thought solves and evades paradox by separating it out -as it were on a plane surface: love ('Innocence') *leads to* law ('Experience'), as law then *leads to* love (through Revolution). Paradox is multivocal; Blake has to break it down into narrative sequence, into the univocal. Though Blake is commonly thought of – and in part rightly – as an enemy of rationalism, in this defining feature of his thought he is a rationalist all through.

Thus, Blake's relation to English Dissent is tortuous and very far from clear. G.E. Bentley has presented evidence, inconclusive but suggestive, that Blake's father about 1769 joined a Baptist church; and this, if true, would clarify the all but unanimous contention of the early biographers that Blake's parents were dissenters, though no one says of what kind. The question is academic, however, for it has come to seem more and more likely – ever since A. L. Morton's *The Everlasting Gospel* of 1958 – that the Dissent which *effectively* influenced Blake was that of the antinomian and heretical sects, the Ranters and Muggletonians, who (as is now clear) survived in clandestine fashion among the artisans and petty tradesmen of London, from their origins in the Cromwellian Commonwealth until Blake's lifetime and after. These sectaries are now attracting much devoted and admiring attention. But it is not denied by their most fervent admirers that what they express is socio-political resentment and aspiration thinly cloaked in religious terminology; and that, as specifically *religious* insights, their ideas are beneath contempt. Thus none of the research currently being pursued into the Muggletonians and others can seriously qualify the impression that in Blake, as – so I shall suggest – in D.H. Lawrence a century later, we have a case of an imaginative genius born into a stratum of religious experience too shallow to sustain him.

John Holloway has shown invaluably how many of Blake's 'Songs of Innocence and of Experience' are cast in the metrical, the rhetorical and stanzaic forms of Watts's and Doddridge's hymns; and indeed the connection with Watts was noticed as early as 1806. But it must be emphasized that the theological content that is poured into these moulds is such as Watts and Doddridge would have been appalled by, and would have denounced as un-Christian.

One may think William Blake a great poet, and an exceptionally engaging person, and still regard with alarm, as a very ominous symptom, the veneration which nowadays is so freely accorded him; for what we see, I suggest, as the aristocratic Anglicanism of George Herbert modulates into the Old Dissent of Richard Baxter and Watts and Doddridge, and then is overtaken by the evangelizing of the Moravians and Wesleyans – is a test case, historically recorded, of what happens when a body of difficult but momentous truths is taken 'to the people'. To those who draw from this record the sanguine conclusion that in the process nothing, or nothing important, was lost – I have nothing to say. For those who believe that something was lost along the way, it is very difficult to determine just where, in the process, the simplifications and intensifications became 'too much' – so as to damage just those truths that were to be simplified and intensified. To speak for myself, I am much persuaded by those who point to the excesses of the Wesleyan meetings – the fallings about, the paroxysms, the 'speaking with tongues', and the preachers' perfervid and foolish rhetoric that provoked such manifestations – as clear symptoms of religious sentiment perverted, and doctrine coarsened out of recognition. But then I encounter the wonderful figure of John Wesley himself, who regretted these grotesque distortions and diagnosed them (as in his comments on the Flemish prodigy, Antoinette Bourignan), who none the less tolerated them as a price that had to be paid; Wesley, whose level-headedness and fastidious though heartfelt taste is manifest on nearly every page of his that has come down to us. What does seem to me certain is that, by the time and to the extent that the process works itself out in Blake, the game is not worth the candle, the price asked (and paid by Blake) is exorbitant. Blake is lamed by this historical process, not – except in the delusory short run – sustained by it; he is not a hero of the democratizing of Scripture, but a martyr to it.

4 Dissent and the Evangelicals, 1800-1850

Horton Davies, in one of his admirable volumes on *Worship and Theology in England,* has shown that George Whitefield was a much better theologian than is commonly supposed. But on the other hand he has to censure, in Whitefield, his 'philippics against book-learning and his pietistical and puritanical assumption that pleasure itself was a pursuit unworthy of a Christian'. Davies points out – what cannot indeed be emphasized too often – that 'Such a philistinism was unthinkable to Wesley, for whom reason, after Scripture, was an avenue of the knowledge of God'. And 'philistinism' seems not too harsh a word for Whitefield, the preacher who declared: 'Our common learning, so much cried up, makes men only so many accomplished fools.' However, when Horton Davies describes this attitude as 'puritanical', he is – while not wrong, for common usage regrettably supports him – certainly misleading, for as we have seen, such dissenters as Watts and Doddridge stand on this issue squarely with Wesley, not with Whitefield – so much so indeed that they have to be defended from the opposite imputation, of being 'cold reasoners'. And the same holds true, perhaps more surprisingly, of dissenters of an earlier, more rugged, kind – of a Richard Baxter or a Matthew Henry, whose *Commentaries* I remember on the bookshelves of my Baptist grandfather. And yet, if we think a little, this should not surprise us; for in Old and New England alike the dissenting ministers were typically martyrs to erudition, as witness the monumental works that they composed. Matthew Henry's *Commentaries* of 1710 certainly constitute such a monument; and it is interesting to see what Henry makes of a Scriptural text that might seem to give colour to an attitude like Whitefield's, the verse from Ecclesiastes which declares: 'For in much wisdom is much grief; and he that increaseth knowledge increaseth sorrow.' Matthew Henry in his comments on this passage interposes a special note, which runs:

> it becomes great men to be studious, and delight themselves most in intellectual pleasures. Where God gives great advantages of getting knowledge, he expects improvements accordingly. It is happy with a

> people, when their princes and noblemen study to excel others as much in wisdom and useful knowledge, as they do in honour and estate; and they may do that service to the commonwealth of learning, by applying themselves to the studies that are proper for them, which meaner persons cannot do.

Did the old Puritan have in mind perhaps such a contemporary as the great Robert Boyle? We cannot be sure; but we *can* be sure that in his mind 'the commonwealth of learning' was not limited to studies like theology and church history, nor yet to those as supplemented by such useful disciplines as accountancy and mechanics. For he is himself glad to call upon the elegant speculations of Sir William Temple when the course of his commentaries has brought him to those books of Scripture which he recognizes without fuss as 'poetical'.

The point, it will be realized, is an important one. Distrust of intellect, of rational discourse and free enquiry, and distrust of the arts – these attitudes, though they can be found among Puritans (for philistines can crop up anywhere), seem not to be characteristic of seventeenth-century Puritanism, and certainly do not characterize its lineal descendant, eighteenth-century Dissent. And yet common usage, as we all know and have just seen, asserts the contrary. How can this be? I will answer brusquely, trusting you to gather from this series of lectures as a whole the evidence on which my answer is grounded: first, the Establishment (in its strict sense, as the Church of England) has in every generation, including our own, disseminated the *canard* that Dissent is of its nature philistine; and, second, in the nineteenth century, Dissent co-operated, by becoming as philistine as the Church had always said it was. In this, English Dissent betrayed its own tradition; and the melancholy story of that betrayal is what I now embark upon.

But the first impetus towards the philistinism of nineteenth-century Dissent came not from Dissent but from inside the Anglican Establishment; and the label to be tied on it is not 'puritanical' but rather 'Evangelical'. This too, however, is a word that must be used with caution. Evangelical with a small 'e' is what every man of God must hope to be, a description in which every one of them should take pride. Even Evangelicalism with a capital 'e' is not altogether right if we take it, as is commonly done, to comprehend Wesleyanism. But the charge lies heavily indeed against the other two branches of what the historian Horton Davies distinguishes as Evangelicalism: that is to say, the Calvinistic Methodism of George Whitefield and the Countess of Huntingdon's Connexion, and second, the closely associated Anglican Evangelicals who 'attained the dimensions of a party in the first three decades of the nineteenth century'. These last have never enjoyed a good press from imaginative writers, nor do they deserve one now from any one concerned with the history of our culture in any sense of that word. Indeed, since the publication of Brown's *Fathers of the Victorians* (1961), the one cultural achievement which it seemed could be laid to their credit, the practical humanitarianism of Wilberforce and his allies, has been so blown upon that it has disappeared, and shows up on the debit side; for Ford shows convincingly that an Evangelical publicist like the famous Hannah More was acting thoroughly in the spirit of Wilberforce himself, when she inculcated the most rigid Tory sentiments in the poor people whom she reached with her tracts. And the Toryism in question is not that of the hearty eighteenth-century squirearchy, nor yet that which was to come with Disraeli, but the openly repressive Toryism of Pitt and Sidmouth and Castlereagh during the French Wars and the post-war wretchedness that exploded in the breaking of the weavers at Peterloo. Politically, indeed, the Evangelicals under Wilberforce not only supported Pitt through thick and thin so long as he worked for the one cause they had set their hearts on, the abolition of the slave trade, but it can be argued that this strategy of bending all energies towards one definable objective – after the slaves were emancipated it became, significantly, foreign missions – had the perhaps intended effect of stifling all protests at more pervasive and inflammable injustices, nearer home.

However that may be, of the philistinism of the Evangelicals there can be no doubt. The monstrous legacy of it is still with us, as ecclesiastical eyesores: the churches that they built, mostly either sham Gothic or Greek Revival. The Roman Catholic architect Pugin, in his pungent *Contrasts* of 1836, spoke of these Anglican neo-Gothic churches as 'Protestant monstrosities in the garb of Catholic antiquity'; and Ruskin, the other great champion of a truly *inward* Gothic revival, declared in *Modern Painters*:

> The group calling themselves Evangelicals ought no longer to render their religion an offence to men of the world by associating it only with the most vulgar forms of art. It is not necessary that they should admit either music or painting into religious service; but if they admit either, the one or the other, let it not be bad music nor bad painting.

As for the *intellectual* philistinism of the Evangelicals, Leslie Stephen speaks with the authority of direct personal and family experience when he says:

> The history of the Evangelical revival illustrates the limits of religious movements which spring up in the absence of any vigorous rivals without a definite philosophical basis. They flourish for a time because they satisfy a real emotional craving; but they have within them the seeds of decay. A form of faith which has no charms for thinkers ends by repelling from itself even the thinkers who have grown up under its influence. In the second generation the abler disciples revolted against

> the strict dogmatism of their fathers, and sought for some more liberal form of creed, or some more potent intellectual narcotic. The belief generated in the lower or middle social strata was utterly uncongenial to the higher currents of thought, and, thus confined within narrow limits, ossified into a set of barren theories, never vivified by contact with genuine thought.

How this worked out in practice may appear from a document relatively early in the history of Evangelicalism, a curious passage in Southey's *Life of Henry Kirke White* (1807), where we read that the friend who converted Kirke White to evangelical principles adduced as proof of his lamentable infidelity his 'having more than once suggested, that the book of *Isaiah* was an *epic,* and that of *Job a dramatic,* poem'. Yet as regards the Book of Job this had been contended for, not only by the famous Robert Lowth, later Lord Bishop of London, in his epoch-making *Lectures on the Sacred Poetry of the Hebrews* (given in 1741 and published in 1753, to be eagerly studied by Christopher Smart), but also at the very beginning of the eighteenth century by the dissenter Matthew Henry. It is plain that, though of course not all Evangelicals were so callow and provincial as this, none the less Evangelicalism was in very crucial ways a putting of the clock back.

Yet it was also very much in tune with the spirit of its times, for it is plainly in its way a profoundly *romantic* movement, as we may see from the poetry of this same Kirke White, the Reverend Charles Simeon's Cambridge prodigy, dead in 1806 at age twenty-one, a sort of Evangelical Chatterton. Kirke White's tragic name is the only one that the Evangelicals might claim to have added to the canon of English poets, though they recruited as it were posthumously both John Newton and William Cowper, co-authors of the *Olney Hymns*.

At this period in fact 'puritanism', if by that we mean a distrust both of open-minded speculation and sensuous pleasure, was to be found at least as much in the Established Church as among the dissenters – inevitably so, since it came in the train of the rejuvenated strict Calvinism which Evangelicalism imbibed from Whitefield and Toplady and (it must be said) Cowper, all of them Anglicans. Nevertheless, it must at once be conceded that even before the eighteenth century was out, there were Evangelical dissenters as well as Evangelical Anglicans, and that they were as philistine as their comrades of the Establishment. The most damning evidence is once again in architecture and furnishings for worship. Surrey Chapel, on the south bank of the Thames, was in being even while John Wesley was alive. It could seat a congregation of 2,000, and organ recitals were given there because the chapel possessed a better organ than any London church. Erik Routley, a historian of Dissent writing for a series called 'English Institutions', says of this development:

> The family has given place here to the massed congregation, and this technique of massed congregations appealed to Dissent in a manner which the Dissenters of the seventeenth century would have found incomprehensible. Preaching gradually developed, in the new large towns, out of the pattern of patient and formal exposition into the pattern of red-hot exhortation and dramatic religious demagogy... To accommodate the great congregations the meeting-houses were often pulled down to make way for large edifices 'in the Gothic style'... in their outward architecture eloquent of the ambition and success of Dissent...

and he decides:

> There was, with all the pomp and circumstance of the new-rich nonconformity, a softness at the centre which too often made the new Puritans content with cheap but pretentious buildings, second- and third-rate music, and a sentimentality in popular religion which a realistic twentieth-century generation has justifiably rejected.

If we ask what created that 'softness at the centre' which infects dissenters and Anglicans alike under the stress of the Evangelical Movement, the answer (I submit) is very clear; it was that 'enthusiasm' which accordingly Watts and Doddridge had been so right to distrust and oppose. Dissent came to it relatively late and in many cases reluctantly, but it was in the end destroyed by it (as a cultural force) far more completely than the Established Church where it originated. It could be controlled, barely, so long as John Wesley was alive; after his death it was defenceless before such homegrown hot-gospellers as George Whitefield or Rowland Hill or (I'm afraid we must say) William Blake.

Nevertheless Dissent *did* put up a struggle. There *were,* until well on into the nineteenth century, distinguished dissenters who clear-sightedly tried to hold fast to their inheritance from previous centuries, even as the tides of feeling round them rose and sank. One may even maintain, looking forward to a figure like the late Victorian writer who called himself 'Mark Rutherford', that the Old Dissent of Isaac Watts survives as a slender thread through all the Victorian generations into our own era. But that case can be argued only with large and damaging qualifications, as we shall see. At any rate, the resistance of Dissent to Evangelicalism is a chapter of our cultural history that so far as I can see remains to be written; and though I can't pretend to write it here and now, it is what I shall be concerned with for the rest of this lecture.

The existence of an Evangelical and an anti-Evangelical wing to Dissent at the start of the nineteenth century is neatly graphed in the fortunes of two important magazines. One, the *Evangelical Magazine,* was founded in 1793 as a joint venture of dissenters and Evangelical Churchmen and 'soon became the most widely circulated religious miscellany in England'. It was denounced by the High Churchman Southey in 1808 and again in 1838 for the deplorably wide influence of its Calvinistic philistinism. In 1805 the *Eclectic Review* was similarly started by dissenters and Churchmen jointly, in hopes of pleasing all denominations 'by entering into a compact of neutrality on disputed points of secondary importance'. But the hope was not realized, the Anglicans withdrew their support after a year, and when a new series was started in 1814 the 'compact of neutrality' was explicitly renounced. Thereafter the *Eclectic Review* was maintained successfully for twenty-three years by Josiah Conder, under whom the regular staff included for several years both Robert Hall and John Foster. It was a very different affair from the *Evangelical Magazine,* devoting not more than a quarter of its space to religious topics and – especially admirable – maintaining a department for reviews of foreign literature. Though its standard for poetry was 'still based on eighteenth-century preferences', it declared *Lyrical Ballads* 'one of the boldest and most fortunate adventures in the field of innovation'.

What provoked the Evangelicals to denounce the *Eclectic* was 'Zeal without Innovation', printed by the *Eclectic* in 1810 and written by Robert Hall the Baptist. Hall had at this time left his ministry in Cambridge and was in Leicester where he was to remain until 1826, five years before he died. But it was during his Cambridge ministry, from 1791 to 1804, that Hall achieved fame; and since the Cambridge of Charles Simeon and poor Kirke White was a centre of the Evangelical infection, it is pleasant to reflect that Hall's powerful antidote was being concocted at the same time, not many yards from Simeon's rooms in King's.

Not that Hall was every inch a Cambridge man. In one sense, of course, he couldn't be, since dissenters couldn't be members of the university. But his affection for the place was in any case something short of besotted. His contemporary and biographer, Gregory, recalls him in 1797 or soon after:

> In him all was at the utmost remove from gloom or moroseness. Even the raillery in which he indulged showed his good-nature, and was exceedingly playful; and, notwithstanding the avowed and lamentable impetuosity in argument to which he was prone, nothing, so far as I ever saw, but conceit, ingrafted upon stupidity, provoked his impatience, and called forth a severity which he scarcely knew how to restrain... And such was his prevailing cheerfulness that he seemed to move and breathe in an atmosphere of hilarity, which indeed his countenance always indicated, except when the pain in his back affected his spirits, and caused his imagination to dwell upon the evils of Cambridgeshire scenery.

This was, in his case, far from a hypothetical grievance. It seriously diminished his happiness at Cambridge, and at length was the main cause of his quitting it. In one of my early interviews with him, before I had been a month at that place, he said to me, 'What do you think of Cambridge, sir?' 'It is a very interesting place'. 'Yes, the place where Bacon, and Barrow, and Newton studied, and where Jeremy Taylor was born, cannot but be *interesting*. But that is not what I mean; what do you say to the scenery, sir?' 'Some of the public buildings are very striking, and the college walks very pleasing; but...' and there I hesitated: he immediately added, 'But there is nothing else to be said. What do you think of the surrounding country, sir? Does it not strike you as very insipid?' 'No, not precisely so'. 'Ay, ay: I had forgotten; you come from a flat country; yet you must love hills; there are no hills here.' I replied, 'Yes, there are; there are Madingley hill, and the Castle hill, and Gogmagog hill'. This amused him exceedingly... '... Gogmagog hill is five miles off, and many who go there are puzzled to say whether it is natural or artificial. 'Tis a dismally flat country, sir; dismally flat. Ely is twelve miles distant, but the road from Cambridge thither scarcely deviates twelve inches from the same level; and that's not very interesting. Before I came to Cambridge I had read in the prize poems, and in some other works of fancy, of 'the banks of the Cam', of 'the sweetly flowing stream', and so on; but when I arrived here I was sadly disappointed. When I first saw the river as I passed over King's College Bridge, I could not help exclaiming, Why the stream is standing still to see people drown themselves! and that, I am sorry to say, is a permanent feeling with me'. I questioned the correctness of this impression, but he immediately rejoined, 'Shocking place for the spirits, sir; I wish you may not find it so; it must be the very focus of suicides...'

If such a passage sounds like a smudged carbon-copy of some page from Boswell's *Life of Johnson*, both Gregory and Hall were aware of it. Taxed with the affectation, Hall admitted it:

> Yes, sir: I aped Johnson, and I preached Johnson; and I am afraid with little more of evangelical sentiment than is to be found in his essays: but it was youthful folly, and it was very great folly. I might as well have attempted to dance a hornpipe in the cumbrous costume of Gog and Magog. My puny thoughts could not sustain the load of the words in which I tried to clothe them.

The evangelical sentiment that Hall there regrets his lack of is, of course, very much evangelical with a small 'e', such as Doddridge, too, would have wished to have. As for the Johnsonian manner, it seems to have been one thing that Hall shared with another Cambridge worthy, the once famous eccentric Dr Samuel Parr, greatly influential in his generation though now hardly remembered. Hall and Parr were intimate from 1799 onwards. Three years before, at the trial of John Binns, a Jacobin who had made contact with the naval mutineers at Spithead and the Nore, Parr is said to have helped get Binns acquitted by sitting directly in front of the jury and scowling with disbelief throughout the case for the prosecution, nodding vigorously at points made for the defence; for Parr's Whiggism – he was called 'the Whig Johnson' – was in the 1790s that of Charles James Fox and of the minority in Parliament which consistently opposed the war with France, and Hall at one time agreed with him, as we see from his *Apology for the Freedom of the Press* (1793), provoked by a riot of Cambridge loyalists who had victimized a local liberal, Musgrave, much as a similar mob in Birmingham had earlier victimized the Unitarian Priestley. Both Parr and Hall moved politically to the Right, as revolutionary France became Bonapartist France; and in 1800 a famous sermon on 'Modern Infidelity Considered' brought down upon Hall charges of political apostasy, just as similar swings over the same period brought the same charges against Wordsworth and Southey and Coleridge. What Hall learned from Samuel Parr was thus not political theory, but (apparently) nothing more momentous than the habit of smoking, to which Parr was notoriously addicted. Concerned about this, Gregory gave Hall a pamphlet against smoking by Adam Clarke, to have it returned with the comment: 'Thank you, sir, for Adam Clarke's pamphlet. I can't refute his arguments, and I can't give up smoking.'

All this adds up to a picture very far indeed from whatever stereotype we may have of the dissenting minister of any century, including our own. And the portrait is not uniformly admirable, nor engaging; there are moments at which Hall and Parr alike may strike us as early examples of a type that has cropped up in every English generation to the present day: pint-size Dr Johnsons, Great Chams of the Senior Combination Rooms (or for that matter of dissenting academies), their inconsistencies and quirks lovingly paraded for the benefit of some non-existent Boswell. But this is too harsh; Robert Hall was perhaps not quite a great man, but he was certainly a very remarkable one, and a man of principle. This shows up in the obvious place, which is also the place where we are least likely to look; that's to say, in his theology. For instance, at a time when the sacraments were largely disregarded in all denominations – in St Paul's Cathedral on Easter Day, 1800, there were just six communicants – Hall, in his definition of the meaning of the Lord's Supper, restated the doctrine of the Eucharist in its full and exacting and mythic grandeur. And the significance of this, for those of us concerned with the imaginative arts (whether we are Believers or not), ought to be obvious; for the moment, the point may be gestured at by my admittedly questionable epithet, 'mythic'. And incidentally, if we are surprised to find such sacramental truths affirmed by a dissenter, this I'm afraid proves only our ignorance; for despite their insistence on 'the preaching of the word', dissenters of the seventeenth and eighteenth centuries, contrary to what is supposed, laid very great stress on the sacrament of the Lord's Supper in particular. As regards Hall's theological position in general, it will be remembered that it was his own father who had helped to wean some of the Baptists from an ultra-Calvinist position, and so, although Edwards on the Will was studied by him repeatedly and admiringly, Hall, when asked if he was Arminian or Calvinist, could reply: 'Neither, sir...' adding however, 'but I believe I recede farther from Arminianism than from Calvinism.' When he adds further: 'I regard the question more as metaphysical than religious', he is being evangelical with a small 'e'.

All in all, I believe we may think that Hall's Johnsonian pretensions were not all affectation, but testified to a measure of real affinity, for the figure which emerges, even from such scanty impressions as these, is distinctly non-Romantic. It should not surprise us to hear that 'he thought Gray's Elegy the finest thing ever written'. In the *Eclectic Review,* we remember, the magazine that Hall wrote for, 'the standard for poetry was still based on eighteenth-century preferences'.

However this may be, we cannot help but think, with the advantage of hindsight, that it was inevitable the conservative Dissent that Hall stood for should have been swamped before the new century had advanced at all far. Part of the reason for this was a sudden accession to the ranks of Dissent by many new schismatic sects; notably the Primitive Methodists in 1812, the Plymouth Brethren in 1827-30, and the Catholic Apostolic Church in 1835. The Methodists, once John Wesley's hand had been removed and their sectarian status had been acknowledged, were particularly addicted to schism; and the Primitive Methodists were only one of several breakaway Methodist churches, though of particular interest to social historians because of their espousal of the cause of the agricultural labourer. Thus assailed on two flanks – by an Evangelical Establishment, and by these proliferating varieties of New Dissent, Old or Orthodox Dissent could not for long hold by its distinctive emphases, especially since it could not profit by Romanticism, as its more charismatic rivals on both flanks were able to do.

Strictly speaking Old Dissent at this period may be held to comprise only two denominations: the Baptists, and the old Independents who now were calling themselves Congregationalists. (Dissent has its snobberies, and even today it is hard for a Congregationalist not to regard the Methodist as a parvenu.) However, there are at least two other churches which can be thought of as borderline cases between the Old Dissent and the New. These are the Unitarians and the Sandemanians, and I want to consider one representative of each of these.

My Unitarian shall be Elizabeth Gaskell, born and raised a Unitarian and married to a Unitarian minister. In her second novel, *Ruth* (1853), Mrs Gaskell showed great courage, not only by dealing compassionately with the scandalous topic of the unmarried mother but, even more outrageously for some readers, by letting her ruined maid's benefactor, a dissenting minister, pass her off as a widow so as to spare her social ostracism. The particular dissenting persuasion of this minister is left unclear, though in fact the original was the Newcastle Unitarian, William Turner. This Unitarian strategy, of consistently presenting themselves as members of Dissent though orthodox Trinitarian Dissent of course disowned them, was first evolved in the 1770s and has done vast damage to Dissent ever since. In any case, the minister who is the hero of *Ruth is* as far as possible from what Mrs Gaskell called in a letter of 1849 'all the cursing evangelicals'. And indeed a Unitarian Evangelical is unthinkable, a sort of *lusus naturae,* for the Unitarians were, and always had been since the days of Joseph Priestley and Richard Price and Mrs Barbauld of the Warrington Academy, an enlightened intellectual minority, particularly strong in those North West Midlands where the Gaskells were in touch with such Unitarian dynasties as the Wedgwoods and later the Darwins. Birmingham was another of their centres. And yet another provincial stronghold of Unitarianism was Norwich, its strength symbolized there by Thomas Ivory's Octagon of 1754-6 – the most elegant meeting-house in England, or perhaps in Europe. From Norwich came Harriet Martineau (1802-76), an even more famous Unitarian bluestocking (and incidentally novelist) than was Mrs Gaskell. It was Harriet's brother James (1805-1900) who was to inspire a Unitarian revival in late Victorian times, for in Elizabeth Gaskell's youth Unitarianism was losing adherents; William Hale White in *The Autobiography of Mark Rutherford* presented it as being spiritually even more sterile than orthodox Dissent, and all the evidence supports him. Meanwhile, as Elizabeth Haldane remarks demurely, 'the sect was small but extraordinarily intellectual and efficient, and if born within it, it was impossible not to gaze at the world from a rather superior angle'. One should set against that Augustine Birrell's testimony that his father, a Liverpool Baptist minister through thirty years, though he admiringly heard both Cardinal Wiseman and Cardinal Manning preach, would have found it unthinkable to enter a Unitarian chapel.

It could be argued, and with justice, that the Unitarians have, in proportion to their numbers and their relatively brief history, made a greater contribution to English culture than all the other dissenting sects put together. Certainly this would be plausible if we proceeded simply by counting heads, enumerating the distinguished individuals who have emerged from among the Unitarians to contribute to the intellectual life of the nation. But, much as we must guard against any sentimentally populist understanding of 'culture', it is undeniable that Unitarians seem in almost every generation to have regarded themselves as an intellectual *élite,* 'gathered' from the world more self-consciously and haughtily than even those other sects which were surest of being 'the elect'. Whereas in some of the other sects – for instance in Congregationalism at certain periods – we find traces of a social *élitism,* this seems never to have been so chillingly exclusive as the intellectual *élite* of the Unitarians. And 'intellectual' can be given another inflection also: the cultural contributions of the Unitarians have been overwhelmingly in speculative thought, in ideas rather than images, arguments rather than fictions, chains of reasoning rather than artifacts. Elizabeth Gaskell is important because she is probably the nearest we can come to finding an exception to this rule. And yet it is generally conceded that even in her case – and one thinks of novels of hers much better than *Ruth* – arguments and ideas, 'causes' and propagandist intentions, lie up too close and manifest below the surface of her stories for us to think of her as a great novelist in the sense in which we are happy to applaud George Eliot or Dickens or Emily Brontë. It is important to get this right. It isn't a matter of setting up cold *head* (the Unitarians) against warm *heart* (the Methodists); that is as unfair to the redoubtably hard-headed Wesley as to the warm-hearted Priestley. None the less, 'rationalist' is certainly what Unitarianism was originally and has remained, with whatever that may imply of imaginative constrictedness and timidity.

I now turn, lastly, to the Sandemanians; and I take as their representative one of the most astonishing geniuses of nineteenth-century England, the scientist (or rather, more properly, the *natural philosopher*) Michael Faraday (1791-1867).

The Sandemanian Church came into being in 1730, founded by an anti-Establishmentarian Scottish Presbyterian minister, John Glas (b. 1695). It was greatly strengthened in 1760 when it was joined by the Inghamites, followers of Benjamin Ingham (1712-72) who, though one of Wesley's earliest associates, broke away and evangelized on his own account, chiefly in the West Riding. The sect takes its name from Robert Sandeman, John Glas's son-in-law (d. 1771), who formulated Glasite doctrine in *Letters on Theron and Aspasia* (Edinburgh, 1757) and *Some Thoughts on Christianity in a Letter to a Friend* (Boston, 1764). William Godwin, the author of *Political Justice* (1793) and of *Caleb Williams* (1794), was brought up as a Sandemanian in Wisbech.

The Sandemanians, though strict in many ways, in others were surprisingly liberal. They did not share, for instance, the traditional dissenting prejudice against the theatre, and Michael Faraday was a theatre-goer. He had no aversion to works of the imagination generally. His wife's niece recalls him in the 1820s:

> My uncle read aloud delightfully. Sometimes he gave us one of Shakespeare's plays or Scott's novels. But of all things I used to like to hear him read 'Childe Harold'; and never shall I forget the way in

> which he read the description of the storm on Lake Leman. He took great pleasure in Byron, and Coleridge's 'Hymn to Mont Blanc' delighted him. When anything touched his feelings as he read – and it happened not unfrequently – he would show it not only in his voice, but by tears in his eyes also.

The dissenters generally treated Lord Byron tenderly – which may appear less odd when one recalls that Byron is formally and stylistically the most conservative of the Romantic poets. More unexpected is the name of Coleridge; Faraday may have imbibed respect for him from his own early mentor and patron, Humphry Davy. But more surprising still is Faraday's tolerance of novels, for instance of the novels of Scott; for in 1821 Coleridge was still protesting that: 'Walter Scott's novels are chargeable with... ministering to the depraved appetite for excitement...' Altogether Faraday's Sandemanian household in the 1820s seems to have been at least as open to the literary culture of that time and earlier as was any establishment household, and a great deal *more* open than Evangelical households.

The demurrer is obvious: wasn't Faraday's Sandemanianism, and indeed his dissenting allegiance generally, merely nominal? The answer is: No. His Victorian biographer is plainly looking through Faraday's own eyes, when he declares:

> The most remarkable event of his life in 1840 was his election as an elder by the Sandemanian Church; he held the office only for three years and a half. During that period when in London he preached on alternate Sundays. This was not entirely a new duty. From the time of his admission into the Church he had been occasionally called upon by the elders to exhort the brethren at the week-day meetings; now, however, it was done regularly...

It is worth pausing here to recall that Faraday was by this time internationally famous and lionized. More to the point, despite the brilliance and profundity of his scientific discoveries, he was not – nor had he ever been – a recluse of the laboratory; on the contrary, he was the interpreter and representative of scientific culture to English society as a whole. In particular, he was a brilliant though scrupulous popularizer of science – principally through his lectures at the Royal Institution which, quite apart from being a crucial source of revenue to that establishment, were highly fashionable and much frequented occasions in the cultural life of early Victorian London. Yet between the accomplished lecturer and the preacher there was a vast gulf:

> The reason why his sermons seemed inferior to his lectures is very evident. There was no eloquence. There was not one word said for

> effect. The overflowing energy and clearness of the lecture-room was replaced by an earnestness of manner, best summed up in the word devoutness. His object seemed to be, to make the most use of the words of Scripture, and to make as little of his own words as he could. Hence a stranger was struck first by the number and rapidity of his references to texts in the Old and New Testaments, and secondly by the devoutness of his manner. These sermons were always extemporary, but they were prepared with great care.

Of the two preaching 'patterns' that Erik Routley cites – on the one hand, 'patient and formal exposition', on the other, 'red-hot exhortation and dramatic religious demagogy' – it is plain which one was favoured by Faraday.

So it should come as no surprise to find him profoundly mistrustful of 'enthusiasm'. This is plain from what he said, as late as 1859, when asked about revivalism:

> The Revivals, &c., cannot trouble the Christian who is taught of God (by His Word and the Holy Spirit) to trust in the promise of salvation through the work of Jesus Christ. He finds his guide in the Word of God, and commits the keeping of his soul into the hands of God. He looks for no assurance beyond what the Word can give him, and if his mind is troubled by the cares and fears which may assail him, he can go nowhere but in prayer to the throne of grace and to Scripture. No outward manifestation, as of a revival, &c., can give either *instruction* or *assurance* to him, nor can any outward opposition or trouble *diminish his confidence* in 'Christ crucified, to the Jews a stumbling-block, and to the Greeks foolishness; but to them who are *called,* Christ the power of God and the wisdom of God'. If his attention is called to the *revivals,* it cannot be that he should feel instruction there or assurance there, other than what he finds in the Scriptures, without reference to them; and it seems to me that any power they may have over his mind other than the Scripture has, must be delusion and a snare. That man in his natural state is greatly influenced by his fellow-creatures and the forms of emotion which are amongst them, is doubtless true, even when it concerns what he considers his eternal welfare. How else would the wonderfully varied and superstitious forms of belief have obtained in the world? What carries the Mormons into the desert, surrounded by trouble and the enmity of those around them? What sustains a spiritual dominion like the Papacy, aided by the nations around it, to proclaim the name of Christ whilst it contradicts His Word – refuses it (the record of the Spirit) to the people – and crushes out with all intolerance the simple obedience of the truth? Man's natural mind is a very unstable thing, and most credulous, and the imagination often rules it

> when reason is thought to be there. Mesmerism has great power over it; so has poetry; so has music; so has the united voice of the multitude; so have many other things: but these things are, so to say, indifferent as respects the *character* of the object they may be used to sustain, and are just as powerful in favour of a bad cause as a good one. Among the contradictory and gross systems of religion, or the numerous and opposed systems of political government, any one of them may be sustained by the use of such agencies as these.

We have already seen that Faraday's apprehension of the profoundly ambiguous effects of poetry upon the imagination does not imply any aversion to poetry, or prejudice against it – quite the contrary. What is notable is his naming as another agency influential on the imagination 'the united voice of the multitude', so averse was Faraday to 'demagogy', and indeed (I think we must say) to mass-democracy. He was in fact strikingly apolitical, yet his modern biographer calls him roundly, and not without justice, a Tory.

In conclusion, it is much to the point to ask how Faraday came by the knowledge and the skills which enabled him to realize his promise as a great scientist. It is common knowledge that in the eighteenth century the dissenting academies taught the rudiments of natural science (and sometimes more than the rudiments) as the universities did not; and so it may seem unsurprising that Faraday should, like the chemist Priestley, have come from among the dissenters. But in fact Michael Faraday's origins were too humble for any academic training at all, and he was self-educated. Let a confessedly 'partial portrait', no more than five years old, describe Faraday's education:

> Perhaps I should mention that Dr. Isaac Watts, now scarcely remembered, and then as a pompous eighteenth-century hymn-writer, was once the authority on self-improvement, on studying hard, on keeping the mind open and free of prejudice, on learning from experience, and so on. Faraday's earliest publication is a small lecture he gave in his twenties, exclusively based on Watts, about means of learning: from observation, from reading, from conversations with people – about their own knowledge, about commonly interesting topics, and so on.

This information is supplied more accurately as well as more elegantly by other biographers; I quote this one, Joseph Agassi, for his memorable expression of what Isaac Watts's reputation has become in the second half of the twentieth century. Faraday's textbook in fact was Watts's *Improvement of the Mind,* of which Johnson said: 'Whoever has the care of instructing others, may be charged with deficience in his duty if this book is not recommended.'

I shall draw on Joseph Agassi for one last observation which, though not much less oddly phrased, is in fact more valuable:

> What is real... in the last analysis, is the dream, says Jorge-Luis Borges. In Faraday's case it was the dream of the philosophic men and their tranquillity and liberalmindedness that was the most real thing. Deep down, Faraday was the last representative of the Age of Reason and as such the link between the classical and the new Enlightenment. But his religious sectarianism and his political conservatism made him a nineteenth-century man.

Agassi cannot really think that 'religious sectarianism' and 'political conservatism' were unknown in the eighteenth century. Yet by saying hastily what he cannot mean, he betrays suppositions which I suspect knock about in the heads of many of us – for instance, that if there were religious sectaries in our eighteenth century, they cannot ever have been 'politically conservative' (unless, perhaps, they were Wesleyans). On the contrary, of course, the distrust of enthusiasm by a dissenter such as Watts that 'pompous eighteenth-century hymn-writer' – inevitably made him opposed to whatever was 'democratical'. And so Agassi is not all in the wrong. The link with the Age of Enlightenment *was* there in Faraday; it was precisely his sectarianism that forged the link and made it hold.

5 Dissent and the Agnostics, 1850-1900

Unless we have a rather exact knowledge of sectarian church history – knowledge that few of us have – we shall misread many Victorian novels. I need not expatiate on this because the case has been made, exhaustively, by Valentine Cunningham in his erudite and disconcerting book, *Everywhere Spoken Against*. I shall briefly consider only one case – that of Bulstrode in George Eliot's *Middlemarch,* particularly as this portrait is related, or has been related by critics, to George Eliot's own religious upbringing. Born to an Anglican household, she seems to have gone first to an Evangelical school run by a Mrs Wallington, and then to the school of the Misses Franklin, daughters of that Francis Franklin who is reputedly the original of Rufus Lyon, a lamentably sentimentalized character in *Felix Holt*. This school is described as 'strongly Calvinistic', on the grounds that the Misses Franklin were Particular Baptists and so, a modern commentator assures us, 'we may presume' that they taught 'Calvinism in its strictest form'. The error here is at least partly the confounding of the Particular Baptists with the Strict and Particular Baptists, followers of William Gadsby (1773-1844) who led a neo-Calvinist reaction within the Baptist Church against what he called 'Fullerism' – that is to say, the middle-of-the-road Calvinism espoused by Robert Hall's contemporary, Andrew Fuller. But in any case the presumption that we are invited to make is unwarranted, for the Particular Baptists 'except for their insistence on Believers' Baptism, are doctrinally and liturgically indistinguishable from the Independents (or Congregationalists)'. The expressions 'General Baptist' and 'Particular Baptist' are in any case misleading, since in the first place the Particulars seem to have outnumbered the Generals at all times through the periods we're concerned with by at least two to one; and second, it was the Arminian General Baptists who in their practices were more 'radical' and 'primitive'. The Particular Baptists seem to have been no less vulnerable than the Independents to Baxterian and other, even deist or Arian, modifications of their Calvinism. These considerations suggest that Particular Baptist attitudes may not have been at all what George Eliot had in mind when creating Nicolas Bulstrode. Of Bulstrode we are told that before he became the effective master of Middlemarch – as banker, businessman and philanthropist – he had belonged to a dissenting church at Highbury; and our commentator assures us: 'the Church was, significantly, Calvinist'. But in fact the Calvinism of Bulstrode's dissenting background is hardly significant at all, since all of orthodox dissent, except for the General Baptists, claimed to be Calvinist in the mid-nineteenth century as in the mid-eighteenth, and the label could be, and was, pasted on to quite 'liberal' doctrines. Moreover, George Eliot herself explicitly warns us not to see in Bulstrode any cautionary example as to one set of doctrines rather than another. 'This implicit reasoning', she says in chapter 61, speaking of Bulstrode's casuistry, 'is essentially no more peculiar to Evangelical belief than the use of wide phrases for narrow motives is peculiar to Englishmen'. We should do well to take her at her word. This is by no means to deny that George Eliot's sympathies in her fiction could take her beyond the positions she might take up in letters or essays; between her essay on 'Evangelical Teaching: Dr. Cumming' and her sympathetic though detached portrait of the Evangelical clergyman Edgar Tryan in 'Janet's Repentance', there is a wide gap, and one that does her credit. The point to be made rather is that in our literary and social historians alike the term 'Calvinistic' is a catch-all bogey-word, possessing, often enough, no strictly accountable meaning at all.

George Eliot of course 'lost her faith'. And in this she was representative of a substantial body of mid-Victorian intellectuals. Another who went the same road was Leslie Stephen. More than once already we have drawn upon Stephen's *History of English Thought in the Eighteenth Century;* and this is no more than just, for Stephen's great work of 1876 deserves its classic status. The chapter of most interest to students of literature is the last; and the degree to which the hundred pages of that chapter survive or withstand changes of taste and opinion over a century is truly remarkable. Certainly Stephen's reading of eighteenth-century literature is infinitely less dated than that of his father-in-law, Thackeray, in *The English Humourists of the Eighteenth Century*. Stephen is at his best when he writes of Doddridge's proposals in 1729 for 'reviving the dissenting interest':

> The general spirit of his advice was that the dissenting minister should try to please everybody. His antagonist seems to have hinted at the propriety of a separation between the bigots and the persons of 'generous sentiments'. Doddridge wished the minister to become 'all things to all men'. That was rather too markedly the leading principle of his own life. The eminent dissenter was on friendly terms with the established clergy, and corresponded with bishops; he had relations with Wesley and the Methodists; he was a spiritual adviser of Lyttelton, and of the converted rake Colonel Gardiner; and his academy, once, at any rate, was honoured by the presence of a duke's

> nephew. Such intimacies, cultivated by the dissenting schoolmaster in a country town, indicated considerable powers of attraction. His life was honourable, independent, and laborious; but we may, perhaps, surmise, without injustice to a good man, that his emotions were rather facile, and that his temptation was to err on the side of complacency. There is a want in his writings of that firmness which is produced by the bracing air of more vigorous times; they show a tendency to flabbiness, and the enthusiasm has but a hollow ring.

This is certainly not the last word on Philip Doddridge; but it is one thoroughly plausible interpretation of the man as we know him through his writings and the record of his life. However, this is conspicuously not true of what Stephen says about Watts:

> In his doctrinal writings there are signs of the diffuse sentimentalism which not infrequently accompanies a feeble constitution... The sermons, however, show something of the old unction. They appeal strongly to the inward witness of the spirit, with a comparative indifference to the ordinary evidential argument. Unlike most of his contemporaries, he addresses the heart rather than the intellect; and in his hands Christianity is not emasculated Deism, but a declaration to man of the means, by which God pleases to work a supernatural change in human nature...

Grateful as we must be to Stephen for rebutting in advance the glib generalizations that Halévy was to make about the dissenters' preaching on the eve of the Wesleyan phenomenon, all the same the betraying sentence here is the first: Watts was of 'a feeble constitution'. But so was Leslie Stephen, until he strenuously over-compensated for it by making himself a boat-club hearty when he was Director of Studies at Trinity Hall, and thereafter by assaulting Alpine peaks with the help of the best guides that money could buy. Lord Annan is surely right to relate this to the fact that Stephen's highest compliment is 'manly'. (So it was also for his contemporaries, Pater and Hopkins; we can only guess at the sexual anxiety that this may point to, in the three of them.) 'Manly' was the epithet that Stephen could apply to the Latitudinarian bishop, Samuel Clarke. He could not apply it to Watts; and this is what flusters him.

As for Stephen's inability to do anything at all with Watts's devotional lyrics, his being completely at a loss to categorize or account for them becomes less surprising when, some pages later, he is speaking of the Wesleyan movement, and remarks: 'The want of a sound foundation in philosophy prevented the growth of any elevated theology, and alienated all cultivated thinkers. *One outward symptom of the deficiency is the absence of any literature possessing more than a purely historical interest.*' Not for the first time in this enquiry, the astonished italics are mine. Charles Wesley's hymns, which to this day are sung every Sunday throughout the English-speaking world, in Protestant churches of whatever denomination, are literature of no more than 'purely historical interest' ? Yes, indeed. Turn to the index to Stephen's massive two volumes and you will find that Charles Wesley, the poet of Methodism, rates not a single entry. For that matter, Stephen roundly asserted: 'Sacred poetry and religious novels belong to a world of their own' – a world, that is, outside literature proper.

When Stephen gets to the end of the eighteenth century and deals with emergent Evangelicalism, he speaks with more authority, and more acceptably. Yet even here he cannot be trusted implicitly:

> The new Puritanism, excluding all the most powerful intellectual elements, was therefore of necessity a faint reflection of the grander Puritanism of the seventeenth century. The morality founded upon it showed the old narrowness without the old intensity. The hatred of the world was too often interpreted into a hatred of all that makes the world beautiful, combined with a hearty appreciation of everything that adds to its material comfort. The tendency which has been the most conspicuous weakness of the creed was the reflection of the tendencies of the English middle classes. Their religious emotions were coloured by the general character of their lives. Protestantism, as it has been developed amongst industrial communities, bears traces of its origin; and though it has produced an heroic type of character, it has always been hostile to the aesthetic development of the race, and to the more delicate forms of religious doctrine.

In that last resounding generalization (which is surely implausible – one thinks, among Stephen's contemporaries, of the undoubtedly puritanical John Ruskin), Stephen is merely parroting a hoary *canard* of the Establishment. Before long a Bishop of Chester was to quote approvingly an authority who declared: 'No doubt the Puritans were often narrow and boorish; they belonged mainly to the middle and lower classes, which in England have never been distinguished by the intellectual graces'; and Froude, writing of Bunyan in the 'English Men of Letters' series, was to present him as 'poet-apostle of the English middle-classes imperfectly educated like himself'.

In particular, of course, Stephen in 1876 was echoing a commination pronounced upon Dissent seven years before in *Culture and Anarchy*. When Matthew Arnold in that book denounced the narrow-mindedness of Dissent in his day, he was in his turn echoing what his father had said thirty years before. 'My fondness for Greek and German literature', wrote Thomas Arnold, 'has made me very keenly alive to the mental defects of the Dissenters as a body; the characteristic faults of the English mind – narrowness of view, and a want of learning and a sound critical spirit –

being exhibited to my mind in the Dissenters almost in caricature.' And it must be said at once that it seems both the Arnolds were right: this was indeed what Dissent had become as distinct from 'what it had always been'. Thus Matthew Arnold's attack, it will be recalled, is focused on a newspaper, the *Nonconformist,* written (he says) 'with great sincerity and ability':

> The motto, the standard, the profession of faith which this organ of theirs carries aloft, is: 'The Dissidence of Dissent and the Protestantism of the Protestant religion'. There is sweetness and light, and an ideal of complete harmonious perfection! One need not go to culture and poetry to find language to judge it. Religion, with its instinct for perfection, supplies language to judge it, language too which is in our mouths every day. 'Finally, be of one mind, united in feeling', says St. Peter. There is an ideal which judges the Puritan ideal: 'The Dissidence of Dissent and the Protestantism of the Protestant religion'!

All the evidence suggests that this condemnation of late Victorian Dissent by the words of Scripture was entirely just. The *Nonconformist,* for instance, the journal that Arnold picks on, was founded and edited through forty years by Edward Miall (1809-81) who, originally a Congregationalist minister, was MP for Rochdale 1852-7 and for Bradford 1869-74. Miall retorted to Arnold obliquely in a House of Commons speech in 1871, advocating disestablishment:

> I wish to say something of the rural parishes of the kingdom. In each of these, we are told, the clergyman, maintained by national endowment, is a living link between the highest and the lowliest of the parishioners – is a cultivated gentleman, located just where there is, if not the greatest need, at any rate the best opportunity, for diffusing both 'sweetness and light' – is the fixed centre in the parish of civilization, of education, of charity, of piety – and I am told that I propose to abolish him and leave the people to fall back again into ignorance and Paganism... These rural parishes have been in the undisturbed spiritual occupation of the clergy of the Church of England for generations past... Well, what, on a large scale, has been the result ? What are the most conspicuous characteristics of our labouring agricultural population? Do they include 'sweetness and light'? Do they include fairly-developed intelligence? Do they include a high state of morality? Do they include affectionate veneration for religion? Are these the most prominent features by which the character of our agricultural population is distinguished, and in respect of which they bear away the palm from the inmates of towns? And the discouraging and painful answers to these queries – are they not to be found in bluebooks, verified as they may be by minute personal observation?

This is effective parliamentary knockabout, but of course two wrongs cannot make a right; and the fact that in every generation perhaps the Anglican clergy have failed to be the *clerisy* that the idea of an Established Church requires them to be – this cannot mean that the very idea of a clerisy, as for instance Coleridge expounded it, is an error and a sham. For our purposes, that idea may be stated thus: since organization for public worship is necessarily a cultural phenomenon, religious leaders necessarily have a cultural responsibility towards their congregations, as well as a religious responsibility. That cultural responsibility extends, at some times and perhaps at all times, to the giving of political advice and political leadership. When the congregations are suffering intolerable economic conditions, such as the rural proletariat undoubtedly was suffering at the time Miall spoke (it was the oppressed and brutalized proletariat from which Thomas Hardy had just struggled to free himself), the responsibility of the clergy to give political leadership must take precedence perhaps over any other cultural duty whatever. And in Miall's time there *was* one body of clergy serving the agricultural labourer in this way. It was not the clergy of the Established Church, but it wasn't (either) the clergy of the middle-class Congregationalism that Miall spoke for. It was the clergy (mostly lay-preachers, in fact) of the Primitive Methodists, who supported Joseph Arch in his struggle to unionize farmworkers.

This is a special case, and not one that Miall had in mind. What *can* be said, however, is that, whereas the Anglican clergy are endowed and established precisely to discharge the duties of a clerisy, the dissenting clergy are not; and hence that when we find dissenting clergy none the less recognizing their cultural as well as their strictly religious duties, they deserve more credit than when we find a parson doing the same. In the first decades of the nineteenth century we find Robert Hall and his associates on the *Eclectic Review* doing just that, precisely as John Wesley did it for his Methodists, and as earlier still Watts and Doddridge had done it for Old Dissent. And small thanks any of them have got, from their own day to the present, from historians of all kinds and all shades of opinion!

However, by 1840 when Thomas Arnold wrote, still more plainly by 1870 when his son wrote, it is clear that the leaders of Dissent had almost universally and almost consciously abandoned any idea that they had cultural responsibilities at all. The proof is indeed where Matthew Arnold found it, in a career such as Edward Miall's. For Miall, the cultural responsibilities of Dissent begin and end with politics, and with politics on a deliberately sectarian basis, so that nearly all the political issues that Miall was heatedly concerned with now seem irrelevant and trivial. It is no more than just that all Miall's Gladstonian politicking brought him nothing that he was working for; for Gladstone consistently out-manoeuvred the nonconformist voters and MPs on whom he depended for his Liberal majorities – it was, for instance, a ludicrous miscalculation on Miall's part to think that Gladstone, that devoted High Anglican, was going to disestablish the Church of England and so give Miall what in 1871 he thought he was on the verge of getting. The nonconformists at Westminster drove Dilke and Parnell out of political life; and it is tempting to say that that seems to be the sum of their achievement.

At any rate, in *Culture and Anarchy* Arnold's harshness towards the dissenters of his day was abundantly justified. However, his attack on them in *St. Paul and Protestantism* was not. It moved William Hale White to unwonted anger in a footnote to his *John Bunyan* (1904): 'There is not perhaps anywhere to be found such a failure to discern the meaning of history as that of Mr. Arnold in dealing with Puritanism and Protestantism generally.' Arnold had contended that 'the Puritans are, and always have been, deficient in the specially Christian sort of righteousness'; and that Puritan theology 'could have proceeded from no one but the born Anglo-Saxon man of business, British or American'. The latter contention, little as it fits the facts of recorded Puritan history (not to speak of those well-known Anglo-American businessmen, Calvin and Zwingli, Melanchthon and Luther), has of course in a sophisticated form entered on a new lease of life, thanks to inaccurate popularizing in the wake of Weber and Tawney. How bad Arnold could be at his worst, when he is every inch what Bridges called him, 'Mr. Kidglove Cocksure', will appear from his address on 'The Church of England' in his *Last Essays on Church and Religion*. Here, too, he speaks of the dissenters:

> Look at one of the ablest of them, who is much before the public, and whose abilities I unfeignedly admire: Mr. Dale. Mr. Dale is really a pugilist, a brilliant pugilist. He has his arena down at Birmingham, where he does his practice with Mr. Chamberlain... and the rest of his band; and then from time to time he comes up to the metropolis, to London, and gives a public exhibition of his skill. And a very powerful performance it often is. And then, the Times observes, that the chief Dissenting ministers are becoming quite the intellectual equals of the ablest of the clergy. Very likely; this sort of practice is just the right thing for bracing a man's intellectual muscles; what I am a little uneasy about is his religious temper. The essence of religion is grace and peace. And though, no doubt, Mr. Dale cultivates grace and peace at other times, when he is not busy with his anti-Church practice, yet his cultivation of grace and peace can be none the better, and must naturally be something the worse, for the time and energy given to his pugilistic interludes. And the more that mankind, instead of placing their religion in all manner of things where it is not, come to place it in sheer goodness, and in grace and peace – and this is the tendency, I think, with the English people – the less favourable will public opinion be to the proceedings of the political Dissenters, and the less has the Church to fear from their pugnacious self-assertion.

Really, the impudence of the fellow! Is Arnold's tone in such a passage suffused with 'grace and peace' ? And does he not realize that the tone of *The Times* is itself insufferable? – the dissenting ministers 'are becoming the intellectual equals of the clergy'! Two hundred years after Richard Baxter, and 150 after Jonathan Edwards, they 'are becoming'! We may well wonder if any dissenter, however benighted, could have been in 1870 more 'sectarian' in tone than this self-appointed champion of the Established Church. Moreover R.W. Dale, though he is a no more inspiring figure than Edward Miall and was for many years as closely associated with Joseph Chamberlain as Miall was with Gladstone, is in fact a figure of an altogether different order – notably, the only prominent dissenting minister to hold by the full uncompromising doctrine of the Eucharist in the second half of the century, as Robert Hall had done in the first half. And as for Arnold's own emasculated theology – 'sheer goodness... grace and peace' – we need only remember an Anglican of a later generation, R.H. Tawney: 'There is a distinctively Christian way of life... This way of life is not, as appears often to be supposed, identical with what is called "goodness".' If in 1870 the dissenting churches make a sorry spectacle, what shall we say of the slackness of an Established Church that could invite Arnold to expound this supercilious milk-and-water to the assembled clergy of London at Sion College?

William Hale White who protested at Arnold's *St. Paul and Protestantism* was the same who wrote fiction under the name Mark Rutherford. No writer is more important if we are looking for what Dissent has been in English culture, what it is now, and what it may become. Accordingly, I want to consider Mark Rutherford in some detail.

> I like the Lutheran service, calm and grave,
> I like its ritual solemn and severe;
> The message of these bare and empty walls
> I bow to, I revere.
>
> But don't you see? Why surely you must know
> That for the last time Faith is with us there.
> She has not crossed the threshold yet to go,
> But all is swept and bare.
>
> She has not crossed the threshold on her way,
> She has not gone for good, and closed the door.
> But yet the hour has struck. Kneel down and pray,
> For you will pray no more.

So wrote the Russian Fyodor Tyutchev (1803-73). And one sees very well that it is the literary equivalent of the bareness and sparseness which Tyutchev responds to, that made the French Protestant André Gide exclaim enthusiastically of *The Autobiography of Mark Rutherford* (1881): 'I do not know any work that is more specifically Protestant...' Moreover I have suggested that the same elusive but astringent quality is what we have to respond to if we are to value Isaac Watts's hymns and psalms as we should. All the same, D.H. Lawrence was not wrong when he remembered this book by Hale White as 'dull'; whereas if we register Watts's poems as dull, the dullness is in ourselves. In other words, despite their common ground and their common aesthetic, to move through a century or more from Watts to Hale White is to be conscious of a very sharp decline. No writing is less appealing than the prose of *The Autobiography of Mark Rutherford;* in all the honest and estimable book, there is hardly a sentence that falls upon the inward ear as memorable or shapely. It is not just that metre and stanza compel Watts's language into shapes that are harmonious; more cripplingly, Hale White explicitly denies himself any of the doctrinal speculations and expositions which time and again, in Watts as in Charles Wesley, make the paradoxes blaze from the page.

Six years later, however, *The Revolution in Tanner's Lane* (1887) is a very different matter. Though there is homespun awkwardness still – for instance a gap of twenty years in the middle of the narrative is very lamely managed – Hale White now permits himself at welcome points a rhetoric which there is little difficulty in recognizing as Dickensian, muted indeed but the better for it. And the book is the narrative not just of a human soul, but of a society, or rather of a society within a society – the society of English Dissent; for *The Revolution in Tanner's Lane* is a historical novel, as is *Adam Bede,* written by that woman whom Hale White knew in his youth and never ceased to revere. I'm afraid we are often not as careful as we should be about reading social history directly out of what are after all works of the imagination. Nevertheless in chapter XVI, the brilliantly sharp yet profoundly sympathetic evocation of the East Midlands community of 'Cowfold' – Cowfold that 'knew no poetry, save Dr. Watts, Pollok's *Course of Time,* and here and there a little of Cowper' – is very plainly put together from distinct recollections by Hale White of accompanying his remarkable father on visits in the vicinity of Bedford, where he grew up. And so no one who reads this chapter need doubt that it is a vividly faithful account of how the sects were disposed in one not untypical provincial community about mid-century. We learn, for instance, how, if Dissent generally was the faith of the relatively unprivileged, within Dissent there were class divisions, in this case between the Congregationalists and the humbler Baptists.

The short narrative *Miriam's Schooling* (1890) is, through its first several chapters, the sharpest and wittiest of Mark Rutherford's stories. Yet it is a delicate contrivance, and must be delicately handled. Who will say, for instance, which way the wit and the irony are cutting when we read this of the heroine, early in the story?

> It must be remembered that although, as before observed, she was naturally truthful, she was so because she was fearless, and had the instinctive tendency to directness possessed by all forceful characters. Her veracity rested on no principle. She was not like Jeanie Deans, that triumph of culture, in whom a generalisation had so far prevailed that it was able to overcome the strongest of passions and prevent a lie even to save a sister's life. Miriam had been brought up in no such divine school. She had heard that lying was wrong, but she had no religion, although she listened to a sermon every Sunday, and consequently the relation in which the several duties and impulses stood to one another was totally different from that which was established in Sir Walter's heroine. By some strange chance, too, tradition, which often takes the place of religion, had no power over her; and although hatred of oppression and of harsh dealing is a very estimable quality, and one which will go a long way towards constructing an ethical system for us, it will not do everything.

Though Mark Rutherford is plainly being ironical at the expense of the Church from whose sermons Miriam learns so little, is he not being ironical also about the Scott who wrote *Heart of Midlothian* and created Jeanie Deans ? We shall tend to think so, if we set beside that 'triumph of culture, in whom a generalisation had so far prevailed', a passage from Hale White's *Examination of the Charge of Apostasy against Wordsworth* (1898) where he says of the political radicalism of the young Wordsworth, from which he is counted an apostate, that it was a matter of abstractions, and therefore accompanied by 'the doubt which infects all abstractions, the suspicion that there are limitations and equally valid counter-abstractions'. The matter is of some importance because Hale White himself can seem to have been an apostate from the radicalism of his youth, and in vindicating Wordsworth he was vindicating himself.

It is possible to read *Miriam's Schooling* as a whole as contending that a mechanical and scientific education is morally more effective than literary and artistic schooling. Not only Felicia Hemans and James Montgomery, but also the music of Verdi and Shakespeare's *Romeo and Juliet,* are presented as doing nothing to remove the flaws from Miriam's character, something that is ultimately effected by the scruple and exactness of her artificer husband, and the clerical astronomer for whom her husband contrives an orrery. Miriam, to be sure, is very carefully presented to us as in many ways a special case. Nevertheless, the value of astronomy (which Hale White set great store by in his own life) is contended for very forcefully, notably in words given to the astronomer:

> 'Now,' continued Mr. Armstrong, 'these are the two great truths

> which I wish you not simply to acknowledge, but to *feel*. If you can once from your own observation realise the way the stars revolve – why some near the pole never set – why some never rise, and why Venus is seen both before the sun and after it – you will have done yourself more real good than if you were to dream for years of immeasurable distances, and what is beyond and beyond and beyond, and all that nonsense. The great beauty of astronomy is not what is incomprehensible in it, but its comprehensibility – its geometrical exactitude. Now you may look.'

It is hard to take this as anything but a re-statement at the end of the nineteenth century of the eighteenth century's 'argument from design'. In the words of the 'Ode' which Addison printed in the *Spectator* for Saturday, 23 August 1712 (thereby fulfilling a promise made to Isaac Watts four days before):

> What though, in solemn silence, all
> Move round the dark, terrestrial ball?
> What though nor real voice nor sound
> Amid their radiant orbs be found?
> In reason's ear they all rejoice,
> And utter forth a glorious voice,
> For ever singing, as they shine,
> 'The hand that made us is divine'.

As elsewhere, so here, what Mark Rutherford utters in his generation is the dry but devout clarity of the eighteenth century. It comes as no surprise that he edited a volume of selections from the *Rambler,* and greatly admired Johnson – an attitude much less common in his day (when Macaulay's tendentious essay on Johnson and Boswell still held the field) than it is today. E.P. Thompson is finely judicious when he writes of 'Mark Rutherford, one of the few men who understood the full desolation of the inner history of 19th century Nonconformity – and who is yet, in himself, evidence of values that somehow survived'. What those values survived from was the cool and accommodating Dissent of the Augustan Age, not the heroic and intransigent Dissent of Jeanie Deans.

Mark Rutherford's disenchantment with radical politics is at its clearest in his *Clara Hapgood* (1896), particularly in chapter XXVI, a discussion with and between two Chartists, and chapter XXVIII, a moving reproof addressed to a Chartist by Giuseppe Mazzini. The book contains other good things – notably, an attack on Evangelicalism all the more devastating for being done in a tone of contemptuous geniality. However, the heroine never says anything that is not stilted, and her heroic sacrifice at the end – of the man she loves to her sister, while she goes off as an active revolutionary under Mazzini – is accordingly hard to believe in.

It was in Mark Rutherford's remaining novel, *Catherine Furze* (1893), that Gide found 'the so specifically Protestant qualities and virtues'. Of Rutherford's style in *Catherine Furze* one can indeed say, with Gide, that it is 'exquisitely transparent, scintillatingly pure', and of his art here that it is 'made of the renunciation of all false riches'. (Gide adds, incidentally: 'He is apolitical, because there is no politics without fraud.')

Very near the centre of *Catherine Furze,* which is set in 1840, is Rutherford's diagnosis of Evangelicalism, in the person of the Cantabrigian and 'Simeonite' rector, Theophilus Cardew; indeed the whole story, from one point of view, is the salvation of Cardew from Evangelicalism, and his 'conversion' to, in effect, Old Dissent. The conversion has to do with manners and with psychology. What is striking is that the psychology to which the Evangelical is converted is very markedly, almost obtrusively, of the eighteenth century. Conversely, the Evangelicalism from which he has to be saved is presented as Romantically subjective:

> The ultra-evangelical school in the Church preserved at that time the religious life of England, though in a very strange form. They believed and felt certain vital truths, although they did not know what was vital and what was not... Evangelicalism, however, to Mr. Cardew was dangerous. He was always prone to self-absorption, and the tendency was much increased by his religion. He lived an entirely interior life, and his joys and sorrows were not those of Abchurch, but of another sphere. Abchurch feared wet weather, drought, ague, rheumatism, loss of money, and, on Sundays, feared hell, but Mr. Cardew's fears were spiritual or even spectral... If anything struck him it remained with him, deduction followed deduction in practice unfortunately as well as in thought, and he was ultimately landed in absurdity or something worse. He saw himself in things, and not as they were. A sunset was just what it might happen to symbolise to him at the time, and his judgments upon events and persons were striking, but they were frequently judgments upon creations of his own imagination, and were not in the least apposite to what was actually before him. The happy, artistic, Shakespearean temper, mirroring the world like a lake, was altogether foreign to him.

The eighteenth century alternative to this is first presented in chapter VI, in the persons of the Misses Ponsonby who, though apparently communicating Anglicans, are carefully said to have 'preserved in their Calvinistic evangelicalism a trace of the Cromwellian Ponsonby, the founder of the race'. It is in relation to their undemonstrative style of life, that Mark Rutherford reflects:

> We mistake our ancestors who read Pope and the *Spectator*. They were

> much like ourselves essentially, but they did not believe that there was nothing in us which should be smothered or strangled. Perhaps some day we shall go back to them, and find that the 'Rape of the Lock' is better worth reading and really more helpful than magazine metaphysics. Anyhow, it is certain that the training which the Misses Ponsonby had received... had an effect upon their character not altogether unwholesome, and prevented any public crying for the moon, or any public charge of injustice against its Maker because it is unattainable.

However, the crucial confrontation is in chapter VII, and it turns upon Johnson's *Rasselas,* on which Cardew's disparaging comments are rejected both by the heroine, and by Cardew's admirable wife, whom he treats cruelly without knowing or intending it. Obviously it would suit my thesis better if the eighteenth century figures appealed to had been Watts and Doddridge rather than Pope and Johnson; none the less I take it that this is an oblique testimony by Hale White to my contention that, just as there is an often noted affinity between Evangelicalism and Romanticism, so there is an affinity just as close but seldom or never remarked, between neo-classicism and Calvinistic Dissent.

I have more to say about Mark Rutherford. And in particular I shall ask next time what it means for us to say, as we are likely to do, that his stories – however we may admire them – somehow don't strike us as truly *novels* at all. Unless I am mistaken, we shall be led, if we try to answer that question, into some very interesting speculations.

Meanwhile, however, I cannot end this lecture by permitting the attractive and admirable figure of William Hale White to conceal from us the depths that in his lifetime English Dissent had sunk to. The representative figure can hardly be other than Charles Haddon Spurgeon (1834-92), a name that I remember being spoken with veneration in the Baptist circles of my boyhood. For by the time the Metropolitan Tabernacle had been built for him, large enough for 5,000 sitting and another 1,000 standing, Spurgeon was minister to probably the largest congregation in Protestant Christendom. 'The boy preacher of Cambridgeshire', of Huguenot stock, son and grandson of Congregational ministers, converted, however, by a Primitive Methodist, Spurgeon joined the Baptists because he found the Scriptures supported the tenet of adult baptism. 'At the age of seventeen he was invited to the pastorate of the Waterbeach Baptist Church and in two years he had doubled the numbers by conversions.' 'Though he was only nineteen when he began his ministry in South London', there too he had 'an immediate and almost embarrassing success'.

If George Whitefield cannot help but be one of the villains of our piece, still less can this be avoided in the case of Spurgeon, who a century later boasted, with justice, of being Whitefield's successor. The histrionics and sentimentalism of Spurgeon in the pulpit are hard to credit. And we must anticipate the objection that such vulgar effects were crucial to the effectiveness of Spurgeon's preaching, since his South London congregation was very largely the poorest of the poor – whereas for instance R.W. Dale's Congregational flock in Birmingham consisted of professional people, civic functionaries, merchants and manufacturers. Such an apology for Spurgeon cannot help but be offensively patronizing; and it is misjudged in other ways, since the evidence is that Spurgeon's vulgarities led him to misinterpret both the Scriptural text and Scriptural doctrine, and to let his exhortatory didacticism swamp out the sacramental aspects of worship. But in any case it is plain that from a standpoint concerned with the cultural implications of English Dissent, Spurgeon's ministry, and the influence he exerted, were disastrous; and that the appropriate *literary* memorial of Spurgeon's ministry deserves to be, what I suppose it already is, Samuel Butler's exasperated lampoon of 1875 (published in the *Spectator,* 1878), 'A Psalm of Montreal':

'The Discobolus is put here because he is vulgar,
He has neither vest nor pants with which to cover his limbs;
I, Sir, am a person of most respectable connections –
My brother-in-law is haberdasher to Mr. Spurgeon.'
O God! O Montreal!

Then I said, 'O brother-in-law to Mr. Spurgeon's haberdasher,
Who seasonest also the skins of Canadian owls,
Thou callest trousers 'pants', whereas I call them 'trousers',
Therefore thou art in hell-fire and may the Lord pity thee!'
O God! O Montreal!

'Preferrest thou the gospel of Montreal to the gospel of Hellas,
The gospel of thy connection with Mr. Spurgeon's haberdasher to
the gospel of the Discobolus?'
Yet none the less blasphemed he beauty saying, 'The Discobolus
hath no gospel,
But my brother-in-law is haberdasher to Mr. Spurgeon.'
O God! O Montreal!

6 Dissent in the Present Century

D.H. Lawrence, as is well known, esteemed Mark Rutherford highly. He wrote to A.W. McLeod in 1912:

> I've read the *Revolution in Tanner's Lane,* and find myself fearfully fond of Rutherford. I used to think him dull, but now I see he is so just and plucky and sound – and yes, perhaps I like his dullness – when one lives in a whirl of melodrama, as I seem to do just now, one is glad of a glass of good porter, like Rutherford.

This isn't exactly a left-handed compliment, but Lawrence's tribute to Rutherford is certainly hedged about with qualifications. Consider only the word 'plucky'. 'Plucky', rather than 'brave' or 'courageous', cannot help but be as patronizing in Lawrence here as it is, for instance, in E.M. Forster's *Two Cheers for Democracy.* Walter Savage Landor disliked 'pluck' and 'plucky', when they first came into use; and there is a valuable gloss on them in Angus Wilson's Ewing Lectures of 1963, *The Wild Garden,* where Wilson speaks of a quality embodied for him in his mother and repeatedly examined in his early stories about 'the resistance of many of my middle-class characters, particularly women, to economic and social decline'. This quality, Wilson says, is one 'to which the period and class English expression "pluck" most satisfactorily applied'; and he says that it 'commanded my deep admiration and compassion; nevertheless it also commanded my irony'. And it is surely true even today that to call somebody 'plucky' is to express, if not irony, then a degree of condescension.

Thus, without bearing down improperly on what is after all only the unconsidered language of a slangy and casual letter, we may reasonably surmise, taking 'plucky' along with 'dull', that if Lawrence esteemed Rutherford he did so only from a distance, as exemplifying a moral stance that, though admirable in its way, certainly wouldn't suffice for Lawrence himself. And the point is of some importance because we are sometimes asked to think that Lawrence was especially well placed, not just for recognizing Rutherford's virtues but for locating them – in a cultural tradition that he shared with Rutherford, that of English Old Dissent. But I believe we have to question how far that tradition was in fact inherited by Lawrence, how far he had access to it. The document most often cited to show that he had such access is his 1928 newspaper article 'Hymns in a Man's Life'. There Lawrence declares: 'So, altogether, I am grateful to my "Congregational" upbringing. The Congregationalists are the oldest Nonconformists, descendants of the Oliver Cromwell Independents. They still had the Puritan tradition of no ritual. But they avoided the personal emotionalism which one found among the Methodists when I was a boy.' However, this is far from conclusive: it touchingly shows Lawrence aware that the tradition existed, but not that he had access to it, or gave it his allegiance. And the same can be said of the awkward and unfinished Rip Van Winkle fable called 'Autobiographical Fragment', posthumously published in *Phoenix;* there, too, Lawrence is careful to distinguish his mother's Congregationalism from 'the Wesleyan Chapel', but there is no evidence that Lawrence understood, as an experienced fact, the cultural and doctrinal differences which ground that distinction in something more substantial than mere taste. Moreover that admirable and irreplaceable witness to Lawrence's early conditioning, Jessie Chambers, is quite explicit that the culture which she speaks of Lawrence and herself as imbibing in the Eastwood Chapel was wholly a *literary* culture. It is quite misleading to speak of it as 'religious' except in the unacceptably broad and nebulous sense that Jessie Chambers intended when she wrote guilelessly to Emile Delavenay: 'Now all this feeling about the value of life and experience, and how the highest and best of it is embodied in art and literature, is in my mind... deeply and inevitably associated with religious feeling. For me, that *is* religion'. If there is any continuity at all between 'the Oliver Cromwell Independents' (those Calvinist Christians) and 'religion' as thus amply understood by Jessie Chambers, it is surely clear that the connections are altogether too tenuous to be dignified with such names as 'tradition' or 'culture' or even 'sub-culture'.

In saying so, I venture – not without trepidation – on to a famous battle-ground where the opposing forces were embodied in T.S. Eliot on the one hand, F.R. Leavis on the other. That historic engagement – and I speak without irony – is best mapped in an article by Dr Leavis, originally in *Scrutiny,* which he reprinted in 1955 as an Appendix to his *D.H. Lawrence, Novelist.* There Leavis recalls the account given of Lawrence in *After Strange Gods,* where Eliot had seen Lawrence as an extreme instance of the 'crippling effect upon men of letters of not having been brought up in the environment of a living and central tradition'. Eliot had spoken of Lawrence's 'lack of intellectual and social training' (as one might speak of toilet-training), and had declared 'that Lawrence started life wholly free from any restriction of tradition or institution'. And as regards Lawrence's mother, Eliot had referred to her 'vague hymn-singing pietism'. After rehearsing these bland judgments by Eliot *ex cathedra,* Leavis is provoked into an understandable but surely very unfortunate piece of chauvinism: 'It is when I come to these things in Mr. Eliot that I find myself saying:

"I am a fellow-countryman of D.H. Lawrence. Mr. Eliot is not...'" The provocation is extreme; Eliot's tone is indeed insupportable. Moreover he is quite plainly wrong: Lawrence *was* brought up in an environment where several traditions were – whether 'central' or not (and whatever 'central' may be thought to mean) – undoubtedly in varying degrees still potent; and thus Lawrence *did* have both 'intellectual and social training'. Leavis is quite right to protest, with justified vehemence, at these comments in the mouth of the Missourian convert to the Church of England.

And yet... 'vague hymn-singing pietism', as a judgment on what Lawrence's mother transmitted to her sons, isn't anything that the historical records permit us to controvert. What in fact went on in the Eastwood Congregational church? That is information that we look for in vain, in Jessie Chambers as in Lawrence himself; and that very absence of testimony, from witnesses as eager and observant as those two, is not far short of damning. The fullest treatment by Lawrence of worship in that church is given (Leavis agrees) in the story, 'Fanny and Annie'. But that does nothing to answer what presents itself as the insistent question: Were the symbolic mysteries of the Faith, such as Lawrence the author of *Apocalypse* can be seen to hunger for, acted out in that church? And in default of evidence to the contrary, we can only fall back on the evidence of general practice in the dissenting churches of the 1890s – to the effect that the mysteries either were not celebrated, or were celebrated in such a way as to emasculate their symbolic significance.

And in that case, Eliot's 'vague hymn-singing pietism' is indeed just about what we are left with. We have seen in earlier lectures that, contrary to what the Anglican Eliot may have believed, it had not always been thus in the practice of the English dissenting churches. But how was it in Eastwood in the 1890s? Dr Leavis contends:

> the religion of Lawrence's mother does not deserve the contempt with which Mr Eliot dismisses it. The Chapel, in the Lawrence circle, was the centre of a strong social life, and the focus of a still persistent cultural tradition that had as its main drive the religious tradition of which Mr Eliot is so contemptuous. To turn, as Lawrence did, the earnestness and moral strenuousness of that tradition to the powering of an intellectual enquiringness was all in the tradition. That the Lawrences were Congregationalists is a relevant point – their Nonconformity was very far from being the debased tin-chapel salvationism that Mr Eliot appears to think it. Congregationalism had a peculiarly strong intellectual tradition...

But alas, most of this surely is beside the point. The purpose of Church or

Chapel is not to be 'the centre of a strong social life', but to be a centre and arena for *worship,* for the enactment of the ultimate mysteries. And certainly Congregationalism had once had 'a peculiarly strong intellectual tradition'. But did that tradition survive into, was it operative in, Eastwood in the 1890s? For lack of evidence to the contrary, I fear we must conclude that it was not, that the Congregationalism of Eastwood was as impoverished, intellectually and symbolically, as it was at that date through most of the kingdom; and accordingly that Lawrence may have been crippled from the first, and throughout his life, from having been born to, and reared in, a religious community that had lost its bearings and reneged on its inheritance. This is quite different from regretfully and impertinently underlining the obvious – that the grown-up Lawrence was never near to accepting the Christian Revelation; it is to question whether that Revelation was ever presented to him in such a form that, when he rejected it, he knew what he was rejecting. It is to the point to observe, as many readers have done, that Lawrence's characteristic rhetoric in verse and prose alike is much nearer to that of the Salvation Army or the Primitive Methodists than to the sinewy sobrieties of Congregationalism at its best. For that in Lawrence's lifetime we go not to him but to Mark Rutherford.

The loss by nineteenth-century Nonconformity of the sacramental and symbolic significance of the Lord's Supper is conveyed quite startlingly by Helen Corke on the first page of her *Lawrence and Apocalypse* (1933), where she recalls her own dissenting childhood:

> In the chapel, which is the House of God, sunlight comes dim through small coloured panes, staining one's white frock rose and blue. Here no one *eats*. Eating and drinking have nothing to do with God, HE is conveyed to my perception by the singing, the silences, the minister's oratorical tone, the presence of the Great Book.

'Eating and drinking have nothing to do with God...' So much for the breaking of the bread, and the drinking of the blood of the Lamb! And a similar disastrous impoverishment shows up in Lawrence himself, in *Apocalypse,* the book that Helen Corke is commenting on. There Lawrence takes it for granted that Protestantism, and especially dissenting Protestantism, is a religion of individualism, of *personal* salvation. And because, so Lawrence maintains, 'the mass of men live and move, think and feel, collectively, and have practically no individual emotions or thoughts at all', the Protestantism of Church and Chapel cannot satisfy the mass of men, whose *collective* religion is articulated in the New Testament only in the Book of Revelation, and in modern worship only by the Salvation Army. Lawrence could not have argued thus if the Congregationalism of his childhood had observed the Lord's Supper in the spirit of Robert Hall, as '*a federal rite*' and 'a solemn recognition of each other as members of Christ'.

But in this as in much else Robert Hall is the exception that proves a sorry rule. The Baptists continued to preserve in its symbolic magnificence that one of the sacraments from which they take their name, but otherwise the decay of the sacraments in dissenting worship is a conspicuous feature of the nineteenth century. And this is particularly true of that central and cardinal rite, the sacrament of the Eucharist or the Lord's Supper. Ultimately the change is theological – the replacement, as in the 1833 Declaration of Faith of the Congregational Union, of a Calvinist or Lutheran understanding of what went on at the Eucharist by a Zwinglian or merely 'memorial' interpretation. (Thus in our century, the Congregationalist P.T. Forsyth, champion of renewed sacramentalism in dissenting worship, would declare that he held 'mere memorialism to be a more fatal error than the Mass, and a far less lovely'.) At a different level of seriousness but no less consequential was the insistence of Temperance crusaders in the later decades of the century that the Communion wine be non-alcoholic, and (still more damaging) the hygienic apprehensions which frowned upon the common cup or chalice, and replaced it by 'unbeautiful stacks of trays with minute cups, suggestive of the laboratory of a chemistry class, or... a doll's tea party'. As in the Barnsley of my boyhood, so today when I take communion in a dissenting church, I find the common cup, that necessary symbol of fellowship, replaced by the separate phials which cannot help but symbolize isolation. For how can I feel myself in love and fellowship with my neighbour when I confess, by the very form of the ceremony which seeks to announce such fellowship, that I'm afraid of catching a loathsome disease from his lips? Lawrence spoke, not without pride, of 'the Puritan tradition of no ritual'. But that tradition is being perverted if it makes us think that considerations like these are frivolous. For our ceremonial actions either have the sort of significance that I've just tried to illustrate, or else they have no significance at all, they are meaningless. Moreover, ceremonial actions *signify* in just the same way as works of art do. This is obvious in the case of such art forms as the dance and hieratic drama, but it is equally true, more elusively and profoundly, of literary art also – particularly of such literary art as Lawrence's own stories. For a symbolic and ceremonial act (or series of such acts) is as near to the centre of *The Captain's Doll* or *The Fox* as it is, more blatantly, in a late story like *The Woman Who Rode Away*. Accordingly, if Puritanism is to be saved from the imputation that it is the enemy of all art whatever, we have to repudiate Lawrence's formula, 'the Puritan tradition of no ritual', and to insist on the contrary that Puritanism implies ritual, but of a singularly austere and frugal kind. The distinction may seem to be a fine one, even lame; the difference may seem to be a difference only of degree. But it is not so, for to minds of a certain temper ceremony, whether in worship or in art, is more meaningful and momentous according as it is more austere. And if Lawrence came to think that his own hunger for ceremonial action could be satisfied only by the Salvation Army or (later) by Aztec blood-sacrifice, the blame may lie at the door of the Congregationalism he was reared in, which could have supplied him with austere versions of the ceremony he craved, but apparently failed to do so.

The same tradition failed Mark Rutherford also. And if we are less conscious of the failure, the thwarting, in his case than in Lawrence's, it is doubtless because in Rutherford's case there was less to thwart. Mark Rutherford (William Hale White) seems at first sight only another late Victorian who lost his faith, like Leslie Stephen except that, less clear-headedly than Stephen, he continued to call himself in some extended sense Christian long after he had lost the right to that title. In fact, however, more justly as well as more charitably, we can see Rutherford gradually putting together as much of the doctrine of Watts and Doddridge as could – so he soberly judged from first-hand experience – stand up to the conditions of nineteenth-century industrialism, as those conditions were experienced not just by the maimed derelicts whom the system cast aside but also by the factory-hand and the overworked clerk who together helped to keep it going. However, what Rutherford has in common with Leslie Stephen – what both of them share with atheists, agnostics and near-agnostics from their day to ours – is that both of them suppose the crux of the religious life to be the mental act of belief, not the physical act of worship. Accordingly the sacraments administered and received enter into their considerations hardly at all. Very telling on this point is a letter that Rutherford wrote in or about 1873 to his schoolboy son. The boy, away at school, had asked reasonably enough why his father, who called himself a Christian, never went to church. His father replied: 'The reason why I do not go to church on Sunday is that I do not know anybody who can teach me anything at church which I want to know. When I lived in London I always went to Mr Morris's. When I am in Exeter I go to your cousin's because I always learn something...' Allowing for the fact that Hale White is here addressing a child, it is consonant with everything we know about him that he should assume the reason for church-going was to 'learn', to 'be told', rather than to *do* something. We've no reason to suppose that he took the Lord's Supper much more often than William Blake did, for whom 'mystery', the name that the Prayer Book gives to that sacrament, is consistently a term of abuse. And in the Congregationalist worship which White knew as a boy in Bedford, which he describes in hostile detail in *The Autobiography of Mark Rutherford,* it is a fact that the Lord's Supper is never mentioned. If in White's youth it was administered only infrequently, as a sort of optional extra, those Congregationalists were a long way indeed from Doddridge, author of the Communion hymn, 'My God, and is thy table spread', in whose church – as in Watts's also – the Friday or Saturday before a Communion Sunday was devoted to special services of preparation.

The lax or impatient ignorance which – even today, and even among dissenters – lumps together all the varieties of Dissent (as if Unitarian and Christadelphian, Primitive Methodist and Congregationalist, were interchangeable labels pasted on to one cultural attitude called 'puritan') obscures from us much of the significance of one undoubted masterpiece of the dissenting tradition, Edmund Gosse's *Father and Son.* First published in 1907, Gosse's extraordinary memoir of his father had been partially anticipated twice over – once by *The Unequal Yoke,* a short novel by Gosse that appeared anonymously in the *English Illustrated Magazine* for 1886, and second, by his biography of his father, *The Life of Philip Henry Gosse, F.R.S.* (1890). It was George Moore who recognized, behind the latter, another story that needed to be told, and pestered Gosse into telling it. In so far as *Father and Son is* now read and remembered, it is either as illustrating the clash between the Christian Revelation and Darwinianism, or else as a book to go on the shelf along with Samuel Butler's *Way of All Flesh* and Augustus Hare's *Life With Mother* – though both the latter tell of childhoods in Evangelical *Anglican* households. Yet Gosse is quite explicit about the particular sort of Dissent that his parents embraced – that of the Plymouth Brethren. Nowhere is this clearer or more pointed than in the intriguing account of how Gosse the schoolboy fell in with an elderly Baptist minister who turned out to be (or to have been) Sheridan Knowles, the celebrated dramatist; and how Knowles instigated the boy to ask his schoolmaster to read some Shakespeare in class, a practice that was abruptly discontinued presumably at the request of Gosse's father who, eminent scientist though he was, 'prided himself on never having read a page of Shakespeare, and on never having entered a theatre but once'. It is clear that in this instance the Old Dissent was less philistine than the New. And yet one of the great and unexpected virtues of Gosse's beautifully tender book is the proof it gives of how a culture and a tradition were transmitted to a child even within a sect so late-come and so rigid as that of the Plymouth Brethren. He tells movingly how he read a hymn by Toplady along with his mother, and how his father and he sang together hymns by the Wesleys – though not, to be sure, 'the hymns of Newman, Faber and Neale':

> It was my father's plan from the first to keep me entirely ignorant of the poetry of the High Church, which deeply offended his Calvinism; he thought that religious truth could be sucked in, like mother's milk, from hymns which were godly and sound, and yet correctly versified; and I was therefore carefully trained in this direction from an early

> date. But my spirit had rebelled against some of these hymns, especially against those written – a mighty multitude – by Horatius Bonar; naughtily refusing to read Bonar's 'I heard the voice of Jesus say' to my mother in our Pimlico lodgings. A secret hostility to this particular form of effusion was already, at the age of seven, beginning to define itself in my brain, side by side with an unctuous infantile conformity.

A household like this, though so fanatical, cannot be called 'philistine'. A child who grew up in it cannot be said to have been aesthetically deprived. Indeed, a seven-year-old who can discriminate between the verse of Wesley and of Bonar is surely a sort of literary prodigy! And Gosse himself believed that appreciation of literature as an art began for him when he was eight, reading and studying with his father the Epistle to the Hebrews.

I believe we must conclude that every sect is a law unto itself, in the sense that each one has a unique relationship to the national and officially received culture. This is at least the hypothesis on which we must proceed, until we can take stock of the cultural bearings of each of them, even over a quite brief period such as the last eighty years. To take the Plymouth Brethren as an example, since it is what Gosse's book has brought us to, a history of their relations to the national culture in the present century would have to take account of General Orde Wingate, leader of the Chindits, killed in the Second World War. And among the documents that would need to be studied is Sybil Wingate's fugitive memoir of the religious culture in which she and her brother were nurtured:

> Of the two great branches of the Christian tradition, the static and the revolutionary, my parents belonged to the second. I do not mean of course that they were politically on the left. Quite the contrary. In so far as they thought about politics at all (which was not very far) they might be described as Conservatives. But their religion was not of the type exemplified in all the great religious Establishments, Roman, Orthodox or Anglican, whose function it is to inspire and direct the existing order of the world but not to change its essential character. Revolutionary Christianity, on the other hand, at least in its pure form, both desires and expects an imminent and total overthrow of the existing order and the substitution of 'a new heaven and a new earth', in which dwelleth 'righteousness'. Sometimes, as in 16th-century Munster, this attitude has flowed over into the directly political realm. More often it has confined itself to the religious sphere and has waited on an immediate Divine intervention. But the fundamental difference remains. Establishment Christianity, like the humorist, is broadly content with things as they are, and does not want a basic change.

> Revolutionary Christianity, like the satirist, is fighting a revolutionary war. Its cry is always 'How long, O Lord, how long' and it expects the reign of Christ upon this earth, and in the near future.
>
> When we, as children, repeated the 96th Psalm, 'Let the field be joyful and all that is therein; then shall all the trees of the wood rejoice before the Lord, for he cometh, for he cometh to judge the earth; He shall judge the world with righteousness and the people with his truth', it was the field outside the window that was to be joyful and the trees at the bottom of the garden that would clap their hands...

If we remember that Orthodox Dissent of the eighteenth and nineteenth centuries denounced 'millenarianism' as a heresy on a par with antinomianism and socinianism, we shall not need further proof of the deep and ancient, and principled, cleavages which divide one sect of English Dissent from others.

Sybil Wingate's testimony – highly intelligent as it surely is, and (as I find it) very affecting also – dates from as late as 1959. And it is not hard to find even more recent and formidable evidence of how stubbornly some of the irreconcilable attitudes of Dissent survive among us – to a degree that is of course never allowed for nor acknowledged by the confident pundits of TV or the public prints, when they tell us about the state of the nation. What persists is not just a system of belief but an intact subculture, with, for instance, its own distinctive tribal rhetoric. Thus, within the last ten years it was natural for a biographer of Charles Haddon Spurgeon to describe the hostility shown to Spurgeon at the start of his ministry by saying: 'Resenting the attacks made on his kingdom, the devil raged against the boy preacher.' And we may set against that the publication in 1972 of a book by an ex-President of the Congregational Church in England and Wales, with the jolly and thoroughly accommodating title, *The Puritan Pleasures of the Detective Story*. English Dissent is a phenomenon as various and as mysteriously unexamined as ever it was.

I am not competent – nor I suspect is any one else – to take stock of this bizarre diversity, its broad quietist middle no less than its salvationist and millenarian extremes. Instead let us look for the last time at the Old or Orthodox Dissent, as the thrust of it, though sadly weakened and more than a little diverted, reaches into our own century in the person of Mark Rutherford. A recent critic has castigated Rutherford for 'luxuriating in epochal gloom', because he believed with Augustine Birrell that somewhere in or near the middle of the nineteenth century Old Dissent had been betrayed by its own adherents. But this is a reader (Valentine Cunningham) who is so little persuaded by Arnold's excoriation of 'the dissidence of dissent', that he can declare: 'Schism is a witness to the vigour of sectarianism: the life-blood of Dissent is dissent.' We have found reasons – for instance, in the weakening of sacramentalism in the dissenting churches – for thinking that Arnold's criticisms cannot be set aside so easily and boldly, and for thinking indeed that Rutherford and Birrell were right to discern a grievous loss of direction by Dissent in their lifetimes. What is at issue, as *Culture and Anarchy* makes very clear, is a strenuous *politicizing* of Dissent, gradually indeed but markedly, through several decades of the nineteenth century. We must tread carefully here, for Dissent in every period has fostered, and could not help but foster, a keen political awareness; and accordingly the leaders of Dissent in every generation – Philip Doddridge in his time, Robert Hall in his – found it necessary to take political stands, and give political 'leads'. Nevertheless, a real change occurs when in 1826 Robert Hall is succeeded at Leicester's Harvey Lane Baptist Chapel by Edward Miall's friend, J.P. Mursell; or when – to take another instance from a later decade – John Angell James in 1859 is replaced, at Carr's Lane, Birmingham, by R.W. Dale. With the extension of the franchise and the lifting of political disabilities from the dissenters, it became possible to organize dissenting sentiment into a powerful pressure group exerting itself first in municipal and local politics and then at Westminster. And the availability of such political leverage makes such late Victorian figures as Miall and Dale into very different creatures from Doddridge or Hall. For the achievement and exercise of this political power, a price had to be paid; and the cost is to be counted in terms of spirituality and culture. To Mark Rutherford, as to Matthew Arnold whom Rutherford so justifiably complained of, it seemed plain that the price paid was excessive. And this I suggest is the right explanation of the words that in his *Clara Hapgood* Mark Rutherford put in the mouth of Mazzini; for Rutherford as he grew older lost faith not just in the radical politics of his youth, but in all politics, in the political arena as such. To be blunt about it, though Rutherford wrote for the *Nonconformist* and was accordingly under obligations to Miall which he recognized, the career of a dissenting politician like Edward Miall came to be as depressing a spectacle for William Hale White as for Matthew Arnold.

And this is an appropriate point at which to risk the suggestion that Mark Rutherford's misgivings about Dissent as a political force have been borne out by subsequent history. For it is too easy to note that Edward Miall was out-manoeuvred by his parliamentary general, Gladstone, and to say that the driving of Dilke and Parnell from public life is the most that parliamentary nonconformity can claim as a political achievement. The nonconformist strength at Westminster was at its greatest not under Gladstone but under the nonconformist Lloyd George; and at least one historian, A.L. Rowse, has seen the presence of R.W. Dale, political ally and spiritual mentor of Joseph Chamberlain, exerting its baleful though high-principled influence over the administration of Joseph's son, Neville, so as to inspire in the 1930s the ruinous and bipartisan policy called 'appeasement'.

Leaving aside such an instance (admittedly debatable) of how politicized Dissent may have worked out in practice, the late apolitical Mark Rutherford cannot help but fall foul of an assumption, very current among us and very much cherished: the assumption that political vigour is the same as cultural vigour, or at least that the first is an infallible register of the second. The history of English Dissent in the nineteenth century, as Mark Rutherford read it, disproves this cherished contention; and I may as well say that I think Rutherford was right. Those who cannot stomach this in Rutherford characteristically get round the difficulty by declaring, in Valentine Cunningham's words, that 'the autobiographical reference is the most important aspect of William Hale White's writing'. That is to say – and elsewhere Valentine Cunningham is quite explicit about it – that Mark Rutherford's books have value as personal testimony or slanted documentary, but certainly not as literature, as imaginative art. Yet it was as *art* that André Gide esteemed them. And the least we can do is to understand what Gide was responding to, before settling for the altogether more contemptuous assessment of Mark Rutherford which presents him as a more or less artless chronicler. And to this, to Mark Rutherford's *art*, I address myself in the few minutes remaining.

Francis Jeffrey, in the *Edinburgh Review* in 1804, distinguished between narratives that 'avoid all details that are not necessary or impressive', and the narratives of Samuel Richardson, with which, so Jeffrey goes on to say, 'we slip, invisible, into the domestic privacy of his characters, and hear and see everything that is done among them, whether it be interesting or otherwise'. Ian Watt quotes this in his *Rise of the Novel,* that masterly study which establishes how the Richardsonian method was in its time an astonishing novelty, foreshadowed only by some of the stories of Defoe; which establishes further how many factors worked together to make it probable that fictional narrative thus conceived should have been implemented just when it was, and not at any other date. Moreover, Ian Watt powerfully implies that fiction written on these principles, which he defines usefully as 'formal realism', has so dominated prose fiction in English in every generation since Richardson's that it is nowadays quite simply what we imagine 'fiction' or 'the novel' to be. This explains how it is that at the present day V.S. Pritchett can declare confidently in a review: 'Of course, Rutherford was not really a novelist'. For Mark Rutherford proceeds quite plainly in the spirit of those story-tellers whom Richardson superseded. From him we learn only those details that are 'necessary or impressive'. In the words of his biographer, Catherine Macdonald Maclean, speaking of his earliest narratives:

> such is the concentration on the theme, such the elimination of every particle of substance not integral to the theme, that at times these

books seem rather to be essences than novels in the accepted sense of the word. In many respects they are more akin to poetry than to prose fiction...

And the same can be said of Mark Rutherford's later fictions, such as *Catherine Furze*. That book, for instance, contains a description of an old meeting-house, which might be profitably compared with a justly celebrated description of what is in fact the Knutsford meeting-house, in Mrs Gaskell's *Ruth*. It is Elizabeth Gaskell's lovingly deliberate dwelling upon her description which does for us what we think a novel should do – it raises the place before our mind's eye, it 'takes us *there*'. Mark Rutherford's writing does not do this, for his is not an illusionistic art, as Mrs Gaskell's is. Whether he knew it or not, he was trying for something quite different from Elizabeth Gaskell, or George Eliot; and because his admiration for George Eliot is well known, it's particularly important that he should not be thought to try for, and fail to achieve, what George Eliot achieved. Ian Watt, who supplied the invaluable term 'formal realism', was the first to allow that it defines only one possible set of conventions for prose fiction; and the conventions that govern Mark Rutherford's fiction are not those, but some others. In the years since he died, more and more writers in many languages have abandoned the conventions of formal realism and tried to create, or to re-create, others; and a generation that can appreciate the fictions of Borges or Samuel Beckett should be well placed for responding to Rutherford's.

If this hypothesis deserves to be taken seriously, I could well be challenged to produce for this alleged relinquishment of formal realism the array of causes or contributory factors – socio-economic, ideological, psychological – that are marshalled by Ian Watt to explain its inception, at the hands of the dissenter Defoe in the first place, and of Richardson in the second. I lack not just the opportunity but also the erudition; and so my suggestion must remain just that. And yet it is worth dwelling for a moment on Catherine Maclean's impression: 'more akin to poetry than to prose fiction'. For it is undeniable that by the time Mark Rutherford died, twentieth-century poetry was indeed set on a course like his, vowed to eliminate all optional superfluities; and it is not hard to imagine the Imagist poet, or the enthusiast for modern poetry in the Imagist tradition, who would take more pleasure in *Catherine Furze* than in *Felix Holt*. (Rutherford's story is, for one thing, so much shorter! And that, in all seriousness, is very much to the point.)

But one may think not of Rutherford's contemporaries, but of Daniel Defoe's. In particular, when Gide says of Mark Rutherford, 'His art is made of the renunciation of all false riches', how can we not think of the dissenting poet who protested: 'It was hard to restrain my verse always within the bounds of my design'? Isaac Watts's poetry has been described as an art of *kenosis* – which *is* a theological term, meaning 'the self-limitation of the divine power and attributes by the Son of God in the Incarnation'. Thus Harry Escott in his *Isaac Watts, Hymnographer* can speak of 'artistic kenosis', and explain this by saying: 'Watts had to lay his poetic glories aside, and dress the profound message of the gospel in homespun verse and the language of the people.' And Mr John Hoyles of Queens' College can declare in his *Waning of the Renaissance:* 'Classicism for Watts was a hard task-master; it demanded from him an artistic kenosis.' *Kenosis* may be an unfortunate word, because hyperbolical; but it certainly comprehends 'renunciation', being indeed the technical term for the most awesome and extreme case of renunciation that we can conceive. Can it be an accident that artistic renunciation, *kenosis* in this sense, is common to Watts, to the French Protestant Gide, and to the lapsed English Calvinist Mark Rutherford? Surely not; it represents, surely, an aesthetic preference and principle integral to the Calvinist tradition, and therefore persisting to inform such as Gide and Mark Rutherford, on whom the religious and dogmatic and (in Gide's case) ethical precepts of Calvinism had ceased to exert much if any claim.

If this be so, we are in the position of thinking that Calvinism in the person of Defoe fomented or nourished 'formal realism', even as Calvinism in the person of Isaac Watts adumbrated an alternative to it. And that should make us pause. What can be said is that Calvinism as a theological system was far more consistently familiar to Watts than to Defoe; and that if the *economic* morality of Calvinism fired the author of *Robinson Crusoe* (as has been contended, but also denied), the *aesthetics* of Calvinism are fulfilled far more clearly in Isaac Watts and, 150 years later – much more partially, but still discernibly – in William Hale White who called himself Mark Rutherford.

Though I see no need for a peroration, yet it is probably in order and advisable, now that I conclude this course of lectures, for me to say something about what I hope they amount to, taken together. I can best do so by reminding you of a point I made in the first of them. I remarked then that the word 'culture' takes on a different colouring according as we take it to be defined chiefly by socio-political groupings and patterns of behaviour, or by religious groupings and beliefs and patterns of worship, or by aesthetic proclivities, patterns and values. I undertook to concentrate on 'culture' in this last sense, by which aesthetic considerations have priority over others, though I allowed that in the nature of the case I should have to attend from time to time to socio-political and religious practices, since these obviously affect aesthetic habits and preferences. I hope you feel that I have kept to my bargain. In the course of my studies I encountered assumptions and contentions of a socio-political kind which I cannot but regard as tendentious to the point of being deliberately misleading. Not without difficulty I have resisted the temptation to expose these falsifications as I have come across them. Some day I may stray from my proper ground so far as to challenge certain received notions about the social and political history of English Dissent over the past three centuries – to ask for instance why, if it was right for Dissent to resist the pretensions of the Crown when the Crown's representatives were squire and parson and bishop, it is wrong for Dissent to oppose them now when the Crown's representatives are the bureaucrats of the Ministry and the Shire Hall. But that enquiry would have to be conducted in a tone more acrimonious than the one I have struggled to maintain, not always successfully, through the last several weeks. 'Simplicity, sobriety, and measure' – these principles which (I have suggested) are characteristic of the dissenters' art from Isaac Watts through to Mark Rutherford are also, surely, the principles that should govern exposition and argument. How to preserve them while not blunting the cutting edge of polemic, when polemic is called for, is no easy matter. But I have done my best; and I thank you for your attention.

Notes

Notes to Lecture 1

p.11 *English Presbyterianism... had by 1800 dissolved almost completely into Unitarianism... The significance of this development... very great...*
In later notes I hope to go some way towards substantiating this contention; for nothing in the whole history of English Dissent seems more important culturally, or in more urgent need of being pondered and understood. For the moment it will suffice to quote the admittedly partial reflections of the Congregationalist Bernard Lord Manning in 1937:

> There were in the century two main currents of religious thought. One was Arian, developing into Socinianism and Unitarianism. The other was evangelical. Leaving aside detail, we may say that English Presbyterians with a few gallant exceptions were swept on by the first current, losing their Calvinism and providing the foundations of the modern Unitarian denomination. Congregationalists were swept on by the second current; and to their Calvinism added Evangelicalism.
>
> Before we offer explanations let us dwell on the greatness of this achievement, an achievement in the sphere of spiritual religion *beside which the political and social deeds of seventeenth-century and nineteenth-century Congregationalism seem almost paltry*. In the day when Presbyterianism was destroyed by Latitudinarian and Unitarian doctrine, and when Anglicanism was riddled by it, our forefathers (after some sad lapses and desperate struggles) kept the faith. This was their first achievement as a tolerated church, and had they done nothing more they would have made the place of their pilgrimage glorious (*Essays in Orthodox Dissent*, 1939, p. 186, italics added).

Manning goes on to argue that one reason why Congregationalism remained Trinitarian was its possession of a Trinitarian liturgy, in the form of the psalms and hymns of Watts.

p.13 *Edwards's doctrine... has never been controverted... but... tacitly laid aside...*
This seems to have already been largely true as long ago as 1901, if we may trust Williston Walker writing in that year about Edwards's *Careful and Strict Enquiry*....

> The volume was, till comparatively recent times, in extensive use, being esteemed by Calvinists generally an unanswerable critique of the Arminian position. It has met, however, with growing dissent, and though not often directly opposed of late years, is largely felt to lie outside the conceptions of modern religious thought; but it has acceptance still, especially with those who hold a necessitarian view of the universe, and may be said never to have had a positive and complete refutation, though suffering a constantly increasing neglect (JONATHAN EDWARDS, from *Ten New England Leaders*, in David Levin (ed.), *Jonathan Edwards: A Profile*, 1969, pp. 110–11).

Walker presumably has in mind chiefly American practices. In England the abandonment of the strict Calvinist position by preachers of intellectual pretensions may have come about gradually between about 1850 and 1887. That is suggested by chapter 7 of *The Revolution in Tanner's Lane* (1887), where the preaching of 'The Reverend Thomas Bradshaw' is Mark

Rutherford's admiring tribute to what he had heard from the Congregationalist Thomas Binney in the Weighhouse Chapel about 1850 (italics mine):

> His discourses were remarkably strong, and of a kind seldom, or indeed never, heard now. They taxed the whole mental powers of his audience, and were utterly unlike the simple stuff which became fashionable with the Evangelistic movement... They will not as a rule bear printing, because the assumption on which they rest is *not now assumed;* but if it be granted, they are unanswerable...

What is at issue here is the vexed question whether a 'moderate' Calvinism is a possibility. So far as I can see, Richard Baxter thought that it was, and that he had worked it out; Watts and Doddridge thought that it was, and that they preached it; after them, Robert Hall and William Carey and Andrew Fuller thought the same; and in the 1830s William Hale White the elder, Mark Rutherford's father, could declare that 'a moderate Calvinism suited him best'. But if Jonathan Edwards has never been refuted, that must mean that none of these attempts to 'moderate' can in the end stand up to the rigour of Edwards's logic. Yet if it be true, as R.W. Dale declared, 'that theologians who begin with Calvin must end with Calvin', and if it follows (as it must) that all these compromise positions are intellectually disreputable compared with Edwards's, one may still contend – as Doddridge for one never tired of doing – that true religion is 'experimental'; that is to say, that it is grounded not on any chain of reasoning but on an irrefutable experience in the act of worship. And if there is no room for that experience in a logical scheme, so much the worse for the logic. However, this is very different from the awkward mish-mash of irreconcilable assumptions – Arminian on the one hand, Calvinist on the other – which was the legacy of the Evangelical Movement. And it was this, as preached from nineteenth-century dissenting pulpits, which brought the mere expression, 'moderate Calvinism', into such disrepute as it had for Mark Rutherford:

> They were taught what was called a 'moderate Calvinism', a phrase not easy to understand. If it had any meaning, it was that predestination, election, and reprobation, were unquestionably true, but they were dogmas about which it was not prudent to say much, for some of the congregation were a little Arminian, and St. James could not be totally neglected.

R.W. Dale said, of such 'moderate Calvinist' preachers: 'They might be assured that, according to the eternal counsels of God, Christ died only for the elect; but they preached as if they thought that He died for every man in the congregation.'

For Mark Rutherford the dilemma was exacerbated because he appears never to have been, in Philip Doddridge's sense, an *experimental* Christian. And so we find in him an eloquent nostalgia for the immoderate Calvinism of Edwards, which he was in love with though he could not believe in it. It seems to be this that lies behind an impassioned digression in chapter 9 of *The Revolution in Tanner's Lane,* when Rutherford reflects on the state of mind of his Calvinist hero, Zachariah Coleman:

> He admitted the unquestionable right of the Almighty to damn three parts of creation to eternal hell if He so willed; why not, then, one sinner like Zachariah Coleman to a weary pilgrimage for thirty or forty years?... At last – and here, through his religion, he carne down to the only consolation possible for him – he said to himself, 'Thus hath He decreed; it is foolish to struggle against His ordinances; we can but submit.' 'A poor gospel,' says his critic. Poor! – yes; but it is genuine; and this at least must be said for Puritanism, that of all the theologies and philosophies it is the most honest in its recognition of the facts; the most real, if we penetrate to the heart of it, in the remedy which it offers.

p. 16 *'The years of Walpole's rule... years of spiritual desolation...'*

When the Master of Balliol can within the last ten years dismiss early Hanoverian culture in a few well-chosen and vindictive generalizations, we can hardly be surprised to hear from a church historian of thirty years ago, speaking of the decades after the Toleration Act of 1689:

> A cold fog of religious indifference descended upon the nation which for a century had been preoccupied with religious questions. It now began to think of other things, such as commerce and science. Religion was displaced from the centre of interest. The eighteenth century was an age of reason. The Deists whittled down the supernatural element in Christianity and reduced its fundamentals to the mere essentials of the natural reason. Philosophy became sceptical under the influence of Locke and Hume. Science made extraordinary progress and attracted to itself great attention. Morality sank to a low level and in all classes of society gambling and drunkenness were rife.

For this authority – A.C. Underwood, whose *History of the English Baptists* (1946) is in fact a mine of curious and intriguing information – there is the excuse that the denominations he is particularly concerned with, the General and the Particular Baptists, do indeed seem to have been sunk in lethargy during this period, though perhaps for reasons peculiar to themselves. In any case there is hardly a history one may consult that does not tell the same groundless tale. There is perhaps not much that the literary historian has to tell the social historian, the historian of ideas, or the church historian, but this much he has to tell them, and has been telling them for fifty years if they would only deign to listen: that the culture which produced and sustained Alexander Pope, a poet of passionate imagination which it is proper to call Shakespearean, just cannot be subjected any longer to such a repeatedly exploded pontification as: 'The eighteenth century was an age of reason.' The most intriguing as well as one of the most extreme statements of this position, as it bears upon Dissent in particular, is Maximin Piette's: 'With the prospect of struggles, tortures and hanging gone, life seemed to lose all its zest. For them religious fervour and persecution were things which went hand in hand. When one ceased, the other likewise disappeared.' Piette wrote as a Roman Catholic, and we may suppose him to be inviting the entirely just reflection that religious fervour which required such outrageous stimulants was not worth very much – which does not prevent the Baptist Underwood from deciding that 'Piette exaggerates little, if at all...'

As for Pope, one way to explain away his fertile presence in an age allegedly sterile is to maintain that he could survive only in spite of his age and in tension with it – as an embattled Tory in an age dominated by Whigs. This argument puts him at the opposite end of the social and political spectrum to the dissenters, Whigs to a man. But as a Roman Catholic, Pope himself was technically a nonconformist; and in Howard Erskine-Hill's *Social Milieu of Alexander Pope* (1975) there is an invaluable portrait of the Baptist financier, Sir John Blunt (1667-1733), who figures in Pope's 'Epistle to Bathurst' as 'Much injur'd Blunt', and Erskine-Hill shows how Pope's sympathies could reach across the sectarian and political divide to enter into the feelings of one who was an outsider like himself. The play of Pope's sympathies, we are persuaded,. is as complex and subtle as a great novelist's: 'Blunt's paradox is like that of a later puritan businessman, Bulstrode in Chapter 71 of George Eliot's *Middlemarch:* he is guilty, but his denunciation of others' guilt is not less true for that reason.'

Blunt, who was largely responsible for the *débâcle* of the South Seas Bubble but was made by Walpole and the Court to seem *solely* responsible for it, might have been fashioned expressly to fit the Weber-Tawney thesis which links protestant Dissent with Capitalism; and accordingly it is worth pausing on him for a moment. It was not left for the present century to see connections between Dissent and speculative finance. A Victorian dissenter, the linguist and traveller Sir John Bowring, in his *Autobiographical Recollections* (1877) reflected:

> In the case of the Jews, persecution drove them from the ordinary pursuits of life to money-making and usury (I attach no disgraceful meaning to the word), just as our Dissenters, tormented by the Test and Corporation Acts, betook themselves to

merchandise and manufactures, and, in both cases, the results have been eminently successful. The Rothschilds and Barings may attribute their present opulence to the sufferings of their forefathers.

But of course Rothschild, Baring and Blunt alike dealt in no merchandise but money; they *manufactured* nothing. (Why Blunt failed, where Baring and Rothschild succeeded, is well brought out by Erskine-Hill.) The distinction which Bowring fails to make had been made, with astonishing acuteness, in Pope's and Blunt's lifetime by the dissenter Defoe, in an essay on 'projectors'; and for an instance of a capitalist (a 'projector') whose activities were valuable and necessary we might take the London Baptist minister, Edward Wallin, who represented the inventor Thomas Newcomen on the syndicate formed in 1716 to exploit the patent protecting the steam engine that Newcomen had invented (see L.T.C. Rolt, *Thomas Newcomen,* 1963). Newcomen (1663-1729) was himself a Baptist, as was his partner John Calley or Cawley in their home town of Dartmouth; and it was Baptists in the Bromsgrove area who some time before 1725 gave Newcomen the chance to construct the working engine which, when he was forty-nine, brought him success. It is not only through literature that we discern Dissent as a close-knit, tribal sub-culture.

Another place where Pope appears to sympathize with a dissenter is in the 'Epilogue to the Satires':

> Let modest Foster, if he will, excell
> Ten metropolitans in preaching well.

This is James Foster, born in Exeter in 1697, who is said to have adopted about 1718 'the arian creed, though he at last settled in what may be denominated low socinianism'. After serving obscure and impoverished congregations in Somerset and Wiltshire, Foster moved to London in 1724 as joint pastor of the General Baptist congregation, Barbican. (That he was of the Arminian *General* Baptists is important.) It was shortly thereafter that he became famous. A manuscript of the time describes his 'evening lecture on the Lord's-day at the Old Jewry': 'Here was a confluence of persons of every rank, station, and quality. Wits, freethinkers, numbers of clergy, who, while they gratified their curiosity, had their prepossessions shaken, and their prejudices loosened.' It is not what one expects to hear of a generation allegedly sunk in religious apathy and Erastianism.

Foster's celebrity was crowned when after the failure of the '45 he attended the Earl of Kilmarnock in the Tower under sentence of death for high treason. Foster subsequently published *An Account of the Late Earl of Kilmarnock after his Sentence, and on the Day of his Execution* (1746), which provoked *Kilmarnock's Ghost* (1747), an attack by Malachi Blake, dissenting minister at Blandford, and also a more formidable rejoinder from the appropriately named John Brine (1703-65), who took the ultra-Calvinist position of refusing to evangelize since to do so would be to meddle with God's absolute prerogative of election when and as He pleased. Bogue and Bennett in their *History of Dissenters* (1809), and Joseph Ivimey in his *History of the English Baptists* (1811-30) are sure that Foster was left without a leg to stand on; but they are all fierce Calvinists, so their testimony is suspect. All the same Foster was a dubious character, and it's not easy to see why Pope should pay him a gratuitous compliment. When Topham Beauclerk put the question in 1780 – 'Why did Pope say this?' – he was told by Doctor Johnson: 'Sir, he hoped it would vex somebody.' This we may be happy to take as conclusive. Yet the significance of James Foster for our present enquiry is considerable. His career shows that Isaac Watts was not alone in his generation of dissenters, in making the dissenting pulpit a rostrum for expounding and recommending the Augustan-Hanoverian cultural compromise. Where perhaps he *was* alone was in doing this while yet escaping – though by a hair's breadth sometimes – such divagations into heresy as Foster fell into or cheerfully embraced.

Certainly Johnson, who had as sharp a nose for heresy as any dissenter, and as hearty a detestation of it, was not likely to overlook the differences between Watts and Foster; as we see he did not from Dr Thomas Campbell's *Diary of a Visit to England in 1775* (Sydney, 1854; ed. J.L. Clifford, Cambridge, 1947), which records that 'when Mrs Thrale quoted something from Foster's *Sermons*, Johnson flew into a passion, and said that Foster was a man of mean ability, and of no original thinking'. Hester Thrale perhaps remembered Johnson's reprimand. At any rate she is to be found, long after she had become Mrs Piozzi and forfeited Johnson's esteem by the change, indeed fifteen years after Johnson had died, annotating Watts's *Philosophical Essays* and writing rather touchingly, against a paragraph by Watts: 'I *think* this was likewise Doctor Johnson's Opinion – I *think* so.' In the margin of another paragraph she exclaims: 'This is like Ajax's Prayer in the Iliad. O admirable Isaac Watts!' So far was Watts still, in 1800, from being read and esteemed only by dissenters and Evangelicals – he was studied still in solid Establishment circles, at least in those which kept alive the memory of Samuel Johnson (see James P.R. Lyell, *Mrs Piozzi and Isaac Watts, Being Annotations in the Autograph of Mrs Piozzi on a Copy of the First Edition of the 'Philosophical Essays ' of Watts*, 1934, pp. 30, 26).

Among the dissenters of Watts's time there were many a great deal more outlandish and unaccountable than James Foster. One engagingly eccentric figure, of great consequence among the dissenters since she was the eldest daughter of General Ireton by Bridget Cromwell, the Protector's daughter, was Mrs Bendish, uncompromisingly devoted to the memory of her grandfather. We are told that she 'looked upon him as the first and greatest of mankind, and also as the best'. Widowed in 1707, Mrs Bendish survived until 1728, living mostly near Yarmouth. A Lowestoft acquaintance recorded, of this formidable lady:

> As the whole of Mrs. B.'s personal economy was not of the common form, her hours of visiting went generally out of the common season. She would very frequently come to visit at nine or ten at night, and sometimes later if the doors were not shut up. On such visits she generally stayed until about one in the morning. Such late visits in those sober times, were considered by her friends as highly inconvenient yet nobody complained of them to her: the respect she universally commanded, gave her a license in this and many other irregularities. Mrs. B. never would suffer a servant to attend her. God, she said, was her guard, and she would have no other! Her dress on these visits, though it was in a taste of her own, was always grave and handsome. At about one in the morning, she used to put herself on the top of her mare, or into the chaise, and set off on her return. When the mare began to move, Mrs B. began to sing a psalm or one of Watts's hymns in a very loud but not a very harmonious key (THOMAS MILNER, *Life, Times, and Correspondence of Watts*, 1845, pp. 294ff).

It is clear that Mrs Bendish, vigilant keeper of the ark of the Cromwellian covenant, did not share the conviction, expressed by romanticizing commentators since her day and into our own, that Watts's more accommodating policies for Dissent represented a betrayal of that intransigent tradition. And for that matter Watts could be intransigent too – as when his loyal poem of 1705 to Queen Anne was given a vicious 'Palinodia' in 1721, because the Queen had let in the Tories ten years before; he would accommodate only up to a point.

Much more of a thorn in Watts's flesh was the notorious John Dunton, who was thought by some of his contemporaries to be not entirely, or not at all times, sane. This is the Dunton who wrote in 1696-7 a monthly paper exposing prostitution, *The Night Walker: or, Evening Rambles in Search after Lewd Women*, in which, according to Ian Watt, 'a virtuous purpose is avowed as strongly and as unconvincingly as it is today by sensational journalists engaged in similar appeals to public lubricity'. A vigorous and imaginative journalist like his greater contemporary Defoe, Dunton's lubricity more than once flickered suggestively about Watts's relations with the once-famous dissenting poetess, Elizabeth Rowe (1674-1737). Dunton's connection with Mrs Rowe went back to the 1690s when, as Elizabeth Singer, she published her early 'pindarick' poems in Dunton's *Athenian Mercury*. Some years later she is to be found engaged in a coquettish correspondence with Matthew Prior, himself of dissenting stock and a master of amorous badinage. Married in 1710, she was widowed five years later, and thenceforward applied herself to living down her early celebrity as 'the Pindarick Lady', becoming instead the Mrs Rowe who was famous throughout the eighteenth century as a protégée of Watts, 'devoted to pious works and devotional poetry'. Watts is said to have wanted to marry her, and to have warned Dunton to stop referring to her. How much he had to fear because of this relationship appears from the sneering *double entendre* in Edward Young's 5th Satire:

> What angels would those be, who thus excel
> In theologics, could they sew as well!
> Yet why should not the fair her text pursue?
> Can she more decently the doctor woo?
> Isaac, a brother of the canting strain,
> When he has knocked at his own skull in vain,
> To beauteous Marcia often will repair,
> With a dark text to light it at the fair.
> O how his pious soul exults to find
> Such love for holy men in womankind!
> Charm 'd with her learning, with what rapture he
> Hangs on her bloom, like an industrious bee;
> Hums round about her, and with all his power
> Extracts sweet wisdom from so fair a flower.

From Young, a parson, Watts could not perhaps expect much else; but from a poet explicitly writing in the dissenting interest he might reasonably ask for more charity. How Dunton complied may be seen from his curious long poem of 1710, 'The Dissenting Doctors: A Poem on the Late Promotion of Mr Daniel Williams, Mr Edmund Calamy, Mr Joshua Oldfield, to the Degree of Doctor of Divinity.' (These doctorates, incidentally, were – as they had to be for more than a century afterwards – Scottish, not English.) The slipperiness of Dunton's tone is remarkable:

> Not Sleep beneath the shade in flowery fields
> To th' weary Traveller more pleasure yields;
> Nor, to assuage his thirst, the living Spring
> In heat of Summer more delight does bring,
> Than unto me thy well-tun'd Numbers do,
> In which thou dost both please and profit too.
> Born in a clime where storms and tempests grow,
> Far from the place where Helicon does flow,
> The Muses travel'd far to bless thy sight,
> And taught thee how to think, and how to write:
> 'Tis Doctor Watts, or farewell Rhyming quite!
> Thou dost not write like those who brand the times,
> And themselves most, with sharp satiric Rhymes;
> Nor does thy Muse with filthy Verses tear
> The modest Virgin 's chaste and tender ear.
> Free from their faults, whate'er thy Muse indites,
> Not Ovid nor Tibullus softer writes:
> The choice of tuneful words t'express our thought,
> By thy example we have first been taught.
> Our English Virgil, and our Pindar too,
> In this, 'tis said, some negligence did shew,
> But you are Doctor to the chiming Crew.
> To thee alone we are beholden more

> Than all the Poets of the Times before.
> Thy Muse, inspir'd with a more pious rage,
> Did first refine the Genius of our Age.
> In thee a clear and female softness shin'd,
> With masculine vigour, force and judgment join'd.

This sounds handsome enough, unless the hyperboles – 'To thee alone we are beholden more/Than all the Poets of the Times before' – are made deliberately ludicrous. But despite the spattering of the page with Ovid and Tibullus, Virgil and Pindar, 'Doctor to the chiming Crew' may well be thought a left-handed compliment. We may well suspect, as we do at times with Defoe, that Dunton himself didn't know whether his tongue was in his cheek, or not. In any case we have read, a few lines earlier:

> The next Dissenter that does preach in Town,
> Who has no Titles got, nor Doctor's Gown
> (But merits more than any Doctor can).
> Is pious, learned, rhyming, modest *Watts*;
> 'He that did tune his harp by Chloris' notes;
> Nay was all ear, when on the banks of Thames
> He listen'd to her sweet harmonious strains;
> Listen'd! – and well he might; for when she sings,
> His zeal did rise on her seraphic wings...'

with the footnote: 'Reader, consult Mr Watts's Poem to Mrs Singer, on the sight of some of her Divine Poems never printed... for your better understanding these five lines...' When the self-appointed literary spokesmen for the dissenting interest were characters as turbulent and unstable as Dunton, or even Defoe, it was not without constant struggle that Watts could maintain simplicity, sobriety, and order as the distinguishing traits of his own life as of his poetry, and of the conduct he inculcated in his congregations.

With admirable loyalty, Johnson is solicitous of Watts's reputation on this vulnerable flank where his name is linked with Mrs Rowe's. For in a little-known review Johnson praised 'the copiousness and luxuriance of Mrs Rowe', together with 'her brightness of imagery, her purity of sentiments'. And he says of her and Watts together: 'They were pure from all the heresies of an age, to which every opinion is become a favourite that the universal Church has hitherto detested... But to them all human eulogies are vain, whom I believe applauded by angels and numbered with the just.' This was in *The Literary Magazine; or Universal Review*, in 1756 (see Boswell's *Life*, edited by Glover, 1901, vol. I, p. 204).

Notes to Lecture 2

On the aesthetic sense of Calvin, and the aesthetics of Calvinism, see Henry. R. Van Til, *The Calvinistic Concept of Culture*, 1959, pp. 107, 109, 111. Brunetière is quoted by Van Til from *The Presbyterian and Reformed Review*, XII, 1901, pp. 392-414.

p. 24 *direct access to the culture which produced* Athalie
Doddridge's reading of Racine is recorded in a letter of 1723:

> Of all their dramatic poets, I have met with none that I admire so much as Racine. It is impossible not to be charmed with the pomp, elegance, and harmony of his language, as well as the majesty, tenderness, and propriety of his sentiments. The whole is conducted with a wonderful mixture of grandeur and simplicity, which sufficiently distinguishes him from the dullness of some tragedians, and the bombast of others.

In the same letter Doddridge recommends Fenelon, whom Watts also admired, saying that 'in his *Posthumous Essays* and his *Letters*, there are many admirable thoughts in practical and experimental religion, and very beautiful and divine sentiments in devotion'. On the other hand Watts no more than Bossuet could look with sympathy on Fenelon's enthusiasm for the mystical quietism of Mme Guyon; and we may suppose him to have that side of Fenelon in mind when he goes on to say that 'sometimes in large paragraphs, or in whole chapters together, you find him in the clouds of mystic divinity, and he never descends within the reach of common ideas or common sense'. There speaks the Watts who was a devoted admirer of Locke. (For the whole of this paragraph, see A.G. Matthews and G.F. Nuttall, 'The Literary Interests of Nonconformists in the 18th Century', *Transactions of the Congregational Historical Society*, vol. 12, 1933-6, pp. 337-8.)

As might be expected, the Wesleyans were less chary of Mme Guyon (and the Quakers, incidentally, co-opted her very eagerly). In John Wesley's *Journal* for 1742, we find him reading her *Torrents Spirituels*, and Henry Bett in his *Hymns of Methodism* recognizes imagery from this book in Charles Wesley's *Hymns and Sacred Poems* of 1749. As late as 1776 John Wesley published *An Extract of the Life of Madame Guion*. Cowper translated her extensively, but when his translations were published posthumously in 1801, his editor William Bull remarked with some agitation: 'To infer that the peculiarities of Madame Guion's theological sentiments, were adopted either by Mr. C. or by the Editor, would be... absurd...'

A more extraordinary case of the French presence in eighteenth-century dissenting and Evangelical concerns is the career in English translation and allusion of a sonnet, 'Grand Dieu, tes jugements... ' by Jacques Vallée, Seigneur des Barreaux (1602-73), a famous libertine whom Pascal described as among those 'who would renounce their reason and become brute beasts', who repented, however, and died in retirement. The full story is extremely complicated, and has been disentangled by the meticulous and indispensable Henry Bett. It encompasses Watts's version, 'The Humble Enquiry'. dated 1695 but not published till the second edition of *Lyra Heroica* (1709); Addison quoting the French sonnet in full in the *Spectator;* attacks on John Wesley, by Thomas Church (1745) and Lavington (1749), for having adapted verses from the French: marginalia to Lavington by Mrs Thrale, ascribing the lines to the French source but with a crucial error; numerous reminiscences of the French lines in Charles Wesley's hymns; and a version by the Evangelical Henry Kirke White, 'Thy judgments, Lord, are just... '

The title of Bishop Lavington's notorious polemic, *The Enthusiasm of Methodists and Papists Compared* (1749-51), hints at how anti-French chauvinism and anti-Papist prejudice could be mustered in some quarters of the Establishment against the often more charitable and cosmopolitan attitudes of dissenters and Wesleyans.

p. 30 *as late as 1960, a historian of Dissent* Erik Routley, *English Religious Dissent,* 1960, p. 137.

Notes to Lecture 3

I quote Lucy Aikin from *Memoirs, Miscellanies and Letters of the Late Lucy Aikin,* edited by Philip Hemery Le Breton, 1864, p. 196. My quotations from and about Halevy's *The Birth of Methodism in England* (originally 1906), together with much of my information about him and his view of Methodism generally, come from the invaluable edition translated and introduced by Bernard Semmel (1971). The letter to Doddridge beginning, 'I will take this occasion...' is reproduced in Duncan Coomer's modest but very useful *English Dissent under the Early Hanoverians* (1946). I have drawn also on Roger Thomas's, 'Philip Doddridge and Liberalism in Religion ', in G. Nuttall (ed.), *Philip Doddridge* (1951). The passages about the Wesley hymns quoted from E. P. Thompson's *Making of the English Working Class* (1964) will be found on pp. 40 and 371-2 of the New York edition. All quotations comparing Charles Wesley with William Blake are from Martha Winburn England in *Hymns Unbidden*

(1966).

p. 33 *Accommodation, yes; but at this rate? And on this scale?*
It was in 1737 that William Law told his fellow non-juror, John Byrom, 'that the Quakers were a subtle worldly-minded people, that they began with the contempt of learning, riches etc., but now were a politic worldly society, and strange people'. Seven years earlier Byrom had decided for himself: 'It is their life, their love of the world, their wisdom as to this generation, their luxury and neglect of that Spirit which they particularly pretend to, which I blame in a Quaker as well as in myself and others' (see Stephen Hobhouse, *William Law and Eighteenth-Century Quakerism*, 1928, pp. 119, 146). To be sure, 'accommodation' among the Quakers took a special form, since the external marks of it were a newly rigid observance of habits of dress, demeanour and address, which served to mark them off at a glance. On this, and on how nevertheless it masked a profound accommodation with the secular spirit of the age, see A. Neave Brayshaw, *The Quakers: Their Story and Message*, 1927, ch. XII.

Lucy Aikin, who quotes not from *The Spleen* but from another of Green's poems, 'The Seeker', had good reason to remember Green's poems, and to recognize their significance, for it was her own father, John Aikin, who in 1796 had re-issued them with an introduction that is still the most just and enthusiastic of all tributes to this poet:

> He had not, like a Gray or a Collins, his mind early fraught with all the stores of classic literature; nor could he devote months and years of learned leisure to the exquisite charms of versification or the refined ornaments of diction. He was a man of business, who had only the intervals of his regular employment to improve his mind by reading and reflection; and his poems appear to have been truly no more than hasty effusions for the amusement of himself and his particular friends. Numbers of works thus produced are born and die in the circle of every year; and it is only by the stamp of real genius that these have been preserved from a similar fate. But nature had bestowed on the author a strong and quick conception, and a wonderful power of bringing together remote ideas so as to produce the most novel and striking effects. No man ever thought more copiously or with more originality; no man ever less fell into the beaten track of commonplace ideas and expressions. That cant of poetical phraseology which is the only resource of an ordinary writer, and which those of a superior class find it difficult to avoid, is scarcely anywhere to be met with in him. He has no hackneyed combinations of substantives and epithets; none of the tropes and figures of a schoolboy's Gradus. Often negligent, sometimes inaccurate, and not unfrequently prosaic, he redeems his defects by a rapid variety of beauties and brilliancies all his own, and affords more food to the understanding or imagination in a line or a couplet, than common writers in half a page (LUCY AIKIN, *Memoir of John Aikin, M.D.*, 1823, vol. 2, pp. 225-7).

Lucy Aikin declared that 'no one, I believe, of all his critical pieces was composed with greater pleasure in his subject than this'. And it is easy to believe her, for Aikin's own copy of verses in rhyming octosyllabics, 'Horatian Philosophy' – by no means a despicable performance – is quite plainly an exercise in Green's manner, and not just in the manner, but in substance too. As Aikin's daughter says, still speaking of Green's poetry:

> While the profusion of uncommon thoughts and witty allusions with which it is studded amused his fancy, the pervading spirit of the whole had much in it to attract his sympathetic approbation. It is that of a philosophy somewhat on the Horatian model, in which habitual serenity of mind is sought by a renunciation of the common objects of ambition, by temperate enjoyments and modest wishes, by the indulgence of a vein of free speculation, and by a general indifference and neutrality in the disputes which chiefly agitate the world (*op. cit.*, pp. 186-7).

And the natural affinity between the Horatian frame of mind and the Quaker at its best, or indeed the Unitarian at its best, is something that deserves pondering, and perhaps study – for instance, as it bears upon a Quaker poet of our day, like Basil Bunting.

John Aikin is an important witness in any case, as the memorialist of those years, in the 1770s and 1780s, when the success of the Unitarian academy at Warrington shifted the intellectual, if not the imaginative, centre of the kingdom from London to an area bounded by Manchester to the east and Liverpool to the west. In both these cities the influence of the Warrington focus of intellectual endeavour persisted through several decades after the Warrington academy had been disbanded. Aikin's memorials of this 'vortex', and of the several personalities that whirled within it, are invaluable precisely because his own equable and Horatian temperament was not shared by his Warrington colleagues; and so our sense of their injudiciousness is gathered from a testimony that is at pains to minimize it. For example, what an unmanageable coxcomb Gilbert Wakefield was, is conveyed between the lines of Aikin's obituary tribute to him (*op. cit.*, pp. 364-5), and is nowhere so unmistakable as in Wakefield's verses responding to the poem with which Aikin welcomed him from prison (*op. cit.*, pp. 237-8):

> Next to that first of comforts to the soul,
> The plaudit of a conscience self-approv'd,
> AIKIN! I deem the gratulation sweet
> Of sympathising friendship, and a Muse
> Terse, uncorrupt, ingenuous, bold and free.

'The plaudit of a conscience self-approv'd' ('Self in benevolence absorb'd and lost', is what Wakefield modestly claims for himself in a later verse) very clearly characterized the Warrington Unitarian Jacobins as a group, Joseph Priestley not excepted. And such self-righteously self-appointed intellectual *élites*, usually ranging themselves on the revolutionary Left, have been a volatile element in English political life from John Aikin's day to ours. Aikin himself, though he pamphleteered in 1790 against Parliament's refusal to revoke the Test Act, was a more admirable and engaging person than the celebrities he chose to memorialize. And his daughter's memoir of him is, though an unexciting book, a worthy one. Nowhere in it, however, do we find anything to set beside what Lucy Aikin confessed to, in a letter of 1831 to Channing, about what it could mean to be brought up an English Unitarian under George III:

> the atmosphere of a sect and a party, which it was my fate to breathe from childhood, narrowed my affections within strait limits. Under the notion of a generous zeal for freedom, truth, and virtue, I cherished a set of prejudices and antipathies which placed beyond the pale of my charity not the few, but the many, the mass of my compatriots. I shudder now to think how *good a hater* I was in the days of my youth. Time and reflection, a wider range of acquaintance, and a calmer state of the public mind, mitigated by degrees my bigotry; but I really knew not what it was to open my heart to the human race until I had drunk deeply into [*sic*] the spirit of your writings (*Memoirs, Miscellanies and Letters*, pp. 243-4).

p. 35 *Halévy … on this point … seems to be quite simply* wrong.
When Halévy seventy years ago, and E.P. Thompson more recently, saw the Methodist evangelists as doing for the dissenting interest what Hanoverian ministers like Watts and Doddridge should have done but didn't, they were only echoing what historians of Dissent have been saying since the beginning of the nineteenth century. Indeed the unanimity on this point is so remarkable that one would be frightened of questioning it, were it not that there is so plainly no agreed mark by which religious decline and religious revival may be measured. What is a sign of demoralization for one historian – for instance, Doddridge allowing Whitefield to preach from his pulpit – is, for another, a symptom of reawakening vigour.

A clear example of the received opinion – and without doubt an influential one – is the second volume of Henry W. Clark's *History of Englísh Nonconformity* (1913), wherein Book III, concerned with the years 1660 to 1736, is entitled, 'The Fading Ideal', and within that span the years 1714 to 1736 are called 'The Darkness before the Dawn', whereas the Methodist years, from 1736 to 1800, are treated of in Book IV under the title, 'The Partial Return to the Ideal'. If we look in Clark for the proof of these contentions we find that, though indeed he pays lip-service to such immeasurable entities as 'feeling' and 'fervour', his ultimate measure is not religious, certainly not doctrinal, *but political;* he is concerned for Church government, and for the relations between that government and the government of the State. Such matters are certainly important; but to look to them for the measure of religious health or decline is surely inadequate and even pedantic. Thus modern readers can hardly be expected to shake their heads in appalled revulsion, as Clark seems to want them to do, when he reveals (*op. cit*., p. 166) that Thomas Abney, Watts's patron, as a London alderman took advantage of the Occasional Conformity Act. And Clark is even less compelling, appeals even more pedantically to a pristine Reformation principle which succeeding years had made inapplicable, when he tries to convict Watts himself of backsliding (pp. 163-4):

> It is worth while in this connection to take a glance at what may be called Congregationalism in a transition stage, as represented in the message sent by Isaac Watts to the Mark Lane Independent Church, when it called him to its pulpit in 1702. Watts had Congregationalism so to say in his blood; for his father was in jail for it when he was born in 1674, and his mother nursed him upon the prison steps; so that the son was from the first too much overshadowed by the Congregational idea to travel as far from it as some were going. Yet, in giving some account of his views to the Mark Lane congregation, although he uses the old language as to every society of saints being a true Church, admits that a Church is not bound to submit itself blindly to its pastor's government, and admits also that in *some* matters a pastor ought to do nothing without the people's consent, he nevertheless declares that in the absence of a pastor a Church is 'incomplete' and without 'power in itself to administer all ordinances among them': there are various hints that the minister is something more than the *primus inter pares* which true Congregationalism holds him... If one were unaware that such a tendency was at work upon a wider stage, Watts's words and clauses might pass unsuspected by, buried as they are among words and clauses of other tenor; but when one knows, then one discerns, in phrases slipped in here and there, how that tendency was claiming occasional visiting rights where it could not as yet hope to be made perfectly at home. And if Watts, for whom Congregational air had been mingled with the earliest breaths he drew, and for whom there was in heredity's cord so marked a Congregational strand – if Watts could go so far, one may conjecture how much further and how much more easily Congregationalists of less high and strenuous ancestry would be led away.

The strain of special pleading in this account is surely obvious; it provokes the retort that precisely because Watts knew at first hand or at one remove what persecution had meant, he had a better right than any subsequent commentator to decide when, and how far, to take note of the maxim *autres temps, autres moeurs*. One may reflect also that a pastor who has in his flock such black sheep as John Dunton is well advised to preserve some residual authority for himself and his office.

Moreover, with all his enthusiasm for the evangelizing of Wesley and Whitefield, Clark is forced to concede that two important dissenting communions – the Particular Baptists and the Quakers – seem to have gone through the eighteenth century largely unaffected by it. More generally, however, no one should want to deny that Dissent *was* affected, and in many ways profitably, by the Wesleyan and Evangelical Revival. This was not denied by R.W. Dale who, however, stands almost alone among historians of Dissent in maintaining that, if much was gained, much also was lost:

> The Revival ... helped to suppress the original type of Independent character. Reserve, a firm self-restraint in habits of expenditure and in amusements, patient, resolute industry, punctuality in the discharge of all obligations, a family life governed by exact method, a keen interest in theology, and a keen interest in politics, a delight in books and in intellectual pursuits of the severer kind, a strict Observance of Sunday – these were the characteristics of the men who had been disciplined by Independent traditions. The great Independents of the Commonwealth who had been formed by other influences were freer and more genial; but in the course of a generation or two the prevailing type of Independent character had taken this austere form. Watts deplored the irregular habits of the Dissenters of his time; but in many Churches the type was still preserved... The authority of the original type of character was still asserted by the public opinion of the Churches. Any serious departure from it was condemned.
>
> But when Congregational Churches began to be thronged with Churchmen who had inherited another ideal of Christian morals and conduct... the whole spirit of the Churches was changed. The moral traditions of Independency were lost. The gravity, severity, and solid strength, to which the habits of an earlier age had formed the members of Congregational Churches, disappeared. The intellectual earnestness also disappeared. Congregationalists ceased to be keen theologians, and they ceased to be keen politicians (R.W. DALE, in A.W.W. Dale (ed.), *History of English Congregationalism*, 1907).

Not everyone will be so attracted as Dale plainly is, by gravity, severity and reserve. However, by his account, what was lost was *culture*, or all those elements of culture which go along with 'intellectual earnestness'.

It was George II who was for the dissenters, and long remained in dissenting tradition, the paragon of princes; and the high-water mark of the dissenters' royalism was when Doddridge and others were active in 1745 in raising levies to oppose the Pretender, despite the civic disabilities which debarred them from serving in arms in any responsible position themselves. George III, though the dissenters had high hopes of him at the start, soon alienated most of them when he identified himself with the policies of Bute; and for the dissenters, conscious of close ties with their fellow sectaries across the Atlantic, the attempt to coerce the American colonies was a bitter pill which many of them (in striking contrast to the Methodists) refused to swallow. The Baptist minister John Collet Ryland scared the schoolboy Robert Hall by the violence with which he declared himself for General Washington; and not many dissenters could be as sorrowfully temperate as John Bowring – a Presbyterian, and grandfather of his celebrated namesake, the Victorian polyglot – when he wrote to his cousin in 1778:

> After the most deliberate consideration of the nature of the quarrel between us, I freely own it appears to me that they are right and we wrong, nor is there anything I more ardently wish for relative to our national concerns than a thorough change both of men and manners in the British Cabinet. Yet, as an Englishman, I by no means wish to see my country vanquished by the arms of France (*Autobiographical Recollections of Sir John Bowring,* 1877, pp. 2-3).

Thenceforward until the end of the century relations between the dissenters and the Crown were strained once again by mutual suspicions. Nevertheless, though the fact is seldom acknowledged, there were in this period dissenters who supported the national policies; and however it may have been earlier in the century, it is not true of this or of later periods that a Tory dissenter is a contradiction in terms:

> Dissenters could always be found who approved of the American War; who petitioned Parliament against the extension of Toleration; who supported Pitt and joined the volunteers during the French Revolution. If we find Richard Price, Joseph Priesdey,

> Robert Hall and Robert Robinson on the one side, there were the Rev. Edward Pickard, the Rev. John Martin, the Rev. John Clayton and the Rev. David Rivers on the other (ANTHONY LINCOLN, *Some Political and Social Ideas of English Dissent, 1763-1800,* 1938, pp. 21-2).

In fact, of the four names cited here as belonging to the less than loyal Opposition in this period, three – Price, Priestley and Robinson – were, or ended up as, heterodox Unitarians quite unrepresentative of Dissent as a whole; and the fourth – Robert Hall, the Baptist – is ranked with them on the score of a couple of youthful polemics which he soon by implication disowned. Of the four 'Tory' names, the most interesting is that of John Clayton (1754-1843).

Clayton was at one time closely associated with the mercurial Sir Harry Trelawney, of the ancient Cornish family, with whom he took Congregationalism into Cornwall, itinerating from the baronet's family seat at Looe. How genteel Dissent could be at this period appears from an account of Sir Harry's being 'publicly set apart to the office of pastor or overseer, in the church of Christ, by the laying on of the hands of the Presbytery':

> This solemnity took place at Southampton, April 22nd, 1777, with more of pomp and circumstance than usually attend services, when administered according to the simple forms of Protestant Dissenters. A large platform was raised, covered with green cloth, and a velvet cushion provided for the young baronet to kneel upon. Constables were in attendance, to guard against disorder and disturbance. The crowd, anxious to witness the celebration of the rite, under circumstances by no means common, was immense and composed of all classes, fashionable and unfashionable, from the town and neighbourhood...

Alas, Sir Harry later went Socinian.

When the Birmingham mob rioted against Joseph Priestley, Clayton preached a sermon, subsequently published, which – says his Victorian biographer – 'embodied some conservative sentiments, which would not be wholly endorsed by many of his brethren then, and still less now'. To this the 27-year-old Robert Hall replied with a pamphlet, *Christianity Consistent with a Love of Freedom* (1791). But Clayton was not to be deflected-

> When the mind of the public was exasperated by party politics, and the horrors of the French Revolution made every ear tingle, and many hearts bleed, he set his face like a flint against what he termed 'the revolutionary mania'; and while barbarous atrocities were practised in a neighbouring land, and corresponding societies, treasonable plots, seditious libels, and furious demagogues, were in activity at home, he felt it to be his duty to insist much on relative obligations – especially those which refer to the subject and the magistrate...
>
> ... he endeavoured to discriminate between the exploded doctrines of passive obedience and non-resistance, and that rational, just, and religious deference to constituted authorities, so indispensable to the liberty, safety, and prosperity of the empire.
>
> The course he took proved offensive to not a few of his ministerial brethren; and to the whole fraternity of Jacobins and revolutionists, who rose up in arms against him, in squibs, pamphlets, and caricatures...
>
> ... He tasked all his strength to stem the torrent of democratic fury (T.M. AVELING, *Memorials of the Clayton Family,* 1867, pp. 145-6).

It comes as no surprise that Clayton, professing these views (which incidentally were firmly upheld in the next generation from the pulpit of his eldest son), was possessed of private means – which at least takes care of any allegation that he was on the Government payroll. Moreover, by 1800 when he was minister of the Weighhouse Chapel in London (where Mark Rutherford was to admire the preaching of his successor, Thomas Binney), his congregations were affluent and genteel, 'for there might have been counted at the doors of the Weighhouse chapel, from sixteen to twenty equipages, or full-appointed gentlemen's carriages, waiting to convey their owners, after public service, to their respective suburban villages'. What is significant is that his biographer Aveling, sixty years later, conveying this information, seems to speak of it as a phenomenon long vanished from the scene. It looks as if an audience for Dissent recognizably similar in social composition to that of Watts survived as late as 1800, but had vanished from dissenting chapels by 1860. If so, it may be that when it vanished it took with it from dissenting households the secular literary culture represented by what John Clayton read with his children (*op. cit.*, p. 100): 'Watts's *Lyrics*, Cowper's *Poems*, the *Odyssey of Homer*, as versified by that author, Pope's *Iliad*, and the *Dramas* of Hannah More.' Already in 1807 David Bogue and James Bennett in their *History of Dissenters* were very suspicious of Watts's versions of the Psalms, and explicitly lamented that Cowper should have spent any of his time on an author so unserious as Homer. Nineteenth century Dissent was by and large to follow their lead, not John Clayton's.

p. 41 *no more incentive from within its ranks to relate the sub-culture to the national culture, than there is on the part of the Establishment...* T.B. Shepherd's *Methodism and the Literature of the Eighteenth Century* (1940), which might seem to address itself to just this topic, fails to live up to the promise of its title. It is particularly barren and perfunctory on the Wesleys' poetry. It has value, however, in directing attention to John Wesley's prose, especially his political and controversial writings like *A Farther Appeal to Men of Reason and Religion*. George Lawton's *John Wesley's English: A Study of his Literary Style* (1962) has more to say on this, but has the opposite defects to Shepherd's book, in that it stays unmanageably close to a card-index concordance to Wesley's works. In both these works may be found hints towards, and material for, a study of Wesleyan prose as carrying forward into the later eighteenth century, for the most part addicted to a more 'Corinthian' and ornamental prose, the easy, trenchant and conversational styles of Swift on the one hand, Robert South on the other – both of them masters whom Wesley appealed to and recommended. Such an investigation would be valuable.

Certainly what might on that showing be claimed for Methodism cannot be claimed for Dissent. By the end of the century dissenters were writing an English that is tumid and glittering; in particular Robert Hall, however estimable on other counts, is nowadays unreadable, though in his own day he was highly praised as an oratorical stylist.

Notes to Lecture 4

For dissenting magazines, see F.E. Mineka, *The Dissidence of Dissent* (1944). Olinthus Gregory's memoir of Robert Hall I read in *The Baptist Library*, 1843, vol. 3, pp. 225-78. For Elizabeth Haldane, see *Mrs Gaskell and her Friends* (1931); and for Augustine Birrell, *Things Past Redress* (1937). For Michael Faraday, see Henry Bence Jones, *The Life and Letters of Faraday*, 2 vols, (1870); L. Pearce Williams, *Michael Faraday: A Biography* (1965); and Joseph Agassi, *Faraday as a National Philosopher* (1971). I am grateful to my friend Robert Conquest for pointing out how Faraday's was a case I ought to take account of.

p. 55 *This Unitarian strategy... first evolved in the 1770s...*
Dr Johnson would not have made the mistake which bedevils historians to the present day, of regarding Unitarians as merely the Left and liberal wing of English Dissent, rather than (what orthodox dissenters have seen in them) pernicious and alarming heretics. Accordingly, Boswell because of his own 'democratical' learnings cannot be trusted when he implies that Johnson was, or would have been, disconcerted by the Unitarian Joseph Towers (1737-99), in his *Letter to Dr Samuel Johnson, Occasioned by his Late Political Publications* (1775), and his *Essay on the Life, Character, and Writings of Dr Samuel Johnson* (1787). It is misleading to have Towers indexed in the Birkbeck/Hill edition of Boswell's

Life, simply as 'dissenting minister'.

The same failure to distinguish the Unitarians from the rest of Dissent marks even an essay so learned and elegant as Anthony Lincoln's *Some Political and Social Ideas of English Dissent, 1763-1800* (1938). Here, having declared (p. 30) of the 'Rational Dissenters' (i.e. Unitarians and their fellow travellers) that, 'equally disliked by Churchmen and orthodox Dissenters, they formed a cultural unit remote from and above the Nonconformist community', Lincoln can none the less decide, with no awareness of inconsistency, that 'the history of significant dissenting opinion in the years 1763-1800 is the history of the Rational Dissenters'. The trap, of course, is precisely in the word 'significant'; Lincoln believes, along with modern commentators generally, that political opinions are necessarily more 'significant' than theological ones. But on that assumption there is no way to explain why David Bogue and James Bennett, or Joseph Ivimey and Robert Hall, or John Wesley and Samuel Johnson, behaved and wrote as they did.

Lincoln is a scrupulous historian, and he presents all the evidence for a quite different reading of events from the one he puts forward himself. (There can hardly be higher praise.) Particularly valuable are the pages he devotes to the matter of the Dissenting Application to Parliament in 1772-3. This is an obscure episode, and no one can be blamed for not knowing about it. And yet it is momentous for understanding the history of the dissenting interest. Lincoln explains the 'new situation' for dissenters, out of which came this appeal for a reconsideration of the Toleration Act.

> Briefly, that new situation was this. The benefits of the Toleration Act could be enjoyed under certain restrictions, the most notable being a compulsory subscription to all save three of the Thirty-nine Articles and certain portions of two others. Similar restrictions hampered dissenting schoolmasters and educationalists. *At the time of the passing of the Toleration Act, the Dissenters had been, for the most part, strictly Calvinist, with few objections of conscience to the Articles themselves* – so few that their dissent was represented by opponents as nothing but a contumacious obstinacy over 'things indifferent'. *So complete had been the revolution in beliefs of English Dissent in the century after 1689, that few of the Applicants of 1772-3 could comply with the subscription required.* Deprived of the protection of the Act, the position of the advanced Dissenters was, on paper at least, full of peril – a peril likely to become a very real one, should the intolerant enthusiasm of the Methodists ever penetrate to the Establishment.

Here the italics are mine, and with good reason. For the sentences italicized show how misleading it is to proceed – as Lincoln himself tries to do, as many since have done, and continue to do – as if the social and political attitudes of dissenters can be studied (in any period, but particularly in the late eighteenth century) in isolation from their *doctrinal* attitudes and convictions. 'Socinian', 'Arian', 'Antinomian', 'Unitarian', 'Trinitarian', 'Calvinist', 'Arminian' – pleasant as it might be to consign these labels to a. realm of 'battles long ago', and of positions long exploded, no responsible historian can afford to regard them thus, since they represent principles for which (as the historical record shows) our forefathers would endure persecution and even martyrdom. Yet so conclusively have they been dismissed into the keeping of specialist disciplines called 'Theology' or 'Divinity' or 'Church History', that it will come as a surprise to many that the 39 Articles of the Church of England constitute a *Calvinist* document, and that at this historical juncture it is a body of dissenters whom we think of as the guardians of the Calvinist doctrines, who *petition to be freed from Calvinist shackles*.

This body of dissenters was, however, unrepresentative. The seventy ministers of the three denominations in London who signed the Application to Parliament of 1772 were wholly out of step with their brethren in the country, as they must have known; and as Lincoln very clearly recounts, it was in fact the provincial dissenters, still mostly Calvinist, who defeated the Application in Parliament in 1773. The consequences were far-reaching: the disunity of Dissent being thus revealed, the Establishment was emboldened to resist in

1790 the far juster demand for a repeal of the Test Act, a demand that was backed by the Calvinist dissenters as well as by the dissenters whom Lincoln calls 'advanced', the Priestleys and Gilbert Wakefields and Robert Robinsons, English *philosophes* who by their arrogance and intemperance thus queered the pitch for Dissent as a whole, permitting the Establishment to pretend for the benefit of the mobs of the 1790s that 'dissenter' meant the same as 'republican' and 'Jacobin'.

This is not the account of these matters that is commonly given by historians of a 'liberal' or 'radical' cast. And indeed I have nowhere seen it plainly asserted that the Arianism of Priestley did far more damage to Dissent than either the hostility of the Establishment or the ambiguous fervour of Methodism. Yet that seems to be the case, and it was moreover damage to dissenting *culture,* for the unabashed philistinism which appears in dissenters of the Regency like Bogue and Bennett, or Joseph Ivimey, quite plainly arises from the reflection that if liberal and philosophical reading leads to Utopian Jacobinism, and to denying the divinity of Christ and the efficacy of the Atonement, then such reading and such interests are what a dissenter must be dissuaded from.

Joseph Priestley himself was perhaps a great man, and a brave one. A more instructively ambiguous figure is Robert Robinson, born at Swaffham in 1734. Anthony Lincoln puts Robinson's *Arcana* of 1773 alongside Furneaux's *Letters to Blackstone as* 'one of the two ablest performances in the literature of Repeal'. 'It surrounds', he says, 'the events of 1772-3 with an atmosphere that can only be described as political romanticism'. And this is meant to be complimentary:

> There is a romantic strain purely English in some dissenting authors of this period, for already Romance was walking in the gardens of England. The personal character and literary qualities of Robert Robinson reveal this blend of candour and sensibility into a humane rationalism...

Robinson, who went on to be Baptist pastor in Cambridge, and to have his biography written by the poet George Dyer, was not always viewed so indulgently. Joseph Ivimey in 1830 in the last volume of his *History of the English Baptists* decided:

> It is not possible to read the memoirs of this celebrated man without perceiving that Mr Robinson became a trifler in regard to serious things, and sceptical as respected the peculiar doctrines of christianity. At first pleading for the innocency of mental error, he was soon found proceeding in the high road towards Socinianism, which he ultimately reached; and, if Dr. Priestley is to be credited, but for this conciliatory scheme, would not have stopped till he had arrived at the dreary regions of infidelity.
>
> It seems almost incredible that the man who at one period of his life wrote the hymns, 'Jesus, lover of my soul', &c. 'Come thou fount of every blessing', &c. and 'Mighty God, while angels bless thee', &c. should have sunk so low as to revile the scripture doctrines of the Trinity and other corresponding truths.

And after quoting from Dyer's *Memoir,* Ivimey observes:

> The concluding part of Mr Robinson's history is indeed most affecting; and there is no way of considering it with any hope respecting his salvation, but that in which the late Dr. Abraham Rees once expressed himself to the writer of this article, that for some time before his death he was evidently *insane*!-

Robinson was certainly exceptional, in that he found his way to Priestleyan 'liberalism' from, of all unlikely quarters, the Particular Baptists, and in Cambridge he took a lot of his Baptist flock with him. Robert Hall, when he succeeded Robinson in 1791, was not able to herd all the Cambridge Baptists back into orthodoxy. Incidentally, William Wordsworth's possession of Dyer's book about Robinson has been adduced to support contentions about the later Wordsworth's religious sentiments, which an accurate idea of what Robinson stood for will by no means bear out.

How the parliamentary events of 1772-3 may be presented – by one who wants to make the new Presbyterians as much part of Dissent as their Calvinist forebears had been – can be seen from Henry W. Clark's *History of English Nonconformity* (vol. 2, 1913):

> It must be confessed... that some non-Presbyterian Nonconformists objected to the Bill granting relief from subscription on the ground that Socinianism would flourish more luxuriantly if the restraints of subscription were removed. Even some who were in favour of the projected change complained that a false colour was being given to the matter by Presbyterian, otherwise Socinian, haste. It is abundantly evident that Presbyterians were far swifter in the race than were the rest. The whole position is perhaps fairly and adequately summed up by saying that in all these things the Presbyterians moved because they were glad and eager to move, while other Nonconformists moved because they must.

But this summary is neither 'fair' nor 'adequate' if it glosses over (as it does) the fact that Presbyterians were potentially and sometimes explicitly republican, whereas the rest of Dissent remained monarchist; nor if it glosses over (as it does) the hostility and resentment felt for the Socinian Presbyterians (or Unitarians – the terms are interchangeable) by the orthodox dissenters. That this was true not only of Calvinist zealots like Bogue and Bennett, but of a moderate like Robert Hall, can be seen from Hall's article in the *Eclectic Review* on Thomas Belsham's *Memoirs of the Late Rev. Theophilus Lindsey* (1812).

p. 55 *as Elizabeth Haldane remarks...*
The superciliousness of the Unitarians is at its most artlessly revealing in the case of Anna Laetitia Aikin, the famous Mrs Barbauld, whose career in the preceding generation set the pattern for both Elizabeth Gaskell and Harriet Martineau. In an extraordinary essay of 1775, Mrs Barbauld declared: 'It is the character of the present age to allow little to sentiment, and all the warm and generous emotions are to be treated as romantic by the supercilious brow of a cold-hearted philosophy.' It is not what we are likely to think of the age that produced Ossian and *The Man of Feeling*. And Mrs Barbauld herself realizes that in so far as 'cold-hearted philosophy' *was* characteristic of the Unitarian Warrington where she had grown up, to just that extent Warrington was out of step with its age. She wants to bring it into step, by adumbrating a characteristically Unitarian *devotion* which shall 'warm' the system of Unitarian belief, and the habits of Unitarian conduct. (Her essay has the title 'Thoughts on the Devotional Taste, and on Sects and Establishments'.) 'Warm', however, is what the Methodists are; and Mrs Barbauld has every sympathy with her Unitarian man of science who, observing what happens at Methodist meetings, decides that devotion had best be left 'to some florid declaimer who professes to work upon the passions of the lower class, where they are so debased by noise and nonsense, that it is no wonder if they move disgust in those of elegant and better-informed minds'. There is, however – Mrs Barbauld urges – 'a devotion, generous, liberal, and humane, the child of more exalted feelings than base minds can enter into'. The 'base minds' of 'the lower class' being thus denied the bare *possibility* of that Christian devotion which the Wesleys were inviting them to (as, of course, parson and pastor had invited them over the years), what must be our astonishment to find Mrs Barbauld and all the Aikins, indeed Unitarians in general, abrogating to themselves the title of 'Democrat' on the basis of having pro-American and later pro-French and of course pro-Negro sympathies! It was the bare-faced impudence of this manoeuvre that made the aged Horace Walpole change his mind about Mrs Barbauld (whom at her debut he had befriended) and in 1791 to explode in indignation, accusing her under the name of 'Deborah', in a letter to Hannah More:

> As I have not your aspen conscience, I cannot forgive the heart of a woman that is party per pale blood and tenderness, that curses our clergy and feels for negroes. Can I forget the 14th of July, when they all contributed their faggot to the fires that her presbytyrants

(as Lord Melcombe called them) tried to light in every Smithfield in the island; and which, as Price and Priesdey applauded in France, it would be folly to suppose they did not only wish, but meant to kindle here? Were they ignorant of the atrocious barbarities, injustice, and violation of oaths committed in France? Did Priestley not know that the clergy there had no option but between starving and perjury?... No, my good friend: *Deborah* may cant rhymes of compassion, but she is a hypocrite; and you shall not make me read her, nor, with all your sympathy and candour, can you esteem her. *Your* compassion for the poor blacks is genuine, sincere from your soul, most amiable; hers a measure of faction (Walpole 's *Letters,* edited by P. Cunningham, 1906, IX, p. 354).

Mrs Barbauld's modern biographer, Betsy Rodgers (*Georgian Chronicle,* 1958, p. 112) is, whether she knows it or not, perpetuating an old and successful deception when she speaks, in relation to this letter from Walpole, of 'his dislike of Dissenters'. Priestley and Price and the Aikins, though they took care to act as if they spoke for Dissent in general, in fact spoke only for that small but influential minority which characteristically pretended to be Presbyterian while being in fact Arian and Unitarian.

Notes to Lecture 5

The critic whom I take to be wrong about George Eliot's Bulstrode is Martin J. Svaglic, 'Religion in the Novels of George Eliot', *Journal of English and Germanic Philology* (1954), reprinted in G.S. Haight (ed.), *A Century of George Eliot Criticism* (1965). For Thomas and Matthew Arnold, and Miall's parliamentary reply to the latter, see David M. Thompson (ed.), *Nonconformity in the Nineteenth Century* (1972). The verses of Tyutchev I quote in the translation by Frances Cornford and Esther Polianowsky Salaman (1943).

p. 65 *It must be said at once that it seems both the Arnolds were right...*
Thirty years after he had collaborated with David Bogue on *The History of Dissenters from the Revolution in 1688, to the Year 1808,* James Bennett, the survivor of the partnership, brought the History up to date with *The History of Dissenters During the Last Thirty Years* (1839). And it is evident that the lapse of years had done nothing to moderate – if anything, it had intensified – the savagely suspicious philistinism of the earlier work. To a mind of this temper Robert Hall could not help but be highly suspect. And in fact Bennett's account of Hall is astonishing in its virulence:

The humble estimate that he formed of himself and his own works, was not mere self-depreciation, but the sentence of sound wisdom. For he was distinguished for taste rather than genius; and excelled in the power of adorning, but not of eliciting truth. Nothing like discovery in mental, moral or theological science is to be found in his works, nor any remarkable proof of intellectual vigour in the highest sense. Some of his most splendid pages are imitations, though plagiarisms they cannot be called; because he so transmuted, and adorned, and improved what he borrowed, as to give him a right to call it his own. His exquisite sensibility to the sublime and beautiful in composition, induced a lofty ambition to excel, which rendered his preparations for the press most laborious, but left him, after all, sincerely dissatisfied with the result; and offended, rather than gratified, by the extravagant praise which his better judgment told him was not true. He wrought into his sentences the trains of thought which led others, as well as himself, to his own conclusions; but which strike the reader as new, because he does not perceive them in the writings of those who are less ambitious of obtaining the approbation of cultivated minds. As a preacher to the literati, he stood alone; but this class of hearers is small, and is usually too conceited to be edified.

So much for 'cultivated minds'! They make up a class that is 'small, and... usually too conceited to be edified'. The espousal of philistinism could hardly be more explicit. Bennett goes on:

> Consciousness of the true character of his mind, led to the miscellaneous and fugitive nature of Mr Hall's works: for, had he attempted a treatise on any great and difficult theme, it would have demonstrated that he was not formed to extricate truth from the involutions that have embarrassed even lofty minds; but was the painter, or the poet, rather than the architect of moral and religious science...
>
> His writings, therefore, are not destined, like those of Edwards, whom he admired... to instruct posterity; but if they are not suffered to lie on the shelf neglected, they will be taken down to rub off the rust. contracted by dealing largely in the compositions of those who valued thoughts as the sons of heaven, and despised words as the daughters of earth.

Bennett, we perceive, is a male chauvinist. But otherwise, this is substantially not unfair: Hall's literary style is meretricious; and his works *do* deserve to lie on the shelf unread, whereas Jonathan Edwards can never cease to fascinate and instruct. But Bennett's revealing distinction – 'the painter, or the poet, rather than the architect' shows that even if Hall had been as good a writer as his age thought him to be, Bennett's verdict would have been the same. This is unmistakable, from the final sentences of his account of Hall:

> Such rarities are, however, fraught with as much danger to the Christian, as benefit to the world. To the communion of which he was a bright ornament, Mr Hall's example would be pernicious, if it led to imitation; for, whatever admiration may be extorted by his printed compositions, it is not in this style that the Gospel should be preached. The rude simplicity of their Bunyan, would secure to the Baptists more effectually the highest honours of usefulness, than the elaborate eloquence of their Hall.

It is *all* the graces of language, not just Robert Hall's, that James Bennett is suspicious of. And accordingly we find him elsewhere explaining, with unmistakable satisfaction (*op. cit.*, p. 306): 'The reading of Dissenters themselves, is very much limited to religious books; for being neither men of leisure nor of wealth, few of them go beyond their favourite hallowed circle. The frequency of preaching among them, and of devotional meetings, leaves them little opportunity, or desire, for a more extensive range.' For conclusive proof of Thomas Arnold's allegation – 'narrowness of view, and a want of learning and a sound critical spirit' – we need go only a few pages further:

> If it be observed, as naturally it may, that the literary mediocrity of most of these publications, says little for the learning or genius of Dissenters; though this is not the object to be proved in a chapter on the state of religion, it may be replied, that the Son of God, when on earth, never visited Athens, to eclipse its philosophers, or Rome, to compete with her orators; but showed the superiority of his character, by confining himself to the paramount interests of eternity, which will retain their worth 'when tongues shall cease, and knowledge shall vanish away'.

This is the voice of that Evangelicalism which, by the received account, rescued eighteenth-century Dissent from stupor and sterility!

It is recognizably the same voice which, thirty years before when Bennett was collaborating with David Bogue, had declared of Isaac Watts (*History of Dissenters*, pp. 111, 473-4): 'This tendency to philosophize upon matters of pure revelation, forms, indeed, the chief fault in the doctor's writings, and may be traced to his connection with the philosophers and literati of the day, whose suffrage to his sentiments he was desirous to gain.' This should be taken along with the historians' exoneration of Thomas Bradbury, of whom it is reported, in a testimony which they quote, that 'he made it his business not only from his own pulpit, but at the Pinner's-hall lecture, to lampoon and satirize the performances of Dr. Watts, and amongst others his hymns and psalms, for which many Christians and churches have reason to bless God'. Bogue and Bennett comment (p. 494): 'Thomas Bradbury... was not the only friend of the Gospel who was prejudiced against the doctor's devotional poetry, and alarmed at the supposed consequences of introducing it into the dissenting worship.' Thus Watts and Hall alike are condemned for having sought the suffrages of 'the literati'.

At such hands Philip Doddridge in his turn could expect to be, at best, damned with faint praise. And so it proves (pp. 482-3):

> He was the soul of every association for religious purposes in the country where he resided; for his heart was too large to be confined to Northampton. He was not equally excellent as a divine; for a mistaken candour often destroyed precision of sentiment, and energy of expression... His publications are deficient in vigour, nor can they be said to evince an exuberance of original thought in the author, or force the profitable labour of thinking upon the reader. Yet they are always serious, respectable, and useful.

Such comments on the luminaries of early Hanoverian Dissent sufficiently show why Bennett thirty years later could allude in passing, when speaking of dissenters' preaching, to 'the inanity that prevailed in the reigns of the first princes of the House of Hanover'.

More far-reaching, however – and quite deliberately so, for Bogue and Bennett are no fools – are the implications of ascribing to Doddridge 'a mistaken candour'. What this means, they had spelled out earlier (p. 384):

> The misapplication of the word candour was more injurious in its effects on religious sentiments, than can now be well conceived. It was supposed to possess indescribable virtues. Candour was sounded from many a pulpit; and like charity, it was supposed to hide a multitude of sins. An orthodox minister who had candour, was to believe that an arian or socinian was a very good man; and that if he was sincere in his opinions, and not rigid in condemning others, he ought not to be condemned himself. The influence of this idea was exceedingly pernicious; for it led to an indifference with respect to truth and error, which depraved both their sentiments and dispositions, which relaxed the springs of Christian integrity and conduct, and gradually brought them to call good evil and evil good, to put light for darkness and darkness for light. This was another of the arian idols. Dr. Doddridge, whose softness of temper led him to more intercourse with ministers of the new opinions than most of his brethren, was sensible of the blindness of this boasted candour, and frequently mentions, with considerable feeling, that its possessors could exercise it to all but those who were the ardent believers of evangelical doctrine.

Though Doddridge is thus at this point exonerated, when on a later page he is charged with 'mistaken candour', Bogue and Bennett mean to accuse him of everything that this passage spells out. The proof is at pages 479-80, where they are unsparing in their castigation of 'the spurious liberality' which 'perverted' Doddridge's seminary at Northampton:

> This inattention to the genuine religion of the youths, which we should call the original sin of the institution, poisoned Doddridge's lectures; for they seem to proceed too much on the idea that the mind of the student was a perfect *tabula rasa,* destitute of sentiments or prepossessions. Had this been the case, we could not approve of the tutors furnishing them with the wrong as well as the right in theology, error as well as truth, and then calling them to make their election. If such conduct be defended under the name of liberality, would it not be still more liberal, to admit persons who were yet speculating whether Christianity, deism, or atheism was most consistent with truth ?

Here, the substitution of 'liberal' for 'candid' may alert us to the fact that in 1976 this is still a live issue – and by no means only in theology. But in any case Robert Hall, who had decided in 1801 for 'devout, liberal, rational, yet fervent piety, of the stamp of Doddridge, who is now my favourite among divines', could not expect to get favourable treatment from such as Bogue and Bennett, who (unfortunately for him) represented the consensus of dissenting opinion in his lifetime, and the future of dissenting sentiment throughout the nineteenth century. The unbridgeable cleavage between them cannot be more precisely pinpointed than in the way the historians single out themselves – on the issue of 'Candour', that central principle of Enlightenment culture, the one that Bogue and Bennett cannot stomach.

And in fact there is evidence to support their contention that 'candour' was indeed the specious pretext by which the Unitarians contrived to subvert English Dissent from within. Thus their contemporary, Joseph Ivimey *(History of the English Baptists,* 1823, vol. 3, p. 400n.), comments that a Baptist congregation was led to accept the Socinian James Foster as their pastor 'by their false notions of candour and catholicism', and Ivimey reproduces the memorial inscription to Foster, which declares that 'notwithstanding the censures which fell upon him, he was candid towards all whom he believed sincere'. This casts a beam of unintended irony on Anthony Lincoln 's judgment that the dissenters ' Application to Parliament in 1772, for the repeal of the Toleration Act, 'as a whole, was sincerely what it professed to be: an appeal to "candour"'. This attempt by Unitarians to speak for a body of sentiment which was, as events showed, overwhelmingly Trinitarian was in fact conspicuously 'uncandid', as the eighteenth century understood 'candour'. It is, I suspect, this discreditable manoeuvre more than anything else which brought candour into such disrepute as it had for George Canning, when he inserted his 'New Morality' into the last number of the *Anti-Jacobin* (1798):

> 'Much may be said on both sides,' hark, I hear
> A well-known voice that murmurs in my ear, -
> The voice of Candour. Hail! most solemn sage,
> Thou drivelling virtue of this moral age,
> Candour – which softens party's headlong rage;
> Candour – which spares its foes; nor e'er descends
> With bigot zeal to combat for its friends.
> Candour – which loves in see-saw strain to tell
> Of acting foolishly, but meaning well;
> Too nice to praise by wholesale, or to blame,
> Convinced that all men's motives are the same;
> And finds, with keen discriminating sight,
> Black's not too black, nor white so very white...

The *Anti-Jacobin,* of course, is hardly a disinterested witness. Yet those who in the twentieth century have seen the duplicity of communist and ex-communist intellectuals will recognize readily enough the sort of people whom Canning is exposing and the rhetorical strategies that they commonly employ. What they brought about seems indisputable: by their manoeuvres, 'candour', which had been for a George Berkeley perhaps the cardinal principle of ethics (see my 'Berkeley and the Style of Dialogue' in H. S. Davies and G. Watson (eds), *The English Mind,* 1964), had become by the end of the century a piece of dangerous *cant.*

p. 68 *Arnold... supercilious milk-and-water to the assembled clergy of London...*
It is plainly Arnold, in a deplorable performance such as this (though the Arnold of *Culture and Anarchy* also), who angered P.T. Forsyth in 1896:

> Culture, aesthetic or even religious, is now the most deadly and subtle enemy of spiritual freedom. It is the growth of culture in the decay of Gospel that the soul's freedom has increasingly to dread. It is there that our Nonconformity is in most danger of being untrue to itself and its mission. We *are* suffering. But it is less from grievance now than from success. We share a prosperity which is passing through variety of interest, refinement of taste, aesthetic emotion, tender pity, kindly careless catholicity, and over-sweet

> reasonableness, to leanness of soul. It is more at home in literature than in Scripture, and in journals more than either. And it tends to substitute charity and its sympathies for grace and its faith. These are tendencies of the time which we have not escaped. I cannot measure the extent to which we have been affected by them, I may only say that, if any churches can thrive on them, it [*sic*] is not ours. To us they are not only dangerous, but fatal. Humanism must indeed find a home in grace which it has never occupied yet. But it is another thing when it becomes a church's note.

Were it not for the distinction of Forsyth's language – consider the mordant accuracy of 'in journals more than either' – we might mistake this for the philistinism of Bogue and Bennett ninety years before, or of Spurgeon even as Forsyth was writing. But it is not so. Forsyth presents a true bill not only against Arnold, but also (prophetically) against thinkers of 'the Arnoldian persuasion' into our own day.

The persevering vindictiveness of Arnold's polemic against Dissent is not always recognized. Already, in his *Essays in Criticism,* he had been unable to applaud the pieties of Eugénie de Guerin without immolating an Englishwoman, Emma Tatham, and sneering at her 'union in church-fellowship with the worshippers at Hawley Square Chapel, Margate':

> Both were fervent Christians, and, so far, the two lives have a real resemblance; but, in the setting of them, what a difference! The Frenchwoman is a Catholic in Languedoc; the Englishwoman is a Protestant at Margate; Margate, that brick-and-mortar image of English Protestantism, representing it in all its prose, all its uncomeliness, – let me add, all its salubrity.

William Hale White and Peter Taylor Forsyth deserve credit for picking up the gauntlet thus tauntingly thrown down, not once but many times.

Forsyth (1848-1921), a Congregationalist theologian who deserves some of the credit given to more modish foreign names like Emil Brunner and Karl Barth, is a very interesting case that deserves study from students of English as well as of Theology. In *Christ on Parnassus* (1911), a book much less impressive than his strictly theological works, Forsyth can be seen still arguing with Arnold, without naming him (p. 232):

> It is said sometimes, with a vague grandeur which captivates half culture, that poetry is religion and religion is poetry; and so we have all the realities of faith melted by the sleight and patter of some voluble conjuror into the final fabric of a vision, an airy, unsubstantial pageant of imagination. This is a loose and vicious use of words. Faith, indeed, is incomplete without imagination, and imagination is baseless without faith. But neither can stand for the other, or do its work.

Here, from a dissenting pulpit, we surely have the Arnoldian programme punctured just as it was by T.E. Hulme when he objected to 'poetry as spilt religion', and as it was to be twenty years later when Eliot lectured on Arnold and Pater in his *Use of Poetry and Use of Criticism* (1933). Forsyth goes on:

> it is a salutary feature of religious feeling that it is abandoning the excessive formlessness which it had assumed in the hands of its most liberal and sentimental champions; and it is seeking to recover, if it has not actually found, an historic positivity which shall not be rigidly formal, a shapeliness which shall not be of iron mould, a system which shall be truly and morally rational, and a law which shall steady and shall not stunt its career.

And Forsyth concludes his *rappel à l'ordre* with the utmost trenchancy:

> To say, then, that religion is poetry would really be, if we measured our words, to re-import into religion with salutary vigour that element of definite and eternal form which seemed in danger of passing into a general being as featureless as the sky, and a catholic emotion as facile as the wind. Undogmatic Christianity is mere music; it is not even poetry.

Music lovers may well chafe at this formulation; a poet cannot fail to realize that this emphasis on 'definite and eternal form' gives to poetry a dignity beyond anything that we find in Matthew Arnold.

Notes to Lecture 6

I quote Jessie Chambers from E. Delavenay, *D.H. Lawrence et la génèse de son oeuvre,* 1969, vol. 2, appendix 4, pp. 695-6. Sybil Wingate's memoir appeared first in the *Spectator* for 29 May 1959, and is reproduced by Derek Tulloch, *Wingate in Peace and War* (1972). 'The devil raged against the boy preacher' is quoted from Ernest W. Bacon, *Spurgeon: Heir of the Puritans,* 1967, p. 50. For A.L. Rowse, see *Appeasement: A Study in Political Decline 1933-39,* 1961, p. 19.

A Gathered Church: the Literature of the English Dissenting Interest, 1700-1930. London and Henley: Routledge & Kegan Paul Ltd, 1978.

Enlightenment and Christian Dissent

The Ward-Phillips Lectures
for 1980

Preface

When the university of Notre Dame honoured me with an invitation to deliver the Ward-Phillips lectures for 1980, I found that I wanted to attempt a sort of sequel to the Clark lectures that I had given in Cambridge in 1976, which were subsequently published as *A Gathered Church* (1978). What sort of sequel should it be, however? On the one hand I could have tied up some of the loose ends left hanging in *A Gathered Church* – of which there were plenty, as my reviewers had pointed out. On the other hand I could have tried to do what I portentously threatened in the last of those lectures – 'to challenge certain received notions about the social and political history of English Dissent over the past three centuries'. In the event I did neither; instead I have covered the same ground as in the Clark lectures, using different examples. In particular, since *A Gathered Church* strayed from the promise of its subtitle, 'The Literature of the English Dissenting Interest, 1700–1930', I have sought to take my examples more exclusively from literature narrowly considered, indeed from poetry.

This means however that the historical scope of my enquiry is even more presumptuous in the four lectures at Notre Dame than in the six at Cambridge: two and a half centuries, more rather than less. Not all the reviewers of *A Gathered Church* were sure that I was aware of my presumption in attempting a survey so sweeping. I assure them that I was, and am. English Nonconformity in the eighteenth century is by itself a broad and fascinating field of historical enquiry, and I am under no illusions that my grasp of the relevant evidence can begin to match that of a specialist in this field, such as Geoffrey F. Nuttall. Similarly, now that I have taken up the challenge of certain reviewers (notably Daniel Jenkins) in trying to assess Robert Browning's place in the historical perspective of English Dissent, I am well aware that specialists in Browning Studies will find my treatment of their poet altogether too bold and sketchy. But since my concern is precisely with the long historical perspective, not with any one moment or phase within that perspective, I hope it may be agreed that some painting in bold strokes is inevitable, and may be condoned. I have tried to make some slight amends by including, among the pieces which I have here appended to the Ward-Phillips lectures, one or two which take a narrower focus – on the period roughly 1770–1800.

I am afraid that my focusing on this span of years will aggravate the offence that I already gave, in *A Gathered Church,* to Unitarians. I am sorry about this, and must ask Unitarian readers to recognize that my enquiry is strictly historical; and that uncovering what I cannot help but see as successful duplicity in the early years of English Unitarianism is not meant to impugn the sincerity and high-mindedness of professing Unitarians at the present day.

This book, like *A Gathered Church,* is undeniably polemical. But those reviewers are wrong who thought, and doubtless will think, that the polemic is in the service of some prejudice political or religious. In my own sense of the matter, the polemic serves no other purpose than to impel us to use certain terms, certain English *words,* strictly and with scruple; to make us aware for instance of what we are doing when we extend the words 'Christian' or 'Dissenter' to comprehend people who deny both Original Sin and the Holy Trinity. Words have meanings, which can be defined; if a word is used in a way that the definition gives no warrant for, one may legitimately protest – not in order to be exclusive, but in order to be precise. In short, I am not aware of 'carrying a torch' for English Nonconformity or for anything else – only for the English language which, like any other writer in that language, I have an interest in keeping crisp, supple, and responsible.

Daniel Jenkins and other reviewers of *A Gathered Church* protested that in my sourness about what English Nonconformity became in the nineteenth century I overlook what they propose as the socio-political achievements of that Nonconformity. The Nonconformist churches, said Mr Jenkins, 'had also to help new social groups to claim their rights'; and 'Dissenters helped to lay the foundations of modern welfare society and to transform the Empire into the Commonwealth'. Well, perhaps so. But my concern was, and is, with our language – with that language when used with most scruple and power, in our poetry. And what has this to do with 'new social groups' claiming 'their rights' – unless one were to ask, in an enquiry which would be quite different from mine, what is meant in this formulation by 'new', by 'social group', and by 'rights'? A concern with what is called 'social justice' may be nobler than what has impelled me; it is at all events quite different.

I am grateful to all those who reviewed *A Gathered Church,* not least those who were most hostile. I have tried to profit from their observations. And I am grateful to the University of Notre Dame, particularly to Professors Tom Werge and John Matthias, for supplying the incentive without which I would not have thought through again my perceptions about English Dissent. To these two, and to others in South Bend, I am moreover indebted for hearty hospitality and flattering attentions.

1 Poetry and the English Enlightenment

There is a trap or a trick – at all events, a problem – in the title I have given to this lecture. For what was 'the English Enlightenment'? 'The Enlightenment' is a category of intellectual history which all of us Anglicists make play with from time to time (though significantly less often than our colleagues in French, in German, and in other languages); but I'm not aware of any book in English that we can point to, which defines 'the English Enlightenment' in a way that commands general assent. The Americans indeed are not so culpable in this respect as the English; for 'the American Enlightenment' has been vigorously discussed and argued about by students of American history, as the English Enlightenment hasn't been. At least one distinguished American historian, Daniel J. Boorstin, has been at pains to argue that there never was any such thing as an American Enlightenment, or else that if there was the Founders of the Republic had no part in it; but Mr Boorstin I think is in a minority, and the consensus is that there was indeed an American Enlightenment, and that the Declaration of Independence and the Constitution of the United States are 'Enlightenment' documents. Henry F. May's admirably thorough book of 1976, *The Enlightenment in America*, detects not one such American Enlightenment, but no less than *four*, to each of which he's prepared to assign dates; thus – 'The Moderate Enlightenment', 1688–1787, 'The Skeptical Enlightenment', 1750–1789, 'The Revolutionary Enlightenment', 1776–1800, and 'The Didactic Enlightenment', 1800–1815. And Garry Wills's *Inventing America* (1978) was concerned with arguing closely that Mr Jefferson's Declaration of Independence derived from the Scottish Enlightenment rather than, as had been thought, from the English thinker John Locke. For yes, there was certainly a *Scottish* Enlightenment, as all of us – Scotsmen and others – are ready to agree; just as there was also by common consent a German Enlightenment, a Russian Enlightenment, a Latin American Enlightenment, and so on, not to speak of an Enlightenment in France where indeed, so many commentators would persuade us, the whole thing began or was concocted. But England, it seems, is the odd one out; for whereas few students of English history explicitly *deny* that the English participated in what was clearly an international movement in the spirit of Western man comparable to what we call two or three centuries earlier, 'the Renaissance', yet among students of English history, whether English or not, the term is rather seldom used and, when it is used (as in Bertrand Bronson's *Facets of the Enlightenment* [1968]), it seems to be no more than a sonorous substitute for 'the Eighteenth Century'. Henry F. May's dates, ranging from the seventeenth century into the nineteenth, suggest that this at all events won't do; indeed, as soon as we turn to studies of the Enlightenment as an international phenomenon, we find it hard to deny that 'the Enlightenment' must encompass Percy Bysshe Shelley in the 1820s, as well as the Englishmen Bacon and Thomas Hobbes in the seventeenth century, not to speak of the Italian Nicolo Macchiavelli in the sixteenth.

All this, it will be seen, puts me in a quandary. Plainly what we have to do with, in this dubiety about an English Enlightenment – was there such a thing? if so when did it happen? how do we define it? – is a redoubtable problem in intellectual history, for the solution of which I would need all of these four lectures, if not indeed many more. And yet what I need, for the quite different investigation that I have in mind, is a working agreement between you and me (not a working *definition,* but rather no more than a shared sense) of what we may take the English Enlightenment to be.

In these circumstances I have no alternative but to be bold – which is to say, impressionistic and personal. And to get the worst impudence over to start with, I offer, to explain some of what I mean by the English Enlightenment, a poem of my own which I call 'In the Geography School':

Fire-drives of Folsom man!
Around the university's
Degree-giving occasion
The stubble burns in Essex.

The great savannahs are
The products of our fires,
All natural resources
Were cultural appraisals

Once. The scarlet doctors
Hark to an Asian age
Of the earliest cultivations
By arms of the China Sea:

Turmeric, and for saffron
The autumnal crocus, plantings

For pigments, not for food
But dyes to fix their stations.

The imagination holds
In the Old World's promontory,
Europe, not by the hues of degree.
It is launched on the *llanos,* the wolds;

And as upon nothing scorched,
No impoverished assemblage,
Ash-groves burnt off, but as
Through an organic household.

Seas. Of grass.
The haze of Indian Summer
Smells of smoke. The Chancellor
And the Vice-Chancellor pass,

The Doctors, the Honorary Fellow,
And the Bachelors of Arts.
A reader in the Library
Whispers, 'Venezuela!'

This poem, I must explain, was written some fifteen years ago, during the period (1964–68) when I was associated with a then new university in England, the University of Essex; and it reflects something of what was in my head as I and my colleagues struggled to set up what it is convenient, though not quite accurate, to describe as a Department of Comparative Literature.

By decisions taken before any of us were appointed, we students of literature and our close associates in the department of Government – along with later some mostly half-hearted sociologists and economists and art-historians – were required to pay particular attention, first, to British experience through the centuries, but secondly, and in parallel, to the historic experience of three regions of the earth's surface: North America, European and Asiatic Russia, and Latin America. Now, as soon as we began to ponder these three regions as cradles of human culture, we were forced to draw some conclusions of a practical sort. The first was very unwelcome and disconcerting: it was that for all practical purposes (since an *undergraduate* curriculum was what we were concerned with) the cultural histories of these three regions began in the second half of the eighteenth century; and it seemed to follow that our studies of English literature, if they were to keep meaningfully in step with study of one of these foreign literatures (and it was clear to us that they should), would have to be disproportionately weighted towards literature of the last 250 years. Thus a very painful sacrifice – of our earlier literature – was exacted from us at the start. On the other hand, I thought, could we not turn this very disadvantage to good account by giving particular attention (as we could hardly avoid doing anyway) to the category or phase of cultural history that goes by the name of 'the Enlightenment' (*die aufklärung, le siecle des lumières*)? Indeed, was it not just here that I and Jean Blondel, the Professor of Government, could begin to meet another of the obligations that had been wished upon us – of breaking down some of the fences customarily erected between the so-called Social Sciences and the so-called Arts? For those social or behavioural sciences – Economics, Political Science, Sociology, along with others that in truth attracted me more, like Anthropology and Cultural Geography – by common consent emerged, in anything like their modern form, out of the climate of ideas that we call (whatever we mean by it) 'the Enlightenment'. And so it seemed that our freshmen could and should, at one and the same time, be given a grounding in eighteenth-century history and be forced into a critical scrutiny of one or another scholarly discipline, introduced indeed to the philosophical problem of just what 'discipline' in this sense means.

But here we ran up against a comically rudimentary difficulty: our university had decided that it could manage without any historians at all! This is hard to believe, but so it was. Of course it has been put right since, but how could the philistine error have arisen in the first place? Only, I think, because both then and since the fashionableness in many fields of what is called 'structuralist' has masked a profound and widespread impatience with the recorded past, simply with the extent and the copiousness of it; and a determination that its awkwardly circumstantial records should in future, so far as possible, gather dust unread. Fortunately Blondel and I had too much respect for the traditional educations we had received – he in France, and I in England – for us to plot our joint curriculum in such structuralist terms. As Jean would say, using a Gallicism that delighted me: 'But that, you know – it is not *amusing*!' So after much difficulty we got the historians we demanded, so that our students should not learn about for instance 'colonialism' without learning also, and more, about colonies and colonists; so that they should not be nourished on more or less neatly matching paradigms and diagrams, but on disparities, particularities, *quiddities*.

And yet this too of course has its dangers. It is all very well and necessary to puncture the presumption of the rationalist, abstracting into diagrams; but on the other hand one mustn't detract from the dignity of the human Reason, by denying that it can responsibly generalize (and *abstract*) from an array of particular cases. Indeed just here, I venture to think, is one urgently persistent problem that 'the Enlightenment' presents us with: in the distinctions that have to be made between the rational and the reasonable, or else between rationalism and rationality. These are the distinctions that the Age of Reason, and its poets, were struggling to make, and they failed, for our intellectual and imaginative life is still maimed by the lack of them – as this excursus into a chapter of my professional past is meant to show. Patriotism, most people would agree, is eminently *reasonable* but a rationalist can show it isn't *rational*. Because we are still mired in these dilemmas, our eighteenth-century ancestors who struggled in the same morass cannot help but be very near to us.

They are near to us in other ways, much nearer I believe than their nineteenth-century successors. How this may be, we see if I remind you of the three foreign areas we at Essex were to take particular note of. North America, South America, Russia – what they have in common is something so blindingly obvious that it can be overlooked: all three name landmasses of continental scale, and by virtue of that in the starkest contrast to what we at Essex had to relate them to – the area of the British Isles, by comparison so exiguous. Accordingly, should not our Essex students first take the measure, physically, of Russia and the Americas; and recognize, then and there, just how *small* the home islands are – how restricted the distances, the range of different terrains and weathers, and conceivably therefore of psychological states, or at least of natural images for such states? Certainly something so massively rudimentary as that was part of what I imagined in the mind of the student in my poem, when he whispered 'Venezuela!' If that student should also wonder at the number and stature of the cultural monuments that the small islands have produced, by comparison with the continents, that would be another factor in a developing equation that we might call 'proportion', and might even name as 'civilization', as 'education'.

There is a magnificent moment in our eighteenth-century poetry where there is registered just this explosive enlargement of an insular or European sense of scale into a scale that is on the contrary continental or oceanic. It uses, it so happens, just that unEnglish word 'savannah' that I made play with in my poem. And it occurs in the second book of Thomson's *Seasons*, where Thomson has pondered what summer must be like in the torrid zone. After an account of tropical fruits, Thomson is suddenly overawed:

> From these the prospect varies. Plains immense
> Lie stretched below, interminable meads
> And vast savannas, where the wandering eye,
> Unfixt, is in a verdant ocean lost.

It is too bad that I cannot go on quoting what is a magnificently composed and consciously ambiguous passage of blank verse. But these four lines sufficiently make the point, which is brought out and discussed very sensitively indeed by Mr John Barrell in his book about Thomson and John Clare, *The Idea of Landscape and the Sense of Place, 1730–1840.* Thomson, indolent and stay-at-home in his life but admirably meticulous and exacting in his art, and venturesome in his imagination, had mastered for the sake of his art the laws of composition that for the sake of *his* art the painter Claude Lorraine had mastered – a way of ordering, and thus *mastering,* whatever landscapes western Europe might present; but faced in imaginative reading with the wholly different non-European landscapes of the savannah, Thomson concedes (wherein his greatness, surely) that the Claudian glass won't serve – the eye is 'wandering', is 'unfixt', is 'lost', it knows no way to *command* a prospect so different from those it has been trained on. And of course this happens elsewhere in *The Seasons;* exuberantly excited by the new continental vistas that Whig maritime and commercial imperialism had opened up for the British imagination, Thomson time and again ascends to a height from which (quite as if he had known what it is like to travel in a jet aircraft) he can look down and, in a perspective undreamed of by Claude Lorraine, see for instance the Orinoco river emptying out into the ocean and staining its blue waters brown. The *shock* of that sudden alteration of scale is caught by Thomson and a few other eighteenth-century poets as it could not be by Victorian poets to whom the imperial vistas were more commonplace.

In thinking along these lines, I was rather keenly aware how I had been myself affected by a sojourn in the western United States, and more remotely by another, twenty-four years earlier, in Arctic Russia – to which was added, while I was at Essex, an altogether more scurrying and less satisfactory visit to South America. What I had experienced, particularly in California and Nevada and Utah, was something astringent and liberating: a wholly non-European sense of how in forbidding and sparsely peopled landscapes the human being has no special privileged status, but must compete for living room and security with nonhuman creatures like scorpions and bodies of water. The proportion that I had taken for granted, between the human and the nonhuman creation, was knocked from under me. And this was frightening, but the fright was salutary; the human race's purchase on the earth's surface and the earth's resources was more precarious than Western Europe was aware of. For the registering of that fright, that *horror* (for the emotion was as intense as that), I find that once again I have to go to the eighteenth century – to Goldsmith, in *The Traveller*:

> Where wild Oswego spreads her swamps around,
> And Niagara stuns with thundering sound...

This, as everyone knows, was elaborated into a famous passage near the end of *The Deserted Village,* about the scenes which attend the expropriated villagers on the other side of the ocean:

> Those poisonous fields with rank luxuriance crowned,
> Where the dark scorpion gathers death around;

Where at each step the stranger fears to wake
The rattling terrors of the vengeful snake;
Where crouching tigers wait their hapless prey,
And savage men more murderous still than they;
While oft in whirls the mad tornado flies,
Mingling the ravaged landscape with the skies.

We are accustomed to snigger at Goldsmith's ignorance of the actual fauna and flora of the state of Georgia, or else with haughty erudition to rebut such misreading by pointing out for instance that Goldsmith, following Buffon, meant by 'tiger' some dozen carnivores, including the cougar. But we would be better employed, much of the time, acknowledging how Goldsmith here articulates the inescapable and natural response of the western European confronting the lethal extremity and luxuriance of the Southern States, even today.

What I had discovered those years ago, and now try to articulate (as I tried in Essex), is the abiding relevance and imaginative richness of Geography, that subject which through school and university I had always thought of as a plodding and fusty occupation for second-rate minds content with memorizing accurately and drawing neatly. What enlightened me – and of course I say 'enlightened' advisedly – was, first, non-European landscapes themselves, but secondly a poet: the six-foot-something Swedish-American Charles Olson, who began his 'Maximus to Gloucester, Letter 27' with:

I come back to the geography of it...

and who ended that poem:

that forever the geography
which leans in
on me I compell
backwards I compell Gloucester
to yield, to
change
        Polis
is this

In Olson's pamphlet, *A Bibliography on America for Ed Dorn* (such texts were in those years available in London and Cambridge – not any more), I read of, and duly noted and followed up, names like Walter Prescott Webb, the historian of the American frontier; and one Anderson, practitioner of an enlightened and undreamed-of discipline called, I suppose, 'palaeo-botany' or 'the history of agriculture'. Above all I encountered the name of the great modern geographer Carl Sauer. And all of the matters canvassed in my poem – that many if not all of the great grasslands of the world were created artificially in prehistory, by primitive hunters using fire to round up and drive the beasts they had to kill; or the possibility that some plants were first cultivated in prehistory not for food but for dyestuffs – came to me first out of Sauer's writings. They intrigued me when I first encountered them, and I sought to promote them enthusiastically in my poem, not as demonstrated or demonstrable truths but on the contrary precisely as 'intriguing' – as learned speculations which could stimulate and release the imagination into looking down undreamed-of perspectives on human history, a history to be read less out of old records than out of landscapes. Years later in California I met Sauer – a sprightly, lean, physically dried-out octogenarian, every inch a Midwesterner and a living link (so I apprehended him) with the immigrant pioneering generations of the great grassland states. He knew, when I asked him, that his work had interested poets; Olson in particular he recalled, 'the big Swede' as he called him, but it was in an inattentively amused tone that he spoke of him, almost impatiently, certainly with condescension. Though he had as a young man fought his own battles with what he called 'positivism', and had even in passing praised poets' apprehensions of 'the areal' (that last very much one of his words, which accordingly, through Olson, finds its way into Edward Dorn's poetry), still Sauer was enough a man of his time and generation to be rather proudly a scientist, interested as he thought only in the ultimately demonstrable, and so committed to dismissing poetry as, in the end or sooner, less than serious. I don't think we know whether the great cultural geographer Montesquieu took a more generous line to the poets whom he stimulated, like Thomas Gray and Goldsmith, than Sauer took towards Olson and Dorn.

At any rate, however it might be with my associates and allies at Essex, I made a new connection here with 'the Enlightenment'. For if I asked myself what poems in English, before those that Olson and Dorn and I were writing, had last gone for imaginative sustenance to geography on an oceanic and continental and millennial scale, I found myself naming those classics of the English Enlightenment: Goldsmith's *The Traveller,* Gray's *Education & Government,* Thomson's *The Seasons;* though also Coleridge's *Ancient Mariner* and some poems by that youthful Wordsworth who, at home in Westmorland, knew the family of Fletcher Christian, leader of the mutineers of the *Bounty,* those who sailed to and populated Pitcairn Island. It was later, after I had left Essex for California, that I came to see how this aspect of the Enlightenment, not its rationalistic arrogance but on the contrary its humbled awe before the revealed plenitude of human terrains and human cultures, was inscribed – as on language by Gray and Montesquieu, Thomson and Goldsmith – so on the maps and charts of the world by Cook and George Vancouver, La Perouse and La Verendrye, Abel Tasman and Vitus Behring. It was the discovery of Melanesian and Polynesian cultures by the great Enlightenment navigators like Cook and Bligh, Bougainville, and the

American John Ledyard (this last read by me, on the prompting of an Edward Dorn poem, inside blizzard-stormed tin walls in Iowa in 1965), which finally exploded, for thoughtful and responsible people in Western Europe, the assumption that cultural and moral and civic standards had been established once and for all, at the start of the Christian era, by three Mediterranean cultures: Greek, and Roman, and Hebrew. In strictly literary histories I am apprised of nothing which can explain, so comprehensively as this does, why at the end of the eighteenth century a classical or neoclassical culture gave way to a culture that we have to call, however uneasily, 'romantic'. The cultural *relativism* that these discoveries induced is famously pinpointed in Diderot's reflections on Tahitian society in his *Supplément à Bougainville*. But Diderot's tendentiously simplified polemic, notoriously a founding document of that great nonsense 'the noble savage', is humanly surpassed by a passage of English poetry when Cowper, in Book I of *The Task*, broods on the fate and feelings of Omai, the South Sea Islander returned to his native shores after being the fashionable toast of a London season:

> But far beyond the rest, and with most cause,
> Thee, gentle savage! whom no love of thee
> Or thine, but curiosity, perhaps,
> Or else vain-glory, prompted us to draw
> Forth from thy native bowers, to show thee here
> With what superior skill we can abuse
> The gifts of Providence, and squander life.
> The dream is past; and thou hast found again
> Thy cocoas and bananas, palms and yams,
> And homestall thatched with leaves. But hast thou found
> Their former charms? And having seen our state,
> Our palaces, our ladies, and our pomp
> Of equipage, our gardens, and our sports,
> And heard our music; are thy simple friends,
> Thy simple fare, and all thy plain delights
> As dear to thee as once? And have thy joys
> Lost nothing by comparison with ours?
> Rude as thou art (for we returned thee rude
> And ignorant, except of outward show),
> I cannot think thee yet so dull of heart
> And spiritless, as never to regret
> Sweets tasted here, and left as soon as known.
> Methinks I see thee straying on the beach,
> And asking of the surge that bathes thy foot
> If ever it has washed our distant shore.
> I see thee weep, and thine are honest tears,

A patriot's for his country: thou art sad
At thought of her forlorn and abject state,
From which no power of thine can raise her up.
Thus fancy paints thee, and, though apt to err,
Perhaps errs little when she paints thee thus.
She tells me too, that duly every morn
Thou climb'st the mountain top, with eager eye
Exploring far and wide the watery waste
For sight of ship from England. Every speck
Seen in the dim horizon turns thee pale
With conflict of contending hopes and fears.
But comes at last the dull and dusky eve,
And sends thee to thy cabin, well prepared
To dream all night of what the day denied.
Alas! expect it not. We found no bait
To tempt us in thy country. Doing good,
Disinterested good, is not our trade.
We travel far, 'tis true, but not for naught;
And must be bribed to compass earth again
By other hopes and richer fruits than yours.

The texture of this blank verse is lax and prosy, as for the most part Thomson's isn't. But if we attend to the sentiments expressed, have we gone beyond them in our attitudes towards what we have been taught to call 'the Third World'? It seems to me we haven't, and that for instance fifteen years ago when Ed Dorn, in a collection programmatically entitled *Geography,* assailed Lyndon Johnson's USA on behalf of the exploited poor of the Banana Republics, Dorn could not move an inch further than Cowper's caustic shame on behalf of Omai. Instead of Diderot's facile opposition between innocent and noble *them,* and hypocritically ignoble *us*, Cowper confronts what we all now realize as the really intractable consequence of European imperialism: a sort of people like Omai, who are no longer either 'them' or 'us', but betwixt-and-between, at home in neither culture but stranded between them.

Here, though, we reach another difficulty in our understanding of what we mean by 'the Enlightenment'. I have called The *Seasons* and Gray's *Education & Government* and *The Traveller* 'classics of the English Enlightenment'; can I say as much of *The Task,* written by a dogmatic and evangelical Calvinist, whose Calvinism is openly expressed in his poem? We may, and I fear do, suppose that Gray's Christianity, and Thomson's, and Goldsmith's, were merely nominal and Erastian though the evidence is far to seek in all these cases, and in Goldsmith's points clearly the opposite way. But the case of Cowper cannot be huddled away in this fashion. And so the question arises quite inescapably: may we suppose that 'the

Enlightenment' is fundamentally, if not indeed by definition, an irreligious, an anti-religious phenomenon? Whether or not we *may* do this, there's no doubt that many of us do; particularly in Marxist circles, where 'the Enlightenment' is commonly invoked as highly commendable, one reason for commending it is that it allegedly refused to smoke 'the opium of the masses'. And thus I have been reproved for wondering if John Wesley, who recommended Christianity as an eminently *reasonable* religion, could be regarded as a figure of the English Enlightenment. But once we begin to apply this standard, we soon find, not just that that devoutly agonized Anglican Samuel Johnson has to be expelled from 'the Enlightenment', but that there is hardly one of our eighteenth-century poets who does not have to be cast likewise into obscurantist darkness. For there is not a one of them whose claims to a properly 'enlightened' infidelity will stand up to inspection. (And what are we to do for instance with that uncomfortably fervent Christian, Christopher Smart?) Unless I am mistaken, we here confront a dilemma which has reverberations far outside the field of English poetry or even of English literature. On the one hand we may decide that 'the Enlightenment' is indeed essentially an antireligious phenomenon, not just anticlerical but antireligious – in which case the English Enlightenment comprises only deists and those Unitarians of whom that excellent writer, our Marxist historian E.P. Thompson, has written that they 'pushed God so far back into his Baconian heaven of first causes that he became, except for purposes of moral incantation, quite ineffectual'; *or else* we refuse an 'Enlightenment' conceived too exclusively on the French model, and declare that there was indeed an English Enlightenment in which, as not in Papist France, Protestant Christianity played a very large, perhaps a directing, role. In the latter case – which is, as will be discerned, the alternative that I prefer – other alleged 'Enlightenments' (the German, the Russian, the Latin American) may breathe a little more freely, being released from the Voltairean straitjacket; and certainly it is only on this understanding that we can save for 'the Enlightenment' any English poet of greater stature than Soame Jenyns.

And if, with this understanding of our eighteenth century as a profoundly *Christian* century, we look for the continuing life of eighteenth century poetry in our own time, we shall not automatically exclude from consideration those poets of our time who write – tormentedly, for the most part – out of the Christian communion. We shall be ready to discern, for instance, a Swiftian and thereby Christian note of self-disgust – a recognizably dry eighteenth-century voice – in this poem, called 'The End', by my English contemporary C.H. Sisson:

> I shall never hear the angelic choir
> Sing, as it assuredly does, I shall walk in hell
> Among tinkers and tailors and other riff-raff.

Another damnation for imagining myself among those
Whose fornications came as easy as winking
And whose pilferings of other people
Were a social bounty which did not stop at themselves.
I knew early what there was to be known about me
Only lacked courage, fortitude, *élan*
And so descended into a consuming whirlpool
Round and round, here I am at the last gurgle.

Where do we locate the antecedents of this plain and passionate asperity, and this driving colloquialism ('tinkers and tailors and other riff-raff'), if not in the eighteenth century of Jonathan Swift?

And yet here we need to pause. Hearing the tone of Swift, we are carried back into the eighteenth century, certainly. But is that the same as saying we are carried back to 'the Enlightenment'? We have already warned ourselves not to use 'the Enlightenment' and 'the eighteenth century' as if they meant the same thing. And if as I have proposed we take the note of the English Enlightenment to be the delighted and awestruck excitement at new vistas and new horizons that we find in Thomson's *Seasons* (vistas and horizons, incidentally, in the mental as well as in the physical world – Thomson was an admirer of Isaac Newton), do we not have to say that this is specifically what we do *not* find in Swift? Much of the time Swift, like his friend Alexander Pope, is rather furiously tugging against, and resisting, just those commercial and scientific and imperialistic developments which so fired the imagination of James Thomson. Much of the time Swift and Pope are castigating their century for departing from the habits of the century before; they are rather consistently backward-looking, both of them. There *may* be texts of Swift which can properly be described as 'of the Enlightenment', and in Pope there certainly are; but in both authors, as I read them, there are many more texts which are not. And so I am constrained to think that the distinction between 'Enlightenment' and 'non-Enlightenment', as I understand those terms, may have to be drawn inside a writer's *oeuvre;* we may judge him as 'of the Enlightenment' at one point, but not at others.

And so there arises the possibility that for the religious poetry of the English Enlightenment we should look not to Swift but to a sector of the Christian communion in England which, as we know, he hated bitterly – to the Protestant Dissenters. Something like this, for instance, from the pen of Swift's contemporary, the great Independent (as we would say, Congregationalist) hymn-writer, Isaac Watts:

Hosanna to the royal son
  Of David's ancient line!
His natures two, his person one,
  Mysterious and divine.

The root of David, here we find,
  And offspring, are the same:
Eternity and time are joined
  In our Immanuel's name.

Blest he that comes to wretched man
  With peaceful news from Heaven!
Hosannas, of the highest strain, .
  To Christ the Lord be given.

Should we, dear Lord, refuse to take
  The Hosanna on our tongues,
The rocks and stones would rise and break
  Their silence into songs. [1]

Neither C.H. Sisson nor any one else in our time writes poems like this. New hymns are composed for us, and at times we contrive to sing them in church without intolerable discomfort. But our serious poets, if they are Christian, write as Sisson does of their solitary and private religious *experience;* whereas Watts writes of and for the communal experience of worship, and so he deals not with self-disgusted desolations nor for that matter with feelingful exaltations, but with Christianity in its public form, as *doctrine*. These are hymns for theologians – because, in those far-off days, religious leaders like Watts were sanguine enough to think that the humblest worshipper could and should be enough of a theologian to understand the tenets of the Faith which he professed. Hence the sinewy intellectualism of this poem – the compressed wit which expresses the paradox of Jesus belonging at once to Eternity and to Time by saying that in him 'The root of David... And offspring, are the same'. This intellectualism, surely, is what makes such a poem at home in 'the Age of Reason'; and Watts's sanguine confidence in the capacities of his fellow Dissenters, something which led him to compose for them schemes of self-education and treatises of logic as well as devotional tracts, is what ranges Watts along with a poet of the Enlightenment like Thomson. In the next generation as much can be claimed for at any rate some of the hymns of Charles Wesley.

In conclusion, however belatedly, I should like to vindicate these poets of the English Enlightenment on that score which, ever since Wordsworth's Preface to *Lyrical Ballads*, has been taken to be their weakest flank – that is to say, their poetic diction. My text shall be, once again, Goldsmith's *The Traveller*:

[1] Text from Toplady's *Psalms and Hymns for Public and Private Worship* (London, 1776). For justification for thus not taking the text of a hymn from its earlier version, see below, 'The Language of the Eighteenth-Century Hymn'.

To men of other minds my fancy flies,
Embosomed in the deep where Holland lies.
Methinks her patient sons before me stand,
Where the broad ocean leans against the land
And, sedulous to stop the coming tide,
Lift the tall rampire's artificial pride.
Onward, methinks, and diligently slow
The firm-connected bulwark seems to grow;
Spreads its long arms amidst the watery roar,
Scoops out an empire and usurps the shore;
While the pent ocean, rising o'er the pile
Sees an amphibious world beneath him smile:
The slow canal, the yellow-blossomed vale,
The willow-tufted bank, the gliding sail,
The crowded mart, the cultivated plain,
A new creation rescued from his reign.

'Where the broad ocean leans against the land...'! Goldsmith here, the agrarian and reactionary Tory, shows himself – unlike those earlier Tories, Pope and Swift – at one with Thomson the exuberant Whig. Goldsmith too could be looking down from a jet aircraft coming in over the Low Countries; and not just looking, but feeling in his own frame (by empathy, therefore – that term so woefully misused in our criticism to replace 'sympathy') the elementary *dynamics* of sea encountering land: 'leans', he says, 'the broad ocean *leans* against the land'. The perception embodied in that verb is a product of abstraction – such abstraction from detail as the jet pilot enjoys, looking down, or the geographer, poring over the physical map. And yet it is profoundly imaginative – the imagination works through the abstraction, and proceeds indeed *by abstraction*. You will see that we have in a fashion come full circle – on to the demands that the human Reason may and must legitimately make, as it goes about its business of abstracting and so generalizing, abstracting from the innumerable details of the physical world so as to contrive the art or science of Geography, or from the multifarious manifestations of the metaphysical world so as to practice the art or science of Theology. The facile opposition that our criticism has made so much play with – between the concrete and the abstract – is here seen for the *ignis fatuus* that it is. Though critics and poetic theorists may have been hung up on this sterile because unfounded antithesis, our good poets never were. Were there world enough and time, I could demonstrate this. For the moment... 'Where the broad ocean leans against the land' – would that I had written such a line!

2 Enlightenment and Dissent

In my first lecture I touched upon several features of what I am venturing to call 'The English Enlightenment'. And I do not want to forget, nor would I have you forget, any of these features. But I want to dwell on one of them in particular: on the point that in England, however it may have been in France, the Enlightenment was not necessarily, still less *essentially,* unchristian. Once we have seized the point that in the Enlightenment the poetic imagination could and did quite naturally work by way of *abstraction,* we perceive that it could hardly stop short of those awesomely abstract, because paradoxical, conceptions that are the matter of theology. Christopher Smart writes, at the end of his 'Hymn for the Nativity of Our Lord and Saviour Jesus Christ':

> Spinks and ouzels sing sublimely
> 'We too have a Saviour born';
> Whiter blossoms burst untimely
> On the blest Mosaic thorn.
>
> God all-bounteous, all creative,
> Whom no ills from good dissuade,
> Is incarnate and a native
> Of the very world he made.

This poem as a whole is very insistently English, because it works – right through to these last stanzas – with the peculiarly English legend of the miraculous Glastonbury thorn, which blossoms only at Christmas, having been planted (so the legend goes) by Joseph of Arimathaea. But there is no way, out of English legend or English history or English landscape, to escape the extraordinarily strenuous conceptualizing that the last two lines demand of us, in order to understand that the same energy which created the entire universe has condescended to become a human baby and therefore 'Is incarnate and a native/ Of the very world he made'. Whether or not we in fact accept this, as an article of faith, is poetically as much beside the point as whether we endorse Oliver Goldsmith's Tory-agrarian diagnosis of what was wrong with England in the 1760s; in either case the leap – not of faith, but of imagination – is breathtaking. In either case the sheer conception is grand and elevating, therefore liberating – whether we conceive of how the ocean *leans* upon the land, or of how a Creator might incarnate himself and so become one of his own creatures. In both cases the evidence of our senses is not denied or contradicted but simply surpassed, leaped over. And so Smart's verses are, just like Goldsmith's, an achievement not indeed of rationalism but of rationality, an instance of just how far the human Reason can go in conceiving the unperceivable and the logically impossible.

And in the Wesleys – in John, but more pertinently in his poet brother Charles, the hymn-writer – we encounter audacities, imaginative abstractings, that in the same way ought to leave us gasping (though apparently they don't):

> Him the angels all adored,
> Their Maker and their King;
> Tidings of their humbled Lord
> They now to mortals bring.
> Emptied of His majesty,
> Of his dazzling glories shorn,
> Being's source begins to be,
> And God Himself is born!

'Being's source begins to be...', 'Is incarnate and a native/ Of the very world he made'... Is it not clear that in both cases (as it happens prompted by the same occasion, the Incarnation) the human intellect – not primarily the sympathies of the human heart, but the energies of human Reason – is stretched to the limit? Was this not also what we found in Isaac Watts's 'Hosanna to Christ'? And is it not clear therefore that all these are entirely appropriate manifestations of what we still laxly call (without attending to what we are saying) the Age of Reason?

Moreover, what are those 'dazzling glories' of which, in Charles Wesley's poem, God is 'shorn' when he condescends to be incarnate, those glories to which after the Crucifixion he returns? What are they but light, 'the Uncreated Light', according to a tradition which reaches back through Dante's *Paradiso* to Scripture itself? *Light* – this is 'Enlightenment'! So how did Unbelievers have the presumption to make of this ancient metaphor *their* peculiar property? And how is it that Believers were and are ready to acquiesce in the impudent takeover? Who says, or who ever proved or could prove, that the light which breaks – on the eighteenth or any other century – is by definition a secular light, not the light of a Divine Intelligence mediated to us through Grace? It is the merest arrogant prejudice that, flying in the face of what we know biographically about Christopher Smart and Charles Wesley, both eager students of the most advanced thought of their time, would deny that they were men of the Enlightenment and their poems products of the Enlightenment.

This prejudice, because it has gone unchallenged for so long, is now very confident. Thus E.P. Thompson, whom I cited in my first lecture, can assure his fellow-Marxists that 'the eighteenth-century Church can scarcely be said to have had an articulated ideology'. And he can be sure, apparently, that no one of his readers will ask: 'What about Christopher Smart and Samuel Johnson, Joseph Butler or George Berkeley or William Law?' Not an articulated ideology among the lot of them, it seems! The same historian can assure us that 'Wesleyanism... was self-consciously anti-Enlightenment'; and can go on to explain that he says this 'not in any pejorative sense, but in the sense that the Wesleys turned their backs upon certain polite and rational modes, and re-emphasized the paternalized responsibilities of the Church for the unenlightened majority.' [1] That the mode of the Wesleyan hymns was not always 'polite' I will concede; on the other hand I have just contended that the mode of at any rate Charles Wesley's hymns was insistently and vehemently 'rational', unless we give to 'rational' an unacceptably restricted sense. And as for 'the paternalized responsibilities of the Church for the unenlightened majority', this seems to mean only that Wesleyan pastors were frequently as solicitous for the worldly welfare of their flocks as were conscientious pastors in the Anglican, the Roman, and the Dissenting communions (though what it really means, I suspect, is that at the time of the American Revolution both the Wesleys were vehement loyalists).

In case you are wondering, I stand before you not as a Methodist (which I am not) nor as a champion of the Wesley brothers (great and pious men though I believe they were, both of them). I take up the cudgels for Wesleyanism only because the prejudice against it is the particular instance that seems to lie across my path as I try to understand what we do mean, and what we might mean, when we talk, in the cultural history of England, of 'the Enlightenment'. It so happens, in fact, that my principal concern is with a quite different body of Christian believers, whom I have just invoked by speaking of 'the Dissenting communions'. Those heirs to the Cromwellian puritans – the Baptists, the Independents (Congregationalists, as they later called themselves), the Quakers, the English as distinct from the Scottish Presbyterians – what happened to them in the eighteenth century? It is after all rather astonishing how little we hear of them, quite suddenly, once we pass the date 1700 in any survey of English history. They have been taken note of, however, particularly by some of our Marxist colleagues, who thereby deserve the gratitude not just of Free Churchmen but of anyone who aspires to the unattainable ideal of disinterested enquiry. E.P. Thompson for instance, who is certainly one of that minority of Marxists who have earned our gratitude on these grounds, is harsh to the Wesleyans only so

[1] E.P. Thompson, reviewing *A Gathered Church* in the *Modern Language Review* 75 (January 1980), p. 165.

as to pay a compliment to what he calls 'Old Dissent'. This appears in his vastly influential work, *The Making of the English Working Class* (1964). Elsewhere he has declared: 'The historian of ideas must see Old Dissent, with its strong intellectual traditions and its mercantile and professional support, as serving increasingly, after 1750, as a vector of the Enlightenment.' [2] Sectarian infighting is a bore, and must be resisted. The important question here is very obvious, and can be posed quite simply: if the Enlightenment is to be understood as a triumph of the secular, infidel intelligence, then how can there be enlisted in its service a body of opinion and sentiment which is explicitly *Christian:* that heterogenous body of Christian belief which, because of developments peculiar to Anglo-American history, gets itself called 'Dissent'? The answer is that in Marxist and more generally 'liberal' ideology it is taken for granted that the complex of beliefs called for instance 'Baptist' is only an untenable way-stage on the journey from unenlightened Belief to enlightened Unbelief. If I refuse to accept this, one reason is that both my parents – strongly 'intellectual' indeed, but neither 'mercantile' nor 'professional' – went to their graves supposing that the Baptist Christianity which they professed was no halfway house but a coherent and consistent system of belief; in short, I suppose, an 'articulated ideology'. I am not prepared to give up my inheritance without a fight; and whereas I have no wish to make converts to their persuasion (which, as it happens, I no longer adhere to myself), nevertheless I won't see their convictions casually laughed out of court, nor smilingly condescended to as an acceptable stage on the way to something more laudable, more 'enlightened'. The acme of Enlightenment on *that* showing is the vehement and explicit anti-Christian, Tom Paine; and sure enough we have seen Tom Paine claimed for Dissent, called 'a Dissenter', for no better reason than that one of his parents was a member of the Society of Friends!

However, let us be grateful. Old Dissent must be seen 'as serving... as a vector of the Enlightenment'. Yes, indeed – the point is an important one, and it is very seldom made, least of all by those supposed heirs of Old Dissent, the 'Free Churchmen' or 'Nonconformists' of our own day. The Baptists for instance of the 1760s and 1770s, whether in the home islands or in the colonies, seem to have been quite often 'enlightened', both in the general sense of that term and even in terms of that time-bounded climate of ideas which we call (when we think about it) *the* Enlightenment. They were very different creatures from the philistine fundamentalists of a later age in the Bible Belt, or in South London and the depressed areas of English industrial cities. Take for an example Isaac Backus of Connecticut, leader of the American Baptists at the Continental Congress and a contumacious thorn in the side of the state church of Massachusetts. Backus was

[2] Ibid.

a devoted admirer of that sage of the Enlightenment, John Locke; and he consistently refused to give up to unbelievers the metaphor of 'enlightenment', of light breaking – as when, in his *Appeal to the Public for Religious Liberty,* he asserted that, whereas 'the state is armed with the *sword* to guard the peace, and the civil rights of all persons and societies, and to punish those who violate the same', on the other hand 'the church is armed with *light and truth,* to pull down the strongholds of iniquity, and to gain souls to Christ, and into his Church...'[3] 'The church is armed with *light*...'! Backus believed that Lockean Reason and scriptural Revelation pointed the same way; but that certainly didn't mean that he denied the authority of Revelation, or was blind to the light that broke from it. And the same is true of his fellow-sectaries on the other side of the ocean, whether they took the part of the American colonists (as many of them did), or loyally supported King George (as rather more of them did than it is now convenient to remember).

How and when and why, in the succeeding century, the dissenting churches became predominantly *un*enlightened is a story that no one seems to have told, doubtless because no one would get any thanks for telling it. Undoubtedly, though for many decades after the Revolution the British and the American dissenting churches worked closely together (for instance in the institution of the first foreign missions – to India and Burma), the American story and the British story are quite distinct. About the British story, I have a few ideas; as regards the American story I know only enough to marvel that so few of us, American or British, know even a little (and cannot easily determine where to go to learn more). Of Isaac Backus, who survived as a staunch Jeffersonian until 1806, William G. McLoughlin has decided: 'it would be erroneous to portray Backus as a man of the Enlightenment in any profound sense. He was not really interested in science and his preoccupation with the reality and direct manifestations of divinity in revivals and conversions predisposed him to favour supernatural explanations for peculiar events.'[4] With this we must agree. But it remains true that the evangelical Christianity which Backus represents was not at all so fundamentally opposed to the Enlightenment as is commonly supposed. McLoughlin makes the point admirably. Baptists like Backus, he declares, 'thought of their "experimental" religion in terms which to them were just as inductive and scientific as the discoveries of Newton, Boyle, or Locke. Experimental piety... stated in religious terms what the Enlightenment philosophers wanted to state primarily in humanistic, secular, or rationalistic terms.'[5] And what is here

[3] O.K. Armstrong and Marjorie Armstrong, *The Baptists in America* (New York, 1979), pp. 93, 97.

[4] William G. McLoughlin, *Isaac Backus and the American Pietistic Tradition* (Boston, 1967), p. 190.

[5] Ibid., p. 232.

claimed for the American 'Great Awakening' is as true of dissenting piety at just the same time in England, where for instance the great Independent Philip Doddridge spoke of 'experimental' religion, and seems to have meant by it just what American Baptists meant. It is not clear what happened to this concept later. But what seems certain is that Enlightenment and Dissent, which supported each other so comfortably for Isaac Backus, had moved very far apart by 1973, when a leader of American Baptists could sum up a personal testament: 'So my conversion was a crisis of faith, the pivotal struggle in a human soul as to who prevails: Christ or culture, God or man, Jesus Christ as Sovereign Will or a people's will.' [6] The implications for a democracy, of this relegation of the 'people's will', is something that I am happy to leave for US citizens to worry about. My point is more simply that the choice of Christ *as against* 'culture' is what, so far as I can see, Isaac Backus would not have understood and so would not have accepted; for him, if I understand him, John Locke belonged to 'culture', but was not for that reason to be spurned by those who declared themselves 'for Christ'.

For the British on the other hand the crucial development, still little understood or remarked upon, is in the last decades of the eighteenth century the precipitate dissolution of English Presbyterianism into Unitarianism, either avowed or (more often) unavowed. The theological implications of this development are crucial; but in our time, when theological questions are by common consent remitted to experts called 'theologians' (how alarmed Isaac Backus would have been!), the implications that take our eye are *political*. And here already the American and the British experiences diverge. For it is natural for Americans, citizens of a republic, to assume that a republican form of government is rational, whereas a monarchical form of government isn't. That was the view of Tom Paine, and of the many English Jacobins who would go most of the way with Paine, if not all the way. But on the other hand there were, and are, British people who hold that monarchy on the British model is just as rational, as *enlightened,* a polity as a republic is. And not only Englishmen have thought so; it was a Frenchman, Montesquieu, who taught that whereas republics depend upon the principle of civic *virtue,* monarchies inculcate and depend on the no less exalted principle of *honour*. And it seems to be Montesquieu who stands behind those lines in *The Traveller* where, emphasizing the point by a renewed address to his brother, Goldsmith deplores attempts being made to limit further under the Constitution the power of the throne, *'regal* power', the power of King George III:

> Yes, brother, curse with me that baleful hour,

[6] *The Baptists in America*, p. 236.

When first ambition struck at regal power;
And thus polluting honour in its source,
Gave wealth to sway the mind with double force.

The power of the throne, of the monarch, is here seen as a necessary bulwark for the nation at large against the otherwise unbridled power of commerce and high finance – 'wealth'; against that 'independence' which demands unrestricted competition in the marketplace, a free-for-all, every man for himself in the struggle for material goods and for power:

That independence Britons prize too high,
Keeps man from man and breaks the social tie;
The self-dependent lordlings stand alone,
All claims that bind and sweeten life unknown;
Here by the bonds of nature feebly held,
Minds combat minds, repelling and repelled.
Ferments arise, imprisoned factions roar,
Repressed ambition struggles round her shore,
Till over-wrought, the general system feels
Its motions stopped or frenzy fire the wheels.

This is the time-honoured case for monarchy, which goes easily into Marxist terminology, arguing that for stability there needs to be one power in the state which stands above and outside the locked and conflicting powers of the class struggle, and that the only such power conceivable is the Crown. There are still British people, though fewer than in the past, who are monarchists on these rational grounds; and of course they do not mean by their monarchism what their American friends are eager to suppose – that the British monarchy is a charmingly ornamental and picturesque excrescence on a form of government that is, basically and essentially, as much a republican form as is the government of the United States. The changing of the guard at Buckingham Palace is a tourist attraction; but that isn't its sole nor its most important significance.

Oliver Goldsmith, to be sure, was no Dissenter, nor with any sympathies in that direction. Yet there have been religious Dissenters who held such views. How could there not have been, since English Dissenters have fought and died for their King (or Queen) and Country just as English Roman Catholics and English Anglicans have? Not all those people were stupid or befuddled about where their true interests lay. And yet the accepted account of them necessarily implies that they were, since the accepted version assumes that the Dissenters were or ought to have been, ever since Oliver Cromwell, republicans. This is for instance the implicit burden of a justly acclaimed work of American historical scholarship, Caroline Robbins's *The Eighteenth-Century Commonwealthman* (1959). That many English Dissenters of the eighteenth century did interpret in this way the heritage that they were proud to own, from the Lord Protector Cromwell and from John Milton, cannot be denied. But not all Dissenters agreed. And if they had only known (as perhaps some of them did) they could have found evidence among their colonial brethren that the Cromwellian legacy did not necessarily work in their favour. John Clarke for instance, born a Londoner in 1609, emigrated to Boston in 1637 and soon found himself rudely disenchanted by the religious intolerance of Massachusetts. Accordingly he fled for succour to the town and plantations of Providence, set up a few years earlier, as just such a refuge, by the Baptist Roger Williams. In 1651 John Clarke returned to his native London to secure from the Lord Protector Cromwell a permanent charter for all the Rhode Island communities. This task occupied John Clarke for twelve years, and when the coveted charter was at last secured it was not from Cromwell but, after Cromwell's death, from the restored monarch Charles II, in private life the most libertine of English kings but in his public policies the shrewdest and one of the most enlightened. Cromwell either evaded Clarke for eight years or else, if the petition was brought to his notice, would not accede to it; and accordingly the first of all the states to attain complete religious freedom received it from the hands of a hereditary monarch. The original charter of Rhode Island (1663) reads: 'Our royal will and pleasure is, that no person within said Colony, at any time hereafter, shall be in any wise molested, punished, disquieted, or called in question for any differences of opinion in matters of religion...'[7] 'Our royal will and pleasure...' – this is Oliver Goldsmith's 'regal power', actively exerted on behalf of minorities which, being outnumbered, could only have been victimized in that sort of condition called 'Freedom' wherein the weakest must go to the wall. In every generation some English Dissenters have learned from this or similar instances, if not indeed from thinking politically in the abstract in the manner of John Locke, to agree with Goldsmith that the throne, the Crown, might be their surest safeguard. Before John Clarke secured the Rhode Island charter, one patriarch of English Dissent, the great Richard Baxter, had dared to say as much to Cromwell directly:

> We took our ancient monarchy to be a blessing, and not an evil to the land, and humbly craved his patience that I might ask him how England had ever forfeited that blessing, and to whom that forfeiture was made.

And in every generation of English Dissent, from Richard Baxter's to ours, there can be heard voices raised in this way, on behalf of monarchist and loyalist principles. For instance:

[7] Ibid., p. 232.

> The mixed form of government under which it is our distinguishing happiness to live, is the noblest monument of political wisdom and justice ever exhibited in the world. By the union of the monarchy, the aristocracy, and the democracy, we are equally protected against the tyranny of an individual, and that worst and heaviest of all scourges, the tyranny of a depraved multitude.

This is a vocabulary for politics that we are not used to: one in which 'democracy' is taken to be a principle or interest in the State, neither more nor less respectable than others which are named as 'aristocracy' and 'monarchy'. And we are not accustomed nowadays to being warned against 'that worst and heaviest of all scourges, the tyranny of a depraved multitude'. This is however the vocabulary of an age; as much the vocabulary of President John Adams as of Oliver Goldsmith and Edmund Burke, and of the English Dissenter whom I quote – the Congregationalist minister Edward Parsons, speaking in 1809 from his pulpit in Salem Chapel, Leeds. Now, when the agencies for depraving the multitude are so much more numerous and potent than they were in 1809 – nowadays we call them 'the media' – it may well be thought that this is a vocabulary that we need to recover. However that may be, this was a vocabulary which, whatever historians may say or imply to the contrary, seemed as natural and proper to many Dissenting Christians as to Christians of the Establishment.

When the existence of this strain in English Dissent is ignored and overlooked, as it habitually is, we can be misled as William Irvine was when he told how the young South London Dissenter, Robert Browning, in the late 1820s came under the influence of the militantly atheistic and republican Shelley on the one hand, and on the other of the Unitarian minister W.J. Fox:

> ... doctrinally, Fox was very little more (or less) than Shelley with his collar turned backward. Both held that evil was at most temporary. Both looked forward to a progress toward perfection, to an infinite felicity in some form. Shelley's atheism was not incompatible with belief in a benevolent, all-pervading Spirit. Fox believed in a God of love. Both were hostile to conventions and institutions. Both maintained that men are basically good and that to be effectually good they need first of all to be free and equal. 'There is a natural alliance,' said Fox, 'between error and slavery, truth and liberty.' In short, both men were deeply indebted to the Enlightenment. [8]

Well, so they were, both of them. No one should want to deny that

[8] William Irvine and Park Honan, *The Book, the Ring, and the Poet* (London, 1974), pp. 28–9.

Shelley's atheism and Fox's Unitarianism were products of what we call 'the Enlightenment', in one of its characteristic manifestations. But on what grounds, or by what principle, do we deny the title 'Enlightenment' to that course of reading which the child Browning had already pursued while still securely within the fold of his parents' Congregationalism: 'Quarles' *Emblems,* Defoe's *Crusoe,* Mandeville's *Bees,* Walpole's *Letters,* "all the works of Voltaire", Junius, many of the Elizabethans, Milton, Pope, Christopher Smart, and of course Byron'? [9]

In this list, which Irvine quotes from Browning's first and most knowledgeable biographer, Mrs Sutherland Orr, can Quarles and Milton, the Elizabethans and Byron, outweigh the presence of such surely 'Enlightenment' authors as Defoe and Mandeville, Walpole and Voltaire, Junius and Christopher Smart? And yet all of these the poet-to-be read about 1820 in the library of his solidly affluent Congregationalist parents in the London suburb of Camberwell. If 'enlightened' means anything other than 'infidel', how can we deny enlightenment on this showing to religious Dissenters like the Browning parents at least as late as 1820 or 1825?

[9] Ibid., p. 7.

3 Robert Browning

I have proposed – no, I have not; I have *asserted* – that whereas in the eighteenth century Dissent was a vector or a vehicle of the Enlightenment (though in ways that force us to rethink just what the 'Enlightenment' was), in the nineteenth century it serves something quite other and less admirable, something indeed that much of the time is directly opposite: unenlightenment. In the nature of the case such a sweeping judgment cannot be demonstrated; which is the reason why I am compelled simply to assert it. The assertion can however be supported by at least circumstantial evidence. Moreover, because we are proceeding on the assumption that the most compelling evidence in all such contentions is the evidence of the arts, and because my own proclivities and training bend me towards that one of the arts which we call literature or more narrowly *poetry,* it must be in that area that we look for evidence of how in the nineteenth century Dissent became unenlightened.

And in this perspective there is no doubt what poet we must scrutinize. It is Robert Browning. Though Browning was never for long a practising member of any Dissenting church, nevertheless Dissent was his family inheritance as it was also the inheritance of the poet he married, Elizabeth Barrett, whose poetry was in her lifetime more highly esteemed than her husband's. Browning indulged a youthful flirtation with Shelleyan atheism, but was already in retreat from that position by the time he met Elizabeth Barrett. And she, during their courtship and the first years of their famous marriage, applied herself to accelerate his retreat to the Dissent that he had imbibed at his mother's knee, that Dissent however considerably modified so as to fall in with the notably 'liberal' variety that she professed herself. And here already we may and must pause: are 'liberal' and 'enlightened' words that go together? It is very commonly assumed that they do, but plainly the two words, like any words but these two more notably than many, are changing their meanings over the centuries; and so we may expect to find that we can with some confidence slide from one to the other when we look at certain periods of our past, but shall go very wrong if we do the same with other periods. So we ought to ask if the two words do or do not happily and justly lie down together when we try to apply them to those decades of the mid-nineteenth century when Robert and Elizabeth Barrett

Browning were living and writing together. In any case there seems to be no doubt that the Brownings conceived themselves to be speaking for the tradition of English religious Dissent, though aware no doubt that they were 'liberalizing' it to a point where much of Dissent would no longer want to own them. And however it may have been in their lifetimes, certainly in the decades after they had died, Dissent was proud to lay claim to them. I speak feelingly here; for it was my mother who first inculcated in me a passion for English poetry, and at her suggestion it was Browning on whom I cut my teenage teeth. It is some tribute to *her* 'liberalism', both in general and more particularly as a far from overbearing or prescriptive parent, that Browning's Dissenting credentials figured not at all in her commendations of him to me, and that it was only many years later that I came to realize how her own Dissenting background had made Robert Browning stand first for her among all the English poets of all periods whom she loved.

And surely Browning is a very strong card to play, in the hand of any scion of English Dissent who wants to claim that the Dissenting tradition was alive and well in England through the reign of Queen Victoria, not just 'alive' (for that we all know about, or should – the vastly increased numbers of the Dissenting faithful, and the political influence they could and did exert) but also 'well' – a hale and sanative element in the public life of the nation, exerting its 'clout' for the most part on behalf of decency and openness and, well, 'enlightenment'. Is not Browning by common consent a great poet? And does not his greatness consist very largely in the frank and masculine vigour of his imagination, the unconstrained and as it often seems unlimited range of his sympathies and his curiosity? Has he not been compared, ever since an early and splendid tribute by his friend of an older generation Walter Savage Landor, with Chaucer, no less? Yes. And it is with a sort of sorrowful deference to my mother's memory that I record my present judgment: Browning is a great poet, and at his tip-top best a Chaucerian poet, great in the way that Chaucer was great. Not the weightiest of Browning's Chaucerian performances, for instance, but among the most sparkling, is 'Up at a Villa – Down in the City'. However, this great Browning is the Browning furthest from Dissent, furthest from those themes and that tone which advertise him as belonging in that lineage. The more narrowly we look at Browning as a poet of religious Dissent, the worse he is. And so we can argue that, great poet though Browning is, he is none the less evidence – indeed, because of his great talents he is singularly compelling evidence – of how by the middle of the nineteenth century Dissent had become a vector of *un*enlightenment.

In passing this judgment I can call upon distinguished authority. For enlightenment was specifically denied to Browning by George Santayana, when he warned that by minds vividly responsive to what Browning has to offer, 'awakening may be mistaken for enlightenment, and the galvanizing of torpid sensations and impulses for wisdom'. This is in Santayana's great essay of 1900, 'The Poetry of Barbarism', in which Browning on one side of the ocean and Walt Whitman on the other are declared to be not just unenlightened but positively, and quite specifically, *barbarous:*

> The 'Soul' which he trusted in was the barbarous soul, the 'Spontaneous Me' of his half-brother Whitman. It was a restless personal impulse, conscious of obscure depths within itself which it fancied to be infinite, and of a certain vague sympathy with wind and cloud and with the universal mutation. It was the soul that might have animated Attila and Alaric when they came down into Italy, a soul not incurious of the tawdriness and corruption of the strange civilization it beheld, but incapable of understanding its original spirit; a soul maintaining in the presence of that noble unappreciated ruin all its own lordliness and energy, and all its native vulgarity.

Santayana's essay enjoys an odd status among us today. It is, most would agree when reminded, a classic of our criticism; and yet it is tacitly set aside whenever we approach either of the poets it deals with, or else it is treated as if it carried no more weight than any of a dozen or more academic hack jobs performed on these poets in the years since. The reason for this, I suspect, is less Santayana's harsh judgment of Browning than his even harsher dealings with Whitman; for Whitman commands more allegiance among us than Browning does, and has been emulated by many more poets, who accordingly would feel Santayana's lash curl about their shoulders as about their master's. Then, too, Santayana's tone and his vocabulary are undeniably haughty; we are democratically uneasy with a criticism that accuses a poet of 'vulgarity', which speaks without embarrassment or apology of 'a person coming to Browning with the habits of a cultivated mind'. It isn't exactly that we deny the existence of vulgarity, or of some minds that are cultivated and others that aren't; but although we know these things, we prefer not to be reminded of them, or not at any rate in the public prints. Moreover Santayana like any one else is open to the rejoinder *ad hominem,* as when we are reminded: 'So speaks a philosopher whose intellect will not allow him to accept literally and dogmatically the Catholicism for which his heart yearns, to whom it is a constant delight to remind us that Christianity rightly conceived is an ecclesiastical tradition of asceticism rather than a way of life attributed to Jesus of Nazareth'. [1] And finally Santayana's way of proceeding is significantly different from that of the best modern criticism. For a good

[1] Kingsbury Badger, '"See the Christ stand!": Browning's Religion' *Boston University Studies in English*, I (1955–6). In P. Drew (ed.), *Robert Browning: A Collection of Critical Essays* (Boston, 1966) p. 75.

modern critic would start with observations about Browning's *style,* and move out from those to generalizations about his temperament and the cast of his mind; whereas Santayana proceeds in the opposite order. But all these concessions made, Santayana's ultimately damning judgment is surely very hard to refute:

> Apart from a certain superficial grotesqueness to which we are soon accustomed, he easily arouses and engages the reader by the pithiness of his phrase, the volume of his passion, the vigour of his moral judgment, the liveliness of his historical fancy. It is obvious that we are in the presence of a great writer, of a great imaginative force, of a master in the expression of emotion. What is perhaps not so obvious, but no less true, is that we are in the presence of a barbaric genius, of a truncated imagination, of a thought and an art inchoate and ill-digested, of a volcanic eruption that tosses itself quite blindly and ineffectually into the sky.

And if we want corroboration, we can find it expressed in more pithy and homely phrase by one who carries even more authority than Santayana because the voice we hear is that of a great poet; one who was Browning's friend, who wrote of him as a person always with affection – Thomas Hardy:

> The longer I live, the more does B[rowning]'s character seem the literary puzzle of the 19th Century. *How* could smug Christian optimism worthy of a dissenting grocer find a place inside a man who was so vast a seer and feeler when on neutral ground? [2]

And Hardy there, with the word 'dissenting' (which Santayana eschews), brings us back to our chief concerns, and to my reluctant contention that Browning is least the seer when he is most the Dissenter. This in turn will prompt questions about why the tradition of Dissent, which in the past had served John Bunyan and Isaac Watts so well, served Browning so ill, in short, why and how Hardy's sneer at a 'dissenting grocer' is justifiable.

The principal exhibit has to be Browning's *Christmas-Eve and Easter-Day,* published 1 April 1850. Would that it were otherwise, for Browning's most fervent admirers have long been apologetic about this poem, and no one wants to bring a large-hearted poet to book for what is a wretched performance, nor to find readers for something that is in everybody's interests better left unread. But it is the poem in which Browning's sympathy with the Dissenting chapels is most explicit, and so it cannot be avoided. I shall pass over it as fast as I can, taking it as manifest that the writing, line by line, displays all of Browning's vices and few or none of his virtues. In the poem Browning takes us in imagination, on

[2] Quoted by Kingsbury Badger, ibid., p. 73.

Christmas Eve of 1849, to London, to Rome, and to Göttingen. Driven by rain squalls into Zion Chapel Meeting, the speaker of the poem listens with the Dissenters to the garbling of scripture by their zealous and vociferous pastor, until the persona either falls asleep or drifts into a distracted reverie. In dream or in reverie he fancies himself transported first to St Peter's in Rome and then to a theology lecture in Göttingen. And in this way we are invited to consider, in the context of the greatest of Christian festivals, the Dissenters' Christianity, the Roman Catholics', and finally a rationalist's. The rationalist in question was conceived very largely on the model of David Friedrich Strauss, whose *Life of Jesus Critically Examined* (1845) was to help shake or destroy the Christian faith of many eminent Victorians, including that of its translator, George Eliot. Browning's was neither shaken nor destroyed, for the sufficient reason that, as Santayana recognized, his 'faith', though it comes with a great head of emotional steam behind it, has virtually no intellectual substance whatever, for Strauss or any other rationalist to unsettle. The most telling witnesses to this are precisely those who, all too faithfully following the directives of their poet, would defend *Christmas-Eve and Easter-Day*, if not as poetry exactly, at least as responsible discourse; who think that Browning can escape the strictures of Santayana or of Hoxie N. Fairchild. Thus 'Browning', says Douglas Bush, 'could not take historical criticism as final, because human reason and knowledge are limited and fallible and because the real evidence is within the soul'. And thus, says Bush, 'in spite of his antagonism to Strauss, Browning's attitude was not altogether different, though his positive faith was less intellectual and more fervent'.[3] The explicit anti-intellectualism here ('less intellectual and more fervent') would obviously cut no ice with Santayana, who had specifically accused Browning of 'contempt for rationality', and had declared that 'a failure of reason is a failure of art and taste'. The real giveaway comes with another apologist, Kingsbury Badger, who explains: 'It is really not Strauss's historical demolition that Browning objects to; it is rather the purely intellectual, emotion-starved, unpoetic substitute that he offers for the Christ of the Evangelists'.[4] The baleful conjunction here (and how sadly familiar it is, surely, to most of us) is of 'intellectual' with 'unpoetic'. Poetry belongs with warm and damp 'emotion', not with cold and dry 'intellect' (for which read 'Reason', 'rationality'). Do I need to remind you how on the contrary, when we glanced in my second lecture at the Christian poetry of Christopher Smart and Charles Wesley, we had specifically to recognize 'not primarily the sympathies of the human heart, but the energies of human Reason'? The difference over a century between Wesley's 'Being's source begins to be,/ And God Himself is born', and Browning's 'Believe in me,/ Who lived and died, yet essen-

[3] Douglas Bush, *Science and English Poetry* (London, 1950), p. 132.
[4] Badger, op. cit., p. 87.

tially/ Am Lord of Life', is the difference between Enlightenment and unEnlightenment. In the eighteenth century our Christian poetry requires of us strenuous thinking; in the nineteenth it demands only *fervour.*

Browning's departure from orthodoxy into Shelleyan atheism, and then his wobbling back into an ambiguous and untenable no-man's-land between Belief and Unbelief, has been explained several times, chiefly by way of his emotional dependence on the two women in his life – his mother, and his wife. And undoubtedly such psychobiographical explanations have their interest and their value. But they need to be supplemented, as they seldom are, by explanations in terms of social history and the history of ideas. Such explanations would have to recreate in some detail the climate of ideas and sentiments in which lived and moved all those, like Browning's mother, who week by week sat at the feet of the Congregationalist George Clayton as he ministered to them at York Street Chapel, Walworth.[5] What seems certain is that York Street Chapel was a very different milieu from that of Zion Chapel in *Christmas-Eve and Easter-Day;* a milieu in which Robert Browning's father may not have been the only member of Mr Clayton's congregation to have on his shelves the letters of Junius and Horace Walpole, and the works of Voltaire, Charles Avison's *Essay on Musical Expression* and Vasari's *Lives of the Painters* and Gerard de Lairesse's *The Art of Painting in All Its Branches.* It would certainly be to the point to identify George Clayton as the son of John Clayton, the Congregationalist minister who in the 1790s had earned the animosity of most of his fellow-ministers by speaking out for Pitt and for war with France, and against the English Jacobins. George Clayton, it appears, preached a Calvinism that had learned to be urbane and genteel without, however, abandoning the crucial tenets of universal depravity and salvation by faith. Early pages of Clyde Binfield's *So Down to Prayers* (London, 1977) show that there were in England in the 1820s and 1830s many more such Calvinists than is usually supposed; Calvinists who thought themselves creatures of an Enlightenment more capacious than the one which Tom Paine and William Godwin and Mary Wollstonecraft had attempted to monopolize.

However, the Brownings by 1850 had read, or were to read, David Strauss and Bishop Colenso and Renan. If we claim Isaac Backus for the Enlightenment because he had read John Locke, or we call the eighteenth-century English Dissenters Watts and Doddridge 'enlightened' because they read Locke and Racine and Fenelon as well as Jonathan Edwards, how can we deny 'enlightenment' to the Brownings who similarly studied the most advanced thinkers of their later day? It is just here that Santayana, remorselessly pressing home his case for the prosecution,

[5] See Clayton's *Course of Sermons on Faith and Practice Delivered at York Street Chapel, Walworth, 1838-39* (London, 1939).

comes to our aid: enlightenment is not a matter of what authors you read, but of the spirit you read them in:

> ... Browning has no idea of an intelligible good which the phases of life might approach and with reference to which they might constitute a progress. His notion is simply that the game of life, the exhilaration of action, is inexhaustible. You may set up your tenpins again after you have bowled them over, and you may keep up the sport for ever. The point is to bring them down as often as possible with a master-stroke and a big bang. That will tend to invigorate in you that self-confidence which in this system passes for faith.

And Santayana presses the point home by attacking the Italianate Browning precisely on the score of that Italian culture which Browning declared to be the university he had studied in, after he had dropped out of that Unitarian and Dissenting institution, the infant University of London, for which his father had entered him. Browning, so Santayana claims, knew nothing of the austere and elevated level of Italian culture represented by the names of Dante and Cavalcanti, Michelangelo and Lorenzo de Medici; and here it may well be thought that Santayana goes too far – one of Browning's later admirers, Ezra Pound, seems to have thought that he did.

What I need to establish is that Browning's development – from a genteel Calvinism, through Shelleyan or Unitarian optimism, to vaguely fideistic fervour – was characteristic of the best minds in Dissent in his lifetime. And that would demand more time than I have, and more learning. I must content myself with one parallel that I hope you will find suggestive – with Thomas Binney, minister of the Weigh-house chapel in London and widely recognized in the 1850s and 1860s as the weightiest and most distinguished representative of the Dissenting churches in England. Moreover, Binney was a poet. He is at any rate the author of one poem that is not known so widely as it deserves, though it survives in our hymnbooks and is sometimes sung in protestant churches. It is a poem too about *enlightenment,* having for its epigraph one of those texts that Christians can appeal to when they refuse to let the metaphor of light be taken over by unbelievers: 'The King of kings, and Lord of lords Who only hath immortality, dwelling in light inapproachable, Whom no man hath seen, nor can see' (I Tim. 5: 15, 16). Binney's poem, accordingly, is entitled: 'Eternal Light':

> Eternal Light! Eternal Light!
>   How pure the soul must be
> When, placed within Thy searching sight,
> It shrinks not, but with calm delight
>   Can live, and look on Thee!

The Spirits that surround Thy throne
May bear the burning bliss;
But that is surely theirs alone,
Since they have never, never known
A fallen world like this.

O how shall I, whose native sphere
Is dark, whose mind is dim,
Before the Ineffable appear,
And on my naked spirit bear
That uncreated beam?

There is a way for man to rise
To that sublime abode,
An Offering and a Sacrifice,
A HOLY SPIRIT's energies,
An advocate with God:

These, these prepare us for the sight
Of holiness above;
The sons of ignorance and night
May dwell in the Eternal Light,
Through the Eternal Love.

I put this before you as an exception to the generalization I risked a few minutes ago, when I said that whereas Christian poetry in our eighteenth century required strenuous thinking, in the nineteenth it demands only fervent feeling. There is thought in Binney's admirably graceful and lucid verses; each stanza clearly enunciates a stage in a well-conducted and interesting argument; and the language, whether touchingly the language of speech as in the second stanza or more elevated and sonorous as in the third, is used responsibly. The poem is admirable in a way that modern criticism, so enamoured of 'complexity', pays too little heed to. And yet the burden of the poem, what it *says,* almost denies the very rationality that so clearly went into its making and its ordering. The light, we note, is *all* in heaven; there is no suggestion that the light of human Reason, fallible as it certainly is and in need of being crucially assisted by Grace, can yet take the human being *some way* towards those crystalline apprehensions which (we admit) are constantly available only to the blest in Eternity. Our native sphere is said to be 'dark', and our minds 'dim'. And so they are, of course; yet we do have the light of Reason to illuminate us, however fitfully. And this is something that Binney's poem leaves out of account. In doing so, it repudiates the belief and aspiration of the Enlightenment.

And in this way we begin to see how the author of this poem could also have expressed himself, less attractively, as follows:

> A whole world-full of modern men, with the thoughts to think and the work to do belonging to their age, have been obliged to listen for weeks and months to the jargon of the schools, to metaphysical distinctions and theological niceties that *they* can only regard as important who draw the pabulum of their internal life from the past – *man's* past, not God's – the times of councils and popes and priests, who suspended eternity on whatever attached importance to themselves! Why, who cares what this council, or that, or the other, thought or determined? What is it to us, who have got something else to think about and do, in this nineteenth century of the Christian redemption (and society nothing like redeemed yet), than to hear what was thought, hundreds of years ago, on matters it may be, which nobody believes, or about which we can judge better ourselves than any old ecclesiastical conclave could judge for us? [6]

This is the voice not of any run-of-the-mill Dissenting rabble-rouser but of the author of 'Eternal Light'; the man who boldly rethought and reformulated a social role for Congregationalism in his day, and also a liturgy for it; the man who under a pseudonym was singled out for commendation in *The Revolution in Tanner's Lane* (1887), that Victorian novel which is most inward with English Nonconformity, written by the very wary and critical and admirable man who wrote under the pseudonym, 'Mark Rutherford'. Before Binney died there had appeared the most searing indictment, by a Victorian, of the characteristic temper of Victorian Nonconformity. This was Matthew Arnold's *Culture and Anarchy* (1869), in which the Victorian Dissenters are assailed as the principal carriers of the virus that Arnold calls 'philistinism', thereby creating the meaning that 'philistine' and 'philistinism' have for us today. And the voice that says, 'We can judge better ourselves than any old ecclesiastical conclave could judge for us', is the very voice of Matthew Arnold's *philistine*. It comes as no surprise that Binney's admiring Victorian biographer should jauntily concede that he had probably never read Jonathan Edwards; or that the sectarian journal of the time, *The Nonconformist,* should in its obituary of Binney give him credit for having cleared out 'much of the ancient dispensation, handed down through six generations of Dissenters'. Binney's voice is hard to distinguish, surely, from that of the American Baptist leader whom we heard, in 1973, opting for Christ *as against* 'culture'.

What Arnold stigmatized as 'philistine' in *Culture and Anarchy* (elsewhere his word for it is 'provincial') is a quality of *tone;* and accordingly it's something which, if people cannot hear it for themselves, they cannot be convinced of. It is to be heard, surely, in what has just been quoted

6. E. Paxton Hood, *Thomas Binney: His Mind, Life, and Opinions* (London, 1874), p. 33. All subsequent quotations are from this source.

from Thomas Binney – a tone that is brutal, overemphatic, overconfident: 'Why, who cares... this council, or that, or the other... What is it to us... something else to think about and do... we can judge better...' Many Victorians seem to have heard it, this tone of voice, as manly, as hearty – in the sense of heartfelt and wholehearted; it seemed to them to have the authority of Thomas Carlyle, and indeed it is surely with Carlyle that it originates. It is certainly not peculiar to Nonconformists, but is to be heard for instance in Dickens (who by the way traduced Binney unforgivably), and oddly enough even in Arnold himself at times. It is the voice at all periods, including our own, of 'modern men, with the thoughts to think and the work to do belonging to their age'. It is, above all, impatient and therefore irreverent. And it is certainly to be heard at times in Browning, as in Charles Kingsley, where Gerard Manley Hopkins heard it and characterized it unforgivingly but vividly when he envisaged a man starting up from the breakfast table, his mouth full of bacon and eggs, declaring that he will stand no damn'd nonsense.

Some who can hear this tone, and are even (a little) offended by it, believe that they can excuse it away by fastening on Arnold's alternative word, 'provincial'. Even leaving aside the literally geographical sense of 'provincial', which can provoke from English people angry or scornful rejoinders about snobbish gentilities of the Home Counties and Oxbridge, apologists for Nonconformity can take the figurative meaning that Arnold attached to the word, the meaning of 'far from the centre' – far from that centre, not locatable on any map, where standards (of social and intellectual behaviour) are set up and kept up. What is that centre (so English Dissenters may ask) if not the Establishment, in England the Church of England? And in this way it is possible to protest that Matthew Arnold berates Nonconformists (Dissenters) for not having access to just that centre which he, as a guardian of the Establishment, has carefully debarred them from. It is a defence, no doubt; but hardly one that English Dissenters can take much pride in. And it is in any case untrue to history. For as Dr Johnson recognized when he wrote about the great Dissenter Isaac Watts (in his *Lives of the Poets*), Dissent in Watts's lifetime, and largely thanks to Watts himself, had contrived to get access to that civilized centre, that imaginary academy, despite its sectarian status. Through Isaac Watts and a few other Dissenting leaders like him, Dissenting Christianity had contrived to participate in that great movement in the mind of Western man which we call, when we think about it, 'the Enlightenment'; and that Dissenting yet Enlightenment culture survived in England into the first years of the reign of Queen Victoria. But what later Dissenters thought of it appears from how Paxton Hood, Binney's Victorian biographer, characterized the regime at the King's Weighhouse of John Clayton, Binney's predecessor there: 'a kind of florid frostwork, in which religious truth was held in a cold crystallization of sanctified Chesterfieldism, for ever fearing to offend'. The obituary in *The Nonconformist* had struck the same note in less Carlylean idiom, saying that Binney came to the King's Weigh-house when 'the age of silk and lavender, and of successful suppression of thought under decorous phrases, was coming to an end'. Nineteenth-century Dissenters *did not want,* they contemptuously threw away, the civility and the enlightenment that eighteenth-century Dissent had achieved. And Robert Browning, though he surely never confronted the issue in just these terms nor made any conscious decision about it, is nevertheless infected by this climate of opinion, and disabled by it more than a little.

Santayana says that 'the essential conception of any rational philosophy' is 'that feeling is to be treated as raw material for thought, and that the destiny of emotion is to pass into objects which shall contain all its value while losing all its formlessness'. And he declares: 'This transformation of sense and emotion into objects agreeable to the intellect, into clear ideas and beautiful things, is the natural work of reason...' This is a view of 'reason' for which we can find no room so long as we are hung up on a dichotomy between intellect supposedly 'cold' and feeling or emotion supposedly 'warm'. To the Victorians it seemed that the rationalism of the Enlightenment had produced systems of thought that were indeed 'cold': atheism, Unitarianism, utilitarianism. And a Victorian like Browning, appalled by the chill that came up from these systems, opted instead for the warmth of feelings that Browning was content *not* to have transformed into 'clear ideas and beautiful things'. Many of us, more than a century later, are on the horns of this same false dilemma, and opt for Browning's solution or evasion. Santayana speaks to us, if we are prepared to listen, by showing that the dilemma is indeed a false one, since 'rationality' is something altogether more ample than 'rationalism'.

It is because we, in our art and our morals and politics, need rather desperately to learn this lesson, that we cannot shuffle off or set aside Santayana's condemnation of Browning in the light of these principles. All the same, those of us who are most persuaded by Santayana's argument as a whole may properly rebel at some of his particular judgments. This one, for instance:

> Love is depicted by Browning with truth, with vehemence, and with the constant conviction that it is the supreme thing in life. The great variety of occasions in which it appears in his pages and the different degrees of elaboration it receives, leave it always of the same quality – the quality of passion. It never sinks into sensuality; in spite of its frequent extreme crudeness, it is always, in Browning's hands, a passion of the imagination, it is always love. On the other hand it never rises into contemplation: mingled as it may be with friendship, with religion, or with various forms of natural tenderness, it always

> remains a passion; it always remains a personal impulse, a hypnotization, with another person for its object or its cause.

We may agree that this is a true description of how Browning treats of love between the sexes and still feel that Browning's achievement in this area deserves far more credit than Santayana will accord it. To stay faithful to passion, without falling on the one hand into sensuality or taking wing on the other hand into some sort of sublimation – we, who have seen how hard it is to maintain this balance, may well feel admiring gratitude to Browning, especially when we recall how many of his most glowing and ardent love-poems (I will instance just one, the beautifully tender 'One Word More') are poems of married love. Some of us are more aware than Santayana seems to have been, of how often apparent sublimations of sexual passion mask impulses of domination and appropriation of the beloved by the lover. Moreover it's by no means clear that Browning was unaware of those Santayana calls 'the real masters of passion and imagination', for whom 'the sudden self-surrender in which he rests was... the starting-point of a life of rational worship', for whom therefore 'love ceased to be a passion and became the energy of contemplation'. With two such 'masters', Dante and Michelangelo, Browning seems to have had dealings far more intimate than Santayana allows for. A later poet who was proud to subscribe himself one of Browning's poetic sons ('*Pourquoi nier son père*?' he said) seems to have been prepared to defend Browning on this flank. This was Ezra Pound, who speaks with authority since he probed behind Dante and Cavalcanti in search of this love that is 'the energy of contemplation', and located it in the 'AMOR' of those Provençal poets whom Dante confessedly learned from; and accordingly no poem by Browning matters more to Pound than the long and early *Sordello*, in which Browning treats of a Provençal poet of Mantua.

However that may be, no one need feel ashamed of discovering in Browning a model of love between the sexes, especially love within wedlock, more worthy of emulation than any model that has been provided since. And of course this model or image is particularly potent because it is mirrored not just in Browning's writings but in his life also, so that it influences people who are not students of literature. The famous 'romance' of his courtship of Elizabeth Barrett, and of how like Perseus he released that Andromeda from her rock and from her dragon of a father, has of course been simplified and falsified into soap opera. But the primary documents – Elizabeth Barrett's love letters and her 'Sonnets from the Portuguese', as well as her husband's letters and poems – are still available and resonant for those who want to go to the sources. We shall next be concerned with a modern British poet for whom these documents resound very loudly indeed.

4 *Two of Browning's Heirs*

The British poet Jack Clemo begins his autobiography published this year (*The Marriage of a Rebel* [London, 1980]) as follows:

> On a Saturday afternoon in July 1947 a small grey-haired woman stood at the tomb of Robert Browning in Westminster Abbey. Through horn-rimmed spectacles her large black eyes probed the shadowy carvings and slabs of Poets' Corner with the nervousness of a country-dweller who was paying her first visit to London. She was alone, and there was an atmosphere of solitude about her: one could not imagine her as a woman who had many friends. It was as though she had spent most of her life grappling with situations so unusual that in her attempts to understand and deal with them she had lost touch with her prosaic working-class neighbours, and with the trends and interests of her own generation. Her sallow face which had never been softened by cosmetics, was deeply lined with suffering, and the big nose and determined jaw suggested that strength of character had developed in her at the expense of superficial charm. But there was no bitterness in her expression. As she bent forward to read the inscription on Browning's tomb her face relaxed in a sort of bewildered gratitude.
>
> The woman was my mother, Eveline Clemo...

And Jack Clemo goes on to explain that the suffering which had grooved his mother's face was largely involved with her caring for her physically afflicted son, himself, whereas her bewildered gratitude to Browning (whom she had hardly read) was because it was from Browning that her son had derived the sustaining conviction that despite his afflictions he would become an author, and that his writing would be bound up, as Browning's was, with happy marriage. Then, in 1947, the first of these unlikely aspirations had been realized, with the acceptance of Clemo's novel, *Wilding Graft*, of which both the title and the motto were taken from Browning's poems; but the second consummation, marriage, was still twenty years in the future.

Jack Clemo is a poet hardly known in the USA though it is twenty years since Daniel Hoffman published a poem about him in the *Transatlantic Review*. His afflictions have been dwelt upon more than he likes; for understandably he resents being presented as a sort of prodigious freak. Briefly, he has been throughout his life intermittently and partially (of late almost totally) blind and deaf. What is more to the point is that he is as authentic a *proletarian* author as modem Britain has produced; and that he is also in our time perhaps the most authentic and distinguished poet to come out of, and to speak for, English Dissenting Protestantism.

The Marriage of a Rebel which is subtitled portentously but accurately 'A Mystical-erotic Quest', is not Clemo's first essay in autobiography. It had been preceded by *Confession of a Rebel* (1949) and by *The Invading Gospel* (1958). No one of these books can be ignored. All can be considered, if we care to take them that way, as necessary commentaries on Clemo's poetry. And it may be objected that poetry of the best sort does not need, does not so depend on, extraneous elucidation by the poet. The objection is just, but it should not be pressed very far. For this poet emerges from, and articulates, a cultural situation so special, both personally and historically, that it is not the poet's fault but rather the fault of avoidable ignorance on our part, if a context for his poems has to be laboriously supplied – and by the poet himself, if no one else volunteers. It has been the assumption, and in part the burden, of these lectures, that the cultural tradition which this poet speaks from – Dissenting Christianity – is habitually and improperly considered, in Britain as in the USA, as an 'underground' tradition, about which the most total ignorance is excusable. But in any case Clemo's Dissenting inheritance, and also his physical disabilities, are only the start; he cuts athwart our expectations in all sorts of other ways. For instance, the sheer fact of his Englishness is in some degree open to question. He is, and not by accident but by inheritance, a Cornishman, a son of that southwestern peninsula of England where he has always lived and lives still, where the inhabitants are well aware of themselves as a Celtic people having ethnically less in common with the English than with the Welshmen of Wales and the Bretons of Britanny, that northwestern peninsula of France which the Cornish in the Dark Ages imperially colonized. Thus Clemo's is a special case in all sorts of ways; and yet I believe he supports and illustrates the thesis that I am urging.

In the first place there can be no doubt that he is an heir of Robert Browning. *The Marriage of a Rebel* tells us how the dog whose companionship meant much to Clemo through some of his most desolate years was named by him 'Plush' after the famous lapdog of Elizabeth Barrett; and the same narrative shows Clemo giving superstitious attention to how the dates of momentous events in his own life corresponded, on the calendar, with dates in the records of the Brownings' courtship and marriage. The internal evidence of his poems tells the same story: a poem called 'The Brownings at Vallombrosa' fittingly illustrates, among a score of other instances, how some idiosyncrasies of Browning's writing – notably, in meter, a headlong readiness to substitute trisyllabic for disyllabic feet, and an obtrusive rhyming which, while it doesn't determine or divert meaning, still draws attention to itself too flagrantly to satisfy such as Santayana – are features of Clemo's practice also. Like Browning Clemo not only is, but seeks to be, in his writing craggy, roughhewn, volcanic. Accordingly we need not expect to find him recovering for the Dissenting tradition that sinewy yet suave polish which it had known, in the Enlightenment, at the hands of Isaac Watts:

> Hosanna to the royal son
> Of David's ancient line!
> His natures two, his person one,
> Mysterious and divine...

No, this is not Clemo's tone at all. And in fact he is very categorical and explicit about this, as we might expect from a writer so self-conscious. In *Confession of a Rebel* he declares:

> It was impossible for me ever to take the cultured, civilized view of human rights – or of anything else. I demanded Christian gusto and scorned the weary dignity of the classic ideal. Ever since my childhood I had detested the Greek spirit and loved the Gothic...

And in *The Invading Gospel* he confesses that 'I liked Wesley's hymns and much of his *Journal*, but his sermons seemed to me as chilled by eighteenth-century rationality as the writings of Edwards and Haldane'. This antipathy to *rationality* (not just to 'rationalism'), which Clemo finds as offensive in the Calvinist Jonathan Edwards as in the Arminian John Wesley, warns us clearly not to look in him for a remarriage between the Dissenting heritage and 'the Enlightenment'. On the other hand, though his demand for what he calls 'Christian gusto' is constant with him, and fervent – he was perhaps the only British man of letters, certainly the only British poet, to respond with enthusiasm to the evangelist Billy Graham – it would not be true to say of him what we have to say much of the time, regretfully, of Browning: that his Christian faith is all fervent feeling, with no intellectual substance. On the contrary there is surely nobility as well as pathos in the story he tells of how, a penurious autodidact in enforced isolation, he became aware in the late 1940s of the achievement of the great Swiss theologian Karl Barth, who regenerated for our time the Calvinist doctrines which the young Clemo had imbibed, mutinously sometimes, at the knee of his mother, bred in the Calvinist variant of Methodism which has always been particularly strong in Cornwall. *The Invading Gospel* is the one of his autobiographies which brings out most clearly how Clemo's Dissent had intellectual sinews, such as Browning's hadn't. And the processional stateliness of Clemo's poem, 'On the Death of Karl Barth', movingly commemorates the great theologian and trail-breaker.

If we say of this, as we might of other poems by Clemo, that it and they are quite unlike other modern poems in English, we may seem to be claiming for their author only the status of an oddity, a curio, perhaps an anomalous survivor. And it is true that none of the categories that usually serve us well with modern poets – 'symbolist' or 'post-symbolist', 'imagist' or 'post-imagist', 'objectivist' or 'objectist', indeed not even the capacious category 'modernist' itself – will help us with this body of poetry. Neither 'symbol' nor 'image' will help us because the habit of Clemo's imagination is constantly and indelibly *allegorical*. Those of us who remember *Maule's Curse,* the late Yvor Winters's study of the Calvinist sensibility in New England, will remember how Winters argued that the allegorical habit – the reading of experience for clues and signs to the Divine purpose – was in that culture endemic and inescapable. Clemo's reading of his own experience is always of this kind; and though his poems are crowded with sensuous details in a way remarkable for a poet whose senses were impaired, those details are to be read in a way quite different from anything we are used to in the symbolist or the imagist ways of writing: every sensuous detail has to be (and usually is, explicitly) *decoded,* allegorically. And before we jump to the conclusion that this is a way of experiencing that we all left behind in seventeenth-century Massachusetts, we need to pause and think whether, for good or ill, this way of reading the universe for 'signs' is not inculcated at the present time, week by week, in various protestant communions, Baptist and other, where, so we may conjecture, this allegorizing habit is still the staple intellectual activity, alike in the pulpit and out of it.

Clemo's finest poem, I think, is his 'Mould of Castile', dedicated to St Teresa of Avila, and closely related throughout to what we know of Teresa's life (1515–82). And incidentally this is only the best of several poems in which Clemo, nonconformist protestant though he is, pays tribute to saints of the Roman Church; 'oecumenical' is what he has always been, in the sense of being ready to go to any Christian Church at all to get the spiritual nourishment that he needs. (It's in this spirit that he can pay tribute to the Anglican C.S. Lewis: 'He was no Calvinist, but Calvinism is a statement of how Christianity works, and fellowship rests on an agreement as to what Christianity is'.) In 'Mould of Castile' Clemo has unshackled himself from all Browningesque precedents in the use of rhyme, meter, and stanza structure:

> A streak of Sappho, it is said,
> Inflamed you, the painted and imperious
> Charmer in velvet robes at Avila;
> But soon your withered young bones rattled
> On convent stones: gaunt postulant,
> You had fled, still dead to God, from a goblin-flare.

No mist or dream had softened
The bold Castilian flint: there was sun-glare
On bull-fights and flashing lizards
And the hot black stems of olives, pungent cistus,
Awaiting the shift and shock, an El Greco storm.

Did you waste thirty years
In fighting the sun, flashing out
With a gay jest between swoons and fears
Of those winged visions? Did election dare
Molest your Spanish pride
To that length, fan a fury of love
That soared, bled in the trap,
Lapped a wilful ease, lastly, in brisk reform?

You were ageing, an enigma still,
When your mules arrived at San Jose,
And a thunder that thrills my flint
In Cornwall now, spread from the wooden waggons,
Filled with your nuns, lurching over calcined plains,
Up primitive mountain-tracks, drifting aground
On river ferries. You and they were bound
For new cells in Elisha's shadow:
Traditional rock like that which my poet-soul,
As wasted and adamant,
Split and gay as yours, descried
Beyond sly bramble, misted kiln
And the dried voluptuary veins.

It should be clear that in this poem the landscape of Castile (which of course the poet had never seen), with its characteristic light and colour, is to be interpreted neither symbolically nor imagistically but allegorically or else emblematically – as is, in the last two lines, the terrain of that industrially mutilated landscape, the China-clay district of Cornwall where Clemo was born and has lived, unresentfully, ever since.

'Mould of Castile' and also 'On the Death of Karl Barth' appeared – along with other instructive pieces like 'Porthmeor Cemetery' and 'Mary Shelley in Geneva' and 'Cookworthy at Carloggas' – in Clemo's collection of 1971, *The Echoing Tip*. His next collection, which is his last to date, *Broad Autumn* (1975), contains other pieces that are striking and memorable. Among these is 'Royal Wedding', about the wedding of the Princess Anne, an occasion that Clemo was party to by way of radio or else television, and thanks to the assistance of his own late-found and devoted wife. This poem, though it includes patches of weak writing, is interesting because it shows how a proletarian religious Dissenter like

Clemo can be a sincerely patriotic monarchist, can find significance and alleviation for his own condition by participating in the rituals of the monarchy. This contention – as I prefer to say, this truth – is very unwelcome to many people in England. On the one hand are those who are or conceive themselves to be of the governing class, to whom it rather commonly seems that properly monarchical sentiments are available only to members of that church, the Church of England, of which the monarch is the head. And on the other hand are those more or less *marxisant* politicians and educators and historians who take it for granted that an unprivileged proletarian like Clemo must nurse sentiments that are antimonarchist, if not republican, at all events socialist.

You will have noticed that Clemo explicitly and with a heavy hand relates the situation of St Teresa to his own situation. And with him this is normal. Places and people, however remote from Jack Clemo, are in his poems sooner or later connected directly and quite explicitly with himself in his own landscape of Cornwall. This is inevitable, given the allegorical cast of his imagination; people and places are scrutinized for clues and keys – and to what if not to himself, his own spiritual and cultural condition? This means that his poetry is very self-centred. How could it be otherwise? Since physical circumstance and historical accident have placed Clemo in a universe so special that hardly anyone shares it with him, how could he not put himself at the centre of it? The consequence is however, that he is very far from sharing a characteristic emphasis of the modernist poetry we associate with the name of T.S Eliot – that is to say, the aspiration towards a poetry that shall be *im*personal, a product of the English language and of the English-speaking peoples, rather than of any one speaker of that language at any one time. To be sure, in this Clemo is not unlike other authors who are sometimes called 'modernist' – D.H. Lawrence, for example, who at one time meant much to him. But this has had the effect of closing to Clemo one kind of poem to which his nonconformist background might have seemed to give him privileged access – the poem that is a hymn. For the congregational hymn, precisely because it is composed so as to be uttered not by an individual but by a congregation or by many congregations, is therefore necessarily, and in a very obvious sense, *impersonal*. This was recognized by Eliot himself, who linked the hymn with (surprisingly) the epigram, saying of both that they are 'extremely objective types of verse'. Accordingly, neither hymn nor epigram is to be found in the poetry of Jack Clemo. Both are to be found however in the work of another of Browning's heirs: Rudyard Kipling. It was with Kipling in mind that T.S. Eliot was led to this reflection. And Rudyard Kipling is the next of the modern poets whom I want to consider – another poet who, though undoubtedly 'modern', is certainly not 'modernist', another poet with whom categories like 'symbolist' and 'imagist' get us nowhere at all.

Kipling of course is a famous riddle; and accordingly he has attracted the attention not just of Eliot but of others among the most powerful and fearless minds of our time, Edmund Wilson and Lionel Trilling, George Orwell and Randall Jarrell and Angus Wilson. I will be bold enough to suggest that the riddle is less riddling than some of these distinguished minds have made out. For instance, Edmund Wilson's momentous essay of 1941, 'The Kipling that Nobody Read', rests on the assumption that Kipling's account of his own boyhood is so tightlipped as to be dishonest; and if we find on the contrary that in Kipling's fragmentary and incomplete autobiography, *Something of Myself* (1937), the account of his boyhood in all its reticence rings true, then most of Wilson's argument slips down like a house of cards. More generally, as I am not the first to notice, the riddle of Kipling is largely created by liberal and humanitarian critics who have decided, without noticing, that literary genius can be allowed to happen only among people who share their social and political sentiments. They suppose that imperialists and racists are, by definition, stupid; Kipling, who was imperialist and racist, wasn't stupid at all, nor philistine either – hence the riddle, which is a riddle only to those political 'liberals' whom Kipling consistently baited and deliberately affronted throughout his writing life. This, we may begin to suspect, is one of those cases where 'liberal' points one way, and 'enlightened' points another.

Kipling was not a son or heir of Robert Browning in quite the straightforward way that we have seen with Jack Clemo. Kipling, no one denies, was astonishingly precocious; and also he profited by exceptionally enlightened schooling (though his grateful acknowledgement of that is another testimony that his critics refuse to accept). Accordingly, almost from the first Browning's influence had to be combined with, or find its place among, the numerous other literary precedents that the omnivorous schoolboy was astonishingly aware of. Nevertheless the primacy of Browning (taking precedence even over Swinbume, whom Eliot makes much of) is sufficiently attested by for instance C.E. Carrington's standard biography, and it shows up, as Carrington astutely notes, not only in poems but in the structure of some of the early and famous stories. Now, Browning was capable of writing poems that are, by whatever standard, objective and impersonal; as witness for instance his much loved yet underrated 'Cavalier Tunes', which were to serve Ezra Pound memorably when Pound was translating some poems of ancient China. Yet in Browning, despite his nonconformist background, such impersonal lyrics never took the form of hymns or of poems that are hymnlike. Accordingly we look in vain in Browning for anything that points to Kipling's hymn or hymnlike 'Recessional' of 1897, perhaps the most famous of all his poems:

God of our fathers, known of old,
  Lord of our far-flung battle-line,
Beneath whose awful Hand we hold
  Dominion over palm and pine –
Lord God of Hosts, be with us yet,
  Lest we forget – lest we forget!

Here we encounter, as distinct from the largely factitious 'riddle' of Kipling, one of the many authentic mysteries about him: when, where, and from whom did he imbibe that awesomely wide yet exact familiarity with the idiom of the Old Testament (in the King James version, of course) which lends authority and resonance to a poem like this, just as it does to its unregarded and orthodox ancestors, hymns by Isaac Watts and Charles Wesley? (The same authority, and the same resonance, are earned by poems that are not hymnlike at all, as well as by many of the famous stories.) To this question, so far as I can see, neither Kipling's own memoirs nor the reputable biographies provide any answer. After all, it is not as if Kipling grew up in a God-fearing and church-going family; on the contrary, Kipling's parents had lapsed from an ancestral Methodism to the point where they very seldom attended any church at all, and equally seldom we may suppose read Scripture together. Where then did the knowledge of Scripture come from? May we dare to suppose that it came from her who is the villain of the story according to Edmund Wilson (though not according to Kipling) – the ogress of Southsea, the cruel foster-mother (described as 'Evangelical' and 'Calvinist', as if the terms were interchangeable) with whom the young Rudyard was boarded out while his parents remained in India? Perish the thought! And yet the question remains: where did Rudyard Kipling, embarrassingly anti-Semite at times in his later life, imbibe his conception of certain races as 'chosen of God', as the 'elect', if not from the Hebrew scriptures of the Old Testament?

I ought to make it clear where I stand, as regards this so celebrated 'Recessional'. It is a poem right enough, a masterly one. It belongs with poetry, not (where Eliot would put it) in a vaguely undefined but somehow subordinate category called 'verse', still less in that fatuous *ad hoc* category dreamed up by George Orwell, 'good bad poetry'. 'Recessional' is a poem, a very *wicked* poem. And I call it wicked not because it enunciates relations between the races of mankind such as I myself do not hold by (and yes, to be sure, we know that 'the lesser breeds without the law' are white Germans, not brown Afghans); but for more strictly artistic reasons – because a form of poetry consecrated to the celebration of Christian charity (as that Charity could and was understood by Isaac Watts and his first auditors) is here perverted to the purposes of *un*Charity. Another way of saying this is that Kipling in this poem cold-bloodedly and expertly touched one after another of the stops that would move an audience of Christian Believers into sympathy with himself, who was a cynical Unbeliever. Nothing is more astonishing – and yet nothing, given the present benign muddle about the boundary between Belief and Unbelief, is more logical – than that this poem, this most shocking of all Kipling's utterances, should be habitually exempted from criticism by those commentators who on other grounds bear hardest on him.

Did Kipling in any case belong to, or have any feelingful connection with, that tradition in English culture which we have identified as 'Dissent'? Edmund Wilson and some other commentators have made much of the fact that his grandfathers on both sides were Methodist ministers; and his cousin Stanley Baldwin, later Prime Minister of Great Britain, declared on one occasion that this inheritance that he shared with Kipling made both of them heirs to a 'puritan' tradition. But once again we may as well trust Kipling himself, who in *Something of Myself* spoke of this Wesleyan tradition in his family as something presented to him only late, and as it were in passing. In any case, it is not at all clear that the Wesleyan (Methodist) persuasion in English history belongs with the Dissenting, the Nonconformist, strain. There are those who will maintain vociferously that it does not, so late come as it is, and, during the lives of the Wesley brothers, so determined not to secede from the Church of England in which it began. The truth seems to be that a Methodist in England is a Dissenter, a Nonconformist, only if he chooses so to regard himself, or so to acquiesce in the opinion that his Anglican neighbours have of him. Jack Clemo declares outright (*The Marriage of a Rebel*, p. 65) that he conceived his Calvinistic Methodism as making of him a Nonconformist. But there is no evidence that the inherited Methodism of the Kiplings and the Baldwins led them to think of themselves in any such light. It was useful to them, however, as a sort of fall-back position, when they got themselves into quandaries and self-contradictions which only a profession of Nonconformity or of 'puritanism' could get them out of. This seems to have happened to Kipling at the time of the war in South Africa, when his poems about that war make such rhetorical play with heroes of the Nonconformist tradition, such as Bunyan and Cromwell. The exceptionally implausible special pleadings that this let him in for is something I have examined elsewhere;[1] and it is all part of the background of 'Recessional'. Even in *Something of Myself,* and certainly in the poems and stories, there is evidence that the Boer War, the war in South Africa, was what coarsened and rigidified Kipling's ideas and made him more or less consciously prostitute his art. From this rigidity, and from this prostitution, the First World War, in which he lost his only son,

[1] See 'Thoughts on Kipling's "Recessional"' below.

shocked him back though less than perfectly.

Though Edmund Wilson is wrongheaded, and also surprisingly ignorant about the *mores* of the British propertied classes before 1914, nevertheless his essay, 'The Kipling That Nobody Read', has the merits of living up to its title and of directing attention to the neglected older Kipling, post-1918. Wilson however was concerned for the storyteller of those years, not the poet. And a case is to be made for the ageing Kipling as a poet. This is the Kipling who is drawn not to the hymn but to the other of the 'objective' and 'impersonal' forms that Eliot identified – the epigram. And Eliot duly included in his *Choice of Kipling's Verse* (1941) the very fine and harrowing sequence, 'Epitaphs of the War'. But the virtues of the epigram inform some other poems, Landorian or Horatian or both, that are too long to be called epigrams proper; and these Eliot represented less generously. In particular he seems to have disapproved of the harmless hoax that Kipling cooked up with the help of A.D. Godley, Orator of Oxford University, when he issued what purported to be translations from a nonexistent Book V of Horace's Odes. And yet some of these poems are a great deal better and more serious than mere japes. It is very interesting to learn from C.E. Carrington that Horace's Odes, more specifically Book III of them, which he was made to study by his schoolmaster F.W. Haslam, is pretty well the only text from ancient Greek or Latin which Kipling knew in the original. (Unlike Browning before him, or the self-educated Thomas Hardy, Kipling knew no classical Greek at all, and little Latin; this is one seldom noticed way in which Kipling was very 'modern' indeed – at his school, which was, as he rightly said, 'before its time', English literature was made to serve the purpose that, through the centuries since the Renaissance, Greek and Latin literature had served. Kipling knows English literature so well because he knows classical literature so little, and in the generations before him there are very few English poets of whom this is true.) At any rate Horace, and the Horatian tone in verse, came to mean much to him. It can be detected as early as 1901, in 'The Reformers'; but most of the poems in this chiselled lapidary manner belong to the years after 1918. One, dated 1920, is 'Lollius', which belongs with the 'spoof' translations, and accordingly does not appear in Eliot's *Choice*:

Why gird at Lollius if he care
    To purchase in the city's sight,
With nard and roses for his hair
    The name of Knight?

Son of unmitigated sires
    Enriched by trade in Afric corn,
His wealth allows, his wife requires,
    Him to be born.

Him slaves shall serve with zeal renewed
 At lesser wage for longer whiles,
And school- and station-masters rude
 Receive with smiles.

His bowels shall be sought in charge
 By learned doctors; all his sons
And nubile daughters shall enlarge
 Their horizons.

For fierce she-Britons, apt to smite
 Their upward-climbing sisters down
Shall smooth their plumes and oft invite
 The brood to town.

For these delights will he disgorge
 The State enormous benefice,
But – by the head of either George –
 He pays not twice!

Whom neither lust for public pelf,
 Nor itch to make orations, vex –
Content to honour his own self
 With his own cheques –

That man is clean. At least, his house
 Springs cleanly from untainted gold –
Not from a conscience or a spouse
 Sold and resold.

Time was, you say, before men knew
 Such arts, and rose by Virtue guided?
The tables rock with laughter – you
 Not least derided.

This represents a sort of poetry so different from what we have become used to that some of us not only take no pleasure in it, but actually cannot make sense of it. It may for all we know be aimed at a particular person, though I think not. On the other hand, of the two 'Georges' in stanza 6, if one is King George V, who was or became Kipling's friend, the other is surely David Lloyd George, Kipling's political enemy, who notoriously when in power 'sold' peerages and other civil distinctions. 'Lollius', who has thus bought his title with money acquired as a war profiteer, is declared in the poem to be more of a fair dealer than others in the State – the orating politicians who sold it to him, or even it may be those with more ancient titles who have preserved their aristocratic status by 'a conscience or a spouse/ Sold and resold'. What is more important is to recognize how the tersely neat Horatian procedures convey a disgusted detachment more lethal than the vehement indignation which had spurred a younger Kipling to fulminate against 'the flannelled fools at the wicket or the muddied oafs at the goals'; and how the same procedures wearily concede that the scoundrelism the poem talks of is not peculiar to Britain in 1920 but is the squalid same through the centuries, how therefore no progress is made. Of many incidental felicities, I would draw attention to two. The first is the very elegant Latinism in line 5, 'unmitigated' (from the Latin *mitis,* 'mild'), where the meaning of 'mitigate' is the one which OED notes as 'now rare' – 'To render (a person, *etc.*) milder; to appease, mollify'. Thus the one word, 'unmitigated', conveys that Lollius is the first of his family to be ennobled, and at the same time exposes contemptuously what it is that people get ennobled for, i.e. to be bought over, to have their fangs drawn. And the second fine stroke to be noted is the extraordinarily deft allusion, at the turn from the seventh into the eighth stanza, to Alexander Pope's Horatian 'Ode on Solitude':

> Happy the man, whose wish and care
> A few paternal acres bound,
> Content to breathe his native air
> In his own ground.

Substituting 'With his own cheques' for 'In his own ground' brilliantly encapsulates 200 years of history which saw England change from being a predominantly landed and agrarian culture into one that is predominantly financial and commercial. It was a historical process that Pope himself saw the start of, in the England of Robert Walpole. To get so much said, simply by making one cadence echo another over two centuries, seems not much short of miraculous.

Such effects, achieved with such disdainful and self-effacing economy, are not to be met with in any of the several styles that Robert Browning practised, and of course they are wholly inconceivable in any of the innumerable Browningesque or Whitmanesque poetasters of our own day. So do we not have at last, in this joining of hands with Pope, a case of Dissenting Christianity joining up again with the Enlightenment? No, we do not, and for two reasons. In the first place, as we have seen, the ancestral Methodism which Kipling inherited, even if he had been far more constantly aware of it than he was (he was baptized in the Church of England), would not of itself give him entry into what we have called 'Dissent'. And in the second place the Alexander Pope who wrote *Essay on Man* may be, and almost certainly is, an author of the Enlightenment, but the Pope who wrote 'Ode on Solitude' and was to write 'Imitations of Horace' can be much less confidently placed in that category. Pope was uncomfortable in his age, and at odds with it; in his Horatian poems he is straining against the historical currents that we call 'the Enlightenment', which his younger contemporary James Thomson was content and eager to be whirled along by. Moreover, Horace after all is a pagan author; pre-Christian as Kipling, at least after 1918, may be thought post-Christian. Horace's urbanely saturnine disenchantment, which Kipling after so many centuries recovers, is even further from the sanguine and expansive temper of the Enlightenment at its most infidel than it is from the more temperate and sober aspirations of the Enlightenment that remained Christian. One sees very clearly how wrong it would be to identify 'the Enlightenment' with 'neoclassicism'.

Thus we must conclude that on the evidence of our poetry the re-wedding of Dissenting 'Revelation' with Enlightenment 'Reason' is as far away as ever it was. Another of Browning's heirs in poetry, the American Ezra Pound, was raised a Presbyterian in Philadelphia, but seems to have taken it no more seriously than Kipling took whatever episcopalian or nonepiscopalian Christianity he was exposed to. (As has been noted, Kipling's Freemasonry, which he linked with Mithraism, seems to have been the focus for such religious apprehensions as he had.) And Ezra Pound, to be sure, valued the Enlightenment and was drawn to it, not just as a system of ideas but more momentously as a governing metaphor; but for him it was specifically a *French* phenomenon, and when his comrade T.S. Eliot directed him to Johnson's *Vanity of Human Wishes,* Pound showed himself (in *Guide to Kulchur*) conspicuously less enthusiastic about it than Eliot was. The American Enlightenment of Jefferson and Adams, which Pound deserves much credit for taking seriously when others didn't, is accordingly for him a distinctly French-influenced and therefore infidel phenomenon. And so we look in vain in Pound for any acknowledgement of those poets – Thomson and Gray, Goldsmith and Smart – whom we have taken as the great voices of an *English* Enlightenment. Thus none of Browning's heirs in poetry, precisely because they *were* Browning's heirs, have been able to put together that homogeneous worldview, at once 'cultured' and Christian, which Browning's mother may have inhabited in the London suburb of Camberwell about 1820.

And yet... 'What do they know of England who only England know?' This famous verse – which, so Kipling tells us, was first formulated by his mother – gives us Kipling's imperialism in its pristine, innocent state, before events in South Africa and his own notoriety as semi-official spokesman led him to encase it in increasingly implausible and unpleasing propositions about the Providential election of some races of mankind before others. And in this, its innocent phase, does it not reach back across two centuries to James Thomson in *The Seasons,* similarly exhorting his countrymen to attain a more than insular vision? And in the making of the British Empire have we not been told how often the Flag followed the Bible? That British dominion in South Africa, for which the Boer War was fought, was achieved reluctantly and with misgiving as inadequate police and military forces were unwillingly committed to protect the intrepid or foolhardy missionaries who had insisted on moving into Dutch and African territories. Moreover, that missionary impetus for good or ill (and there are anthropologists who will tell us of the 'ill') was spearheaded by Dissenters; William Carey, the Baptist shoemaker, was the first of them all. In this way, the Empire was very much originally a Nonconformists' empire; and when, in World War Two, the leader of the Chindits in Burma was a member of the Plymouth Brethren, General Orde Wingate, history rather weirdly brought round its revenges. The White Man's Burden was through many generations, for Briton and American alike, the burden of the Holy Scriptures. This consideration opens up a historical perspective which I confess I find myself daunted by. It has, at any rate, a lot to do with Dissenting Christianity and with Rudyard Kipling, and something to do with 'Enlightenment'. I leave it to be explored by those who are more energetic, and more intrepid, than I am.

Dissentient Voice: The Ward-Phillips Lectures for 1980 with some Related Pieces. Notre Dame & London: University of Notre Dame Press, 1982.

Related Pieces

1 *The Language of the Eighteenth Century Hymn*

In a way that neither I nor the sponsors of this seminar could have foreseen, my talk has achieved a surprising topicality. In the London *Daily Telegraph* for 7 February this year (1977) appeared a news item under the headline, 'MP "could do better than Betjeman"'. And the story below told of a Tory MP, a Mr Nicholas Fairbairn, objecting to the Jubilee Hymn composed by the Poet Laureate Sir John Betjeman and Mr Malcolm Williamson, Master of the Queen's Music, to celebrate the twenty-fifth anniversary of the accession of Queen Elizabeth II. 'It is', said Mr Fairbairn, 'absolutely pathetic. It is the most banal, ninth-rate piece of children's verse. It has none of the mystery of poetry about it'. And the bold politician undertook to do better in three hours than Sir John had managed to do in three months. Next day, the newspaper followed up the story under the headline, '"My words are for music", says upset Poet Laureate'. His verses, said Sir John, were *never* to be considered apart from their music, and through his agent he told the press and the breathless populace: 'Hymns are not good poems, nor is "God Save the Queen"'.

For our special purposes I believe we must ignore the Poet Laureate's declared wishes, and briefly consider his verses shorn of the music that will attend or embellish or decently obscure them when the hymn is rendered by sixty thousand schoolchildren next July in Liverpool. They are arranged in five quatrains with a chorus. And here they are, chorus first:

> For our Monarch and her people,
> United yet and free,
> Let the bells from every steeple
> Ring out loud the Jubilee.
>
> In days of disillusion,
> However low we've been
> To fire us and inspire us
> God gave to us our Queen.
>
> She acceded, young and dutiful
> To a much-loved father's throne;

Serene and kind and beautiful
She holds us as her own.

And twenty-five years later
So sure her reign has been
That our great events are greater
For the presence of our Queen.

Hers the grace the Church has prayed for,
Ours the joy that she is here.
Let the bells do what they're made for!
Ring out thanks both loud and clear.

From that look of dedication
In those eyes profoundly blue
We know her coronation
As a sacrament and true.

I experience in any case a certain embarrassment at reading these loyal verses to an audience of presumably staunch republicans (with a small r, of course). And I cannot overcome my embarrassment sufficiently to give you the other text that I have with me – which is to say, the product of Mr Fairbairn's feverish three hours with the Muse. I cannot forbear, however, informing you that Mr Fairbairn's afflatus permitted him the daring stroke of addressing his sovereign as 'Queen glorious, Queen *frail*', and also as 'Queen of the British, so valiant and *vain*'. At the height of his transports moreover he addresses her as 'Our lassie' – which may have something to do with the fact that Mr Fairbairn sits for a Scottish constituency. At any rate, this poet's audacity as to epithets – 'frail' and 'vain' – may give us a clue what to listen for as we hear the hymn of the past with which Sir John Betjeman explicitly challenges comparison – that is to say, 'God Save the Queen', the national anthem, which is (he tells us) as far from being 'a good poem', as is his own Jubilee Hymn. I give this in the form it had when first printed in full in *The Gentleman's Magazine* for October 1745 under the title, 'A Loyal Song, Sung at the Theatres':

God save great George our King,
Long live our noble King;
  God save the King.
Send him victorious,
Happy and glorious,
Long to reign over us;
  God save the King.

O Lord our God arise,
Scatter his enemies,
  And make them fall.

Confound their politicks,
Frustrate their knavish tricks;
On him our hopes we fix;
    O, save us all.

Thy choicest gifts in store
On George be pleased to pour;
    Long may he reign.
May he defend our laws,
And ever give us cause
To say with heart and voice,
    God save the King.

Here the only epithets that are ascribed to the monarch are 'great' and 'noble' – the latter, I believe, not crediting him with nobility as a moral virtue but asserting only that he is of noble (meaning, exalted) lineage. The other epithets – 'victorious', 'glorious, ' and 'happy' (that last I suspect, more in the sense of 'lucky' than in our modern sense) – are not ascribed to him, but prayed for on his behalf. And now let me remind you of Sir John Betjeman's epithets for *his* sovereign: she is, he says (or in some cases, she *has been)* 'young and dutiful', also 'Serene and kind and beautiful', and her eyes are 'profoundly blue'. Of these epithets the most just and the most affecting, to my mind, is 'serene' – which is more affecting, one may think, than any of the attributes given by the poet to her ancestor, George II. Remarkably, serenity is almost the first quality attributed to Her Majesty by the rival poet, Nicholas Fairbairn; and one sees why – to be unflurried, rigorously consistent in her public demeanour, conspicuously removed above the jar and din of partisan policies and ideologies, is required of a twentieth-century monarch far more urgently than of an eighteenth-century one. There is a lot of history in and behind the choice of this word; and that is certainly one of the things that we ask of words in poetry. As for the other epithets... 'kind'? Well, yes – it is better no doubt to have a kind Queen than an unkind one, though in twentieth century circumstances it is much less important for her to be kind than to be 'serene', or to be 'dutiful', which last may be regarded as the *sine qua non*. But 'beautiful'... ? I shall not be so ungallant as to ask if this word is accurate. But it *is* to the point to ask how important it is that the monarch be handsome. And surely we must reply: the comeliness or uncomeliness of a monarch matters hardly at all. As for her being blue-eyed rather than grey-eyed or hazel-eyed, or her being profoundly rather than shallowly blue-eyed... to regard this as anything but a sentimental irrelevance would lay one open to charges of *racism,* perhaps.

I hope it is clear that these are serious questions to ask, and that the answers to them have a lot to do with how we judge the *poetic* merit of such verses as these. And my point is a very simple one – that the author of the stanzas to George II took seriously both the monarchical system of government and the divine providence which it assumes as necessary to it. That the head of state be 'great' (i.e. with notable powers at his disposal), that he be 'victorious' (over foreign enemies), and that he be 'glorious' (that last, I take it, comprehending all that the Renaissance meant when it asked that its princes be 'magnificent'), above all that the monarch be 'happy' (fortunate, blest with good luck) – these are indeed the things to be wished and prayed for, in all seriousness, as his being blue-eyed or hazel-eyed emphatically is not. Sir John Betjeman, though we happen to know that he is both a convinced monarchist and a devout Anglican, is less than serious about these matters in his verses. And thus I believe we may say that the National Anthem may or may not be 'a good poem' (I hold that in its modest measure it is), but that certainly it is nearer to that status than is Sir John's Jubilee Hymn, since it passes the first and minimal test of taking seriously what its words say, *each* of those words, severally and together.

How far we can consider it an eighteenth-century hymn is what we may next consider. Certainly it is not what would first spring to our minds as an example of that category. And the extraordinary possibility that it was first composed in French in 1686 by Mme. de Brinon, to music by Lully, and sung to Louis XIV, though this notion was magisterially dismissed eighty or more years ago by the great hymnologist Julian, is still current – as you may satisfy yourselves by consulting *The Sun King* (1966) by the late Nancy Mitford. It is nowadays often ascribed to the obscure and wretched Henry Carey (1687?–1743), and an eighteenth-century correspondent claimed to have heard it sung by Carey in a Cornhill tavern in 1740, to celebrate Admiral Vernon's defeat of the Spaniards at Portobello in the Caribbean. But Carey's son didn't claim it for his father until 1795, and accordingly the ascription to Carey has been much disputed. However, just such dubiety is (I suggest) of the nature of the congregational hymn. For the hymn, like the ballad or the folk-lyric, is transmitted to us by oral tradition rather than through the channels of copyright. With eighteenth-century hymns this may seem not to be the case. After all, if in church we are using *Hymns Ancient and Modern* and we are directed to a hymn beginning, 'O Thou, before the world began/ Ordained a Sacrifice for man…', we may look to the name at the head or the end in our hymnbook, and find there the name of Charles Wesley. But what appeared over Wesley's name in *Hymns for the Lord's Supper* (1745) was a hymn beginning:

> O Thou Eternal Victim slain,
> A sacrifice for guilty man…

which is a great deal more disconcerting. And in 1745 the second stanza ran:

Thy Offering still continues new,
The vesture keeps its bloody hue,
Thou stand'st the ever-slaughter'd Lamb,
Thy Priesthood still remains the same,
Thy years, O god, can never fail,
Thy goodness is unchangeable...

whereas *Hymns Ancient and Modern* has huddled the bloody purchase out of sight, and gives us, for 'The vesture keeps its bloody hue', the inoffensive though ungrammatical 'Before the righteous Father's view'.

The point is obvious enough, and familiar to all of us: though in the eighteenth century a hymn-writer normally subscribed his name under the hymns he composed, this has never meant – and the author cannot have conceived it *would* mean – what it means in the case of a secular poet. To this day, ministers of religion and choirmasters and even individual worshippers have no compunction about keeping a name like Isaac Watts at the foot of a hymn, even though in singing and often enough in reprinting that composition they habitually leave out certain verses and completely change others. Thus – to stay with the Anglican *Hymns Ancient and Modern* – one of the most famous and popular of Watts's hymns 'When I survey the wond'rous Cross', appears in that hymnbook shorn of its fourth quatrain:

His dying Crimson like a Robe
Spread o'er his Body on the Tree,
Then am I dead to all the Globe,
And all the Globe is dead to me.

To my mind this omission, by muting the elaboration of the emblematic motif of the Redeemer's blood, emasculates the piece quite grievously. And, it has the additional disadvantage of concealing how far Watts, English Dissenter though he was, was happy to emulate the iconography of the Roman Catholic Counter-Reformation, as he had studied it for instance in the Latin poems of 'the Christian Horace', the seventeenth-century Polish Jesuit Matthew Casimire Sarbiewski.

The question is what we should do about this. As literary scholars, our first impulse is to protest in outrage, and apply ourselves to reestablishing an exact canon and an uncorrupted text. But I'm not at all sure that we should act on our first impulses. For when a text like this ceases to be 'corrupted', it ceases to be alive as a still germinating presence in the ongoing consciousness of the English-speaking peoples. We must beware of stacking away on library shelves a text of which the living place is still in tattered hymnals, on insecure music stands, and in the inexact memories of infrequent worshippers. When a few months ago I was castigating an English audience for consistently ignoring Isaac Watts, and thereby perpetuating the outrageous fiction that eighteenth-century poetry was barren of devotional lyrics, my good friend Professor Frank Kermode argued very forcibly that to instate Watts's hymns and his versions of the psalms as texts for study along with Thomson's *Seasons* and Pope's *Imitations of Horace* would be to do a notable disservice to Watts, and also (more important) to the still not extinguished trains of thought and feeling which Watts pre-eminently articulated for the English-speaking peoples. (And incidentally, in case the point needs to be made, my use of that expression, 'the English-speaking peoples', is deliberate; Watts, like Doddridge and Charles Wesley also, is a continuing presence in the experience of the American people – as witness the extraordinary liberties taken with Watts's texts by American Unitarians at the end of the eighteenth century. And what goes for American culture is true also of for instance Australian, even, I discover with pleasure, of a considerable number of people in the subcontinent of India.) This is a hard pill for the scholarly conscience to swallow – that the selfless devotion of the scholarly editor may be a kiss of death. Yet I think the point is well taken. And this is the reason for insisting that the congregational hymn belongs with anonymous and oral forms of poetry like the ballad. The literary scholar must learn to deal with them as he has learned to deal with the ramifying versions of Child's Border Ballads, where we do not suppose that a relatively late version recorded in the Appalachians or the Ozarks is an inferior because corrupt version of some pristine original which alone, if we can recover it, merits a scholarly *imprimatur*.

At this point it is useful to go back for a moment to my clippings from the *Daily Telegraph*, where we read how the Master of the Queen's Music rallied to help his beleaguered collaborator by declaring that Sir John's words were 'deceptively simple', and testifying that 'Sir John has simplified and simplified it and has written it specifically to be sung'. For it was Isaac Watts who first seemed to insist on simplicity as of the essence of hymn writing. Watts wrote:

> In many of these composures, I have just permitted my verse to rise above a flat and indolent style; yet I hope it is every where supported above the just contempt of the critics: though I am sensible that I have often subdued it below their esteem; because I would neither indulge any bold metaphors, nor admit of hard words, nor tempt the ignorant worshipper to sing without his understanding.

And in his 'Short Essay toward the Improvement of Psalmody', Watts is more vehement: 'It was hard to sink every line to the level of a whole congregation, and yet to keep it above contempt'. On the one hand this shows that Watts, in his anxiety to keep his compositions 'above contempt', 'above the just contempt of the critics', certainly did not agree with Sir John Betjeman that 'hymns are not good poems', that the poet who turns to writing hymns thereupon abandons all his aspirations and scruples as a poet. (And Watts, it must be said, was making a real sacrifice; for there are among his *juvenilia* poems which show he was capable of writing in a very bold and exuberant style.) What is more important, however, is to recognize that in considering literary style there is no concept more complicated than 'simplicity'. Are we after all right to assume that when Watts calls his verse style 'flat and indolent' (or rather, elevated by just one degree above that), he means what we would mean by 'simple'? Or again, when he speaks of his effort 'to sink every line to the level of a whole congregation', did he mean what the Master of the Queen's Music means when he says that Sir John 'has simplified and simplified it'? Watts and Mr Malcolm Williamson *may* be saying the same thing, and again they may not.

For a test case we may turn to one of Watts's hymns which enables us, as happens very rarely with him, to glimpse him actually in the act of composition. For it was amended by Watts after his first edition had appeared. It is a hymn to which he gave the title, 'The Passion and Exaltation of Christ', and I think it is seldom or never sung – for reasons which are significant, though not hard to find. In the first edition it ran like this:

Thus saith the Ruler of the Skies,
Awake my dreadful Sword;
Awake my Wrath, and Smite the Man
That's Fellow to a God.

Vengeance receiv'd the dread Command,
And armed down she flys,
Jesus submits t'his Father's Hand,
And bows his Head and dies.

But oh! the Wisdom and the Grace
That join with Vengeance now!
He dies to save our Guilty Race,
And yet he rises too.

A Person so divine was he
Who yielded to be slain,
That he could give his Soul away,
And take his Life again.

Live, glorious Lord, and reign on high,
Let every Nation sing,
And Angels sound with endless Joy
The Saviour and the King.

This is one of the pieces by Watts which cannot help but remind us that, despite the accommodating blandness of his demeanour and conduct in

Hanoverian London, he was doctrinally as Calvinist as his master Richard Baxter (though not enough, incidentally, to satisfy Jonathan Edwards). It is one of many pieces which, when we remember them, make us boggle at Elie Halévy declaring, of Hanoverian Dissenting ministers like Watts, that 'they preached a doctrine more and more like that of Aristotle or Cicero, instead of Christianity according to Saint Paul'. We shall have to look a long way in Aristotle or Cicero before we encounter the vengeful God who irrupts into Watts's first stanza, with *'Awake my dreadful Sword;/ Awake my Wrath, and Smite the Man/ That's Fellow to a God'*. And for Watts the fearsomeness of a God smiting humankind by smiting not man but the God-Man, Jesus, is, even so, not rammed home forcefully enough. For in later editions the first stanza read:

> Thus said the Ruler of the Skies,
> *Awake my dreadful Sword;*
> *Awake my Wrath, and smite the Man*
> *My fellow,* saith the Lord

The question arises: Is this ferocious emendation in the direction of greater simplicity? And I think we have to say that it is, that the second version seals off any loopholes by which to evade the fearsomeness of what Watts is saying. But if so, the simplicity is as far as possible from what A.E. Housman had in mind forty years ago when, after quoting four lines of Watts, he declared fatuously, 'That simple verse, bad rhyme and all, is poetry beyond Pope'. On the contrary, where Watts is concerned, what we call 'simplicity' is more properly *clarity*. In this poem as a whole the language is made transparent in order that we shall not blink; and what we cannot blink is less the fearsomeness of what he is saying, than its irrationality or (better still) its meta-rationality. What Watts's clarity forces his readers and hearers to confront is the irrationality that is *paradox:* the central paradox of the God-man breeding inevitably the corollary paradoxes by which to die is to rise, and to give the soul away is to take life back. The language is 'simplified'; but there is nowhere any simplifying of the content, which is *doctrine,* paradoxical as Christian doctrine necessarily is.

And it is no insult to Sir John Betjeman to deduce that the simplifying which *he* conscientiously pursued can hardly have been of this sort. He was simplifying not just language but doctrine also. For the 'doctrine' of monarchy involves, if it is not blasphemous to say so, a paradox of the same sort, if not of the same order, as the paradox of Jesus the God-man. To apprehend the Queen-woman involves a movement of the mind on two levels at once: humanly, Elizabeth is a woman of her time basically like any other, having for instance blue eyes rather than hazel eyes; but emblematically or mythically she is also, and at the same time, the United Kingdom personified. The humble Christians for whom Watts wrote were, he judged, capable of the intellectual and imaginative athletics which this involved; the hearers of the Jubilee Hymn are not, so the Poet Laureate seems to decide. And of course he is prudent to think so, since rationalizing intellectuals through many generations have shown themselves incapable of it.

Watts and Philip Doddridge and the Wesleys were sophisticated and learned men who deliberately purged their language of everything that would make it inaccessible to men and women who were less sophisticated and less learned than they were. And in the process, as they must have realized, they denied themselves the Shakespearean or Popian splendours that depend upon allusion and mysterious resonance and obliquity. They imposed upon themselves the same self-denying ordinance that after them William Wordsworth was to observe when he wrote his *Lyrical Ballads*. And the same is true of William Cowper, at least of the Cowper who wrote religious poems. Yet Cowper stands apart. Although 'God moves in a mysterious way' and the still lovelier 'Sometimes a light surprises/ The Christian when he sings' are poems by Cowper which have been adopted as greatly cherished hymns, hymnologists have rightly pointed out that they are hymns only with a difference. Indeed, though I have described the eighteenth-century hymns as devotional Lyrics, and think that I was right to do so, yet 'devotional lyric' fits Cowper's Olney hymns more purely and exactly than any others. For the congregational hymn as we find it in Watts or Wesley or Doddridge or Toplady is necessarily public utterance, whereas 'Sometimes a light surprises' is a wistful private musing. Partly the difference is that the other men were ministers, leaders of congregations, where Cowper was merely one of those who sat at their feet. This has the effect that whereas all the other hymns have at their centre the exposition of scriptural doctrine (that being indeed what gives them intellectual sinews and verbal precision), at the centre of Cowper's hymns is not doctrine, but *experience* – as we recognize when we reflect that as God moves 'in his mysterious way', among the 'wonders' that he performs is the peculiar fate of intermittent suicidal depression with which he has visited his poet.

In any case, there is at least one outstanding hymn-writer of the eighteenth century who seems to present us with a different language from the purged but still educated and elegant English of the eighteenth-century gentleman. This is John Newton, Cowper's collaborator on the Olney Hymns. [1]

There are few nowadays to whom the Reverend John Newton is even a name. And among those few there are some, I fear, for whom the name conjures up a grotesque image, both comic and horrifying, of a Pecksniffian

[1] From this point to the end of my paper, I reproduce verbatim what I wrote on pp. 24-9 of my anthology, *Augustan Lyric* (London, 1974).

hypocrite who walked the planks of his slave ship in the Atlantic, reflecting aloud, for the sake of the human cattle chained to their gratings below, 'Glorious things of thee are spoken/ Zion, city of our God'; a monster of complacency who later, after a well-publicized 'conversion', harried into insanity his parishioner William Cowper, by hellfire sermons expounding Calvinist doctrine at its most rigid and ferocious.

In fact Newton, as the captain of a slave ship, was as humane as possible by the standards, and given the conditions, of the slave trade in his day. His conversion was publicized much later, precisely to give ammunition to those who wanted the slave trade outlawed. The records of the Evangelical Movement show that, far from being an extremist, Newton continually tried to mediate between the Calvinist and the Arminian wings. And as for Cowper, he had known suicidal fits of insane melancholia before he ever met Newton, and the seeds of it were in congenital hypochondria. But all this, it will seem, is to plead no more than mitigating circumstances. By the standards of his day, both in his first profession and his second one, John Newton was temperate and enlightened – very well; but then (it will be said) the standards of his day were abominable. It is better to take the bull by the horns and admit that Newton was a remarkably simple, even an obtuse man. This at least saves him from the charge of hypocrisy. He was sincere within his limits, which were narrow.

Long before humanitarian feeling and the political genius of William Wilberforce made the slave trade a burning issue of social morality, men like James Thomson and William Shenstone had perceived the monstrous anomaly of Sunday services at sea for the crews of slave ships. But Newton, self-educated, represents a much less sophisticated level of society than Thomson or Shenstone or his own friend, Cowper. And for the historian, just that is his irreplaceable value. Newton on his last voyage committed to his diary his fears of an insurrection among his slaves:

> We have not been wanting in care to keep it out of their power, yet (as the best mere human precaution is insufficient to guard against everything) they had found means to provide themselves with knives and other dangerous weapons and were just ripe for mischief. So true it is that except the Lord keep the city the watchman watcheth in vain!

We find it hard to credit a simplicity which could in all good faith subscribe that last pious reflection. Yet it's just this naiveté which, later in Newton's life, produced his best hymns:

> The prophet's sons, in times of old,
> Though to appearance poor,
> Were rich without possessing gold,
> And honour'd, though obscure.

In peace their daily bread they eat,
    By honest labour earn'd;
While daily at Elisha's feet
    They grace and wisdom learn'd.

The prophet's presence cheer'd their toil,
    They watch'd the words he spoke,
Whether they turn'd the furrow'd soil,
    Or fell'd the spreading oak.

Once, as they listened to his theme,
    Their conference was stopp'd;
For one beneath the yielding stream,
    A borrow'd Axe had dropp'd.

'Alas! it was not mine,' he said
    'How shall I make it good?'
Elisha heard, and when he pray'd,
    The iron swam like wood.

If God, in such a small affair,
    A miracle performs,
It shows his condescending care
    Of poor unworthy worms.

Though kings and nations in his view
    Are but as motes and dust,
His eye and ear are fix'd on you,
    Who in his mercy trust.

Not one concern of ours is small,
    If we belong to him;
To teach us this, the Lord of all
    Once made the iron swim.

This disconcerting *literalness* in the reading of the Christian Revelation was something that more complex and self-conscious writers like Isaac Watts and George Herbert (they were Newton's favourite poets) strove to attain by strenuous moral and artistic discipline. Those who know Newton from his logs and diaries, from his 'Authentic Narrative' (of his own conversion), from his innumerable letters, will realize that for him on the contrary this naiveté was natural. The absence of conscious intention and strategy, the lack of pressure and strain behind the ultimate transparency, certainly makes Newton's hymns inferior, as poems, to the poems of Herbert and the best hymns of Watts and Cowper. Yet the product speaks for itself. Its poetic virtues are minimal perhaps, yet real and rare, and moral as much as literary. For it is honesty, the refusal to slip anything over on the reader or the congregation, which pins down the miracle at its most literal, by *rhyme:*

'Alas! it was not mine', he said,
  'How shall I make it good?'
Elisha heard, and when he pray'd
  The iron swam like wood.

And it is the same wide-eyed concern to get the point home at its most astounding which justifies what seems at first sight a clear case of that bane of eighteenth-century poetry, the superfluous because 'stock' epithet: 'For one beneath the yielding stream/A borrow'd axe had dropp'd.' It is of the nature of streams to 'yield'. This one didn't – and that's just the point; simple enough in all conscience, but in its very simplicity massively disconcerting.

The tang of colloquial idiom is everywhere in Newton:

The Manna, favour'd Israel's meat,
  Was gather'd day by day;
When all the host was serv'd, the heat
  Melted the rest away.

In vain to hoard it up they try'd,
  Against tomorrow came;
It then bred worms and putrify'd,
  And proved their sin and shame.

'Twas daily bread, and would not keep,
  But must be still renew'd;
Faith should not want a hoard or heap,
  But trust the Lord for food.

The truths by which the soul is fed,
  Must thus be had afresh;
For notions resting in the head
  Will only feed the flesh.

However true, they have no life
  Or unction to impart;
They breed the worms of pride and strife,
  But cannot cheer the heart.

Nor can the best experience past
  The life of faith maintain;
The brightest hope will faint at last,
  Unless supply'd again.

Dear Lord, while we in pray'r are found,
  Do thou the Manna give;

Oh! let it fall on all around,
  That we may eat and live.

''Twas daily bread, and would not keep...', 'Must thus be had afresh...' – this is the language of the eighteenth-century small shopkeeper and thrifty housewife, an idiom which has not got into English poetry at all, except through the hymnbook. Perhaps Newton's most audacious and brilliant use of the colloquial is, on an off-rhyme, at the end of 'By the poor widow's oil and meal':

Then let not doubts your mind assail,
  Remember God has said,
'The cruse and barrel shall not fail,
  My people shall be fed.'

And thus, though faint it often seems,
  He keeps their grace alive;
Supply'd by his refreshing streams,
  Their dying hopes revive.

Though in ourselves we have no stock,
  The Lord is nigh to save;
The door flies open when we knock,
  And 'tis but ask and have.

The people who spoke this language – and John Newton who wrote for them, because he was one of them – are much stranger to us than their social betters whom we encounter in poetry so much more often. They were, for instance, much more callous, in a way which our humanitarianism finds hard to forgive, which is however easy to understand when we consider that they were only one defaulting creditor away from Gin Lane or the Debtor's Prison, only one press-gang away from the floating slums that were the British warships. They had, in any case, compensating virtues. In particular they saw piety and religious observance in terms of history which was literally true, and doctrine that was to be explained, and then accepted or rejected, not explained away or allowed to dissolve behind a mist of emotional indulgence. At their most fervent, their fervour was always related to the literally true and the doctrinally exact. As a result they produced a body of religious poetry which is the least *religiose* of any that one can think of.

This address was first delivered at the William Andrews Clark Memorial Library, Los Angeles, on 5 March, 1977. It has been published, along with a lecture by Robert Stevenson on 'The Eighteenth-Century Hymn Tune', as *English Hymnology in the Eighteenth Century* (Los Angeles, 1980). Reprinted in *Dissentient Voice*.

2 *An Episode in the History of Candour*

I believe I can supply a footnote, or perhaps several footnotes, to a document already a quarter-century old, William Empson's *The Structure of Complex Words* (1951). In chapter 15 of this book Empson considered the semantic history of two English words, 'sensible' and 'candid'. Respecting the latter he was intrigued by an exchange in Jane Austen's *Pride and Prejudice:*

> 'I would wish not to be hasty in censuring any one; but I always speak as I think.'
>
> 'I know you do, and it is *that* which makes the wonder. With *your* good sense, to be so honestly blind to the follies and nonsense of others! Affectation of candour is common enough – one meets it everywhere. But to be candid without affection or design – to take the good of everyone's character and make it still better, and say nothing of the bad – belongs to you alone'.

Empson remarks of this, very justly:

> Jane Austen's use of the word here... is very far from the unquestioning use which could assert an equation in the word as normal. It examines rather sceptically just what kind of truth-telling is involved, and the result is a definition... A candid person picks out the good points in a person's character and ignores the bad ones...

In other words, in the 1790s, if one were in any way scrupulous and alert and honest as a speaker or writer of English, one had to recognize that 'candour' and 'candid' were suspect words, very problematical.

Even a few years before, this had not been the case. Dr Johnson had defined 'candour' in his *Dictionary* as 'Freedom from malice, favourable disposition, kindliness; "sweetness of temper, kindness".' And in the Preface to his Shakespeare (1765) he uses the term firmly and without qualification, as if usage had not yet distorted or perverted it. Thus, of those who had quarrelled with Warburton's annotations to Shakespeare Johnson writes:

> Let me however do them justice. One is a wit, and one a scholar. They have both shown acuteness sufficient in the discovery of faults, and have both advanced some probable interpretations of obscure passages; but when they aspire to conjecture and emendation, it appears how falsely we all estimate our own abilities, and the little which they have been able to perform might have taught them more candour to the endeavours of others.

And here we need to pause.

For 'candour' and 'candid', like some other words in our language, have so changed in meaning that their current meaning, now in the twentieth century, can seem to be one hundred and eighty degrees away from the meaning that they had two hundred years ago. Nowadays, when an acquaintance begins, 'To speak candidly…', we brace ourselves; because we know that what he will go on to say, about a third person or more probably about ourselves, is something disparaging: 'I think you were wrong…'; or, 'I think you behaved rather badly…'. In the eighteenth century, as Johnson's definition and his usage makes clear, the expectation was precisely the opposite: 'To speak candidly…' introduced a statement of the order of, 'Though he may seem to have behaved badly, I believe he meant well'; or, 'You are not so much in the wrong as you think'. In the eighteenth century a *candid* person was one who habitually gave others the benefit of the doubt, who thought the best of others until he was compelled to think worse. In this sense, 'candour' was for the eighteenth century the name of a very lofty virtue indeed – equivalent indeed to the virtue of Christian *charity*. And in fact, in 1768 the biblical scholar Edward Harwood, translating the First Epistle to the Corinthians, translated 'charity' by 'candour', when for 'Charity beareth all things, believeth all things, hopeth all things, endureth all things', he wrote of 'Benevolence' that it 'throws a vail of candour over all things'. This is very plain from another sentence from Johnson's Preface to Shakespeare, where he says of previous commentators, 'They have all been treated by me with candour, which they have not been careful of observing to one another…'; and then goes on to say, 'It is not easy to discover from what cause the acrimony of a scholiast can naturally proceed'.

The puzzle of course, for us as for Empson, is to understand why inside thirty years 'candour' and 'candid', such firm and respectable words for Doctor Johnson, had become such besmirched and questionable words as they clearly were for Jane Austen. The *NED* gives an example from 1798 which Empson took note of, from George Canning's 'New Morality' in the *Anti-Jacobin:*

> 'Much may be said on both sides,' hark, I hear
> A well-known voice that murmurs in my ear, –
> The voice of Candour. Hail! most solemn sage,

Thou drivelling virtue of this moral age,
Candour – which softens party's headlong rage;
Candour – which spares its foes; nor e'er descends
With bigot zeal to combat for its friends.
Candour – which loves in see-saw strain to tell
Of acting foolishly, but meaning well;
Too nice to praise by wholesale, or to blame,
Convinced that all men's motives are the same;
And finds, with keen discriminating sight,
Black's not too black, nor white so very white...

Give me the avow'd, th'erect, the manly foe.
Bold I can meet – perhaps may turn his blow;
But of all plagues, good Heav'n, thy wrath can send,
Save, save, oh! save me from the Candid Friend!

William Empson commented with honest puzzlement:

> One would suppose that the Victorian fear of outspokenness was the strongest enemy of the grace of the word, and it is hard to invent a reason why the song should appear as early as 1798. Perhaps it is part of the feeling that the Augustan settlement had become artificial; the word presumes a code of manners which had become vulgarised, and the attack on it is a sort of minor parallel to the attack on Poetic Diction.

Rather plainly, both of the explanations that Empson here offers are snatched at desperately; he doesn't believe in either of them himself – and for good reason. For the Victorians, as we know, were a great deal more outspoken on some things than we can afford to be – for instance, on whether, in order to be a Christian, you have to believe in the Holy Trinity. And as for 'the Augustan settlement', it had split in two a full thirty years before, when Goldsmith and Johnson took arms against Thomas Gray and his imitators. A historical explanation that is worth anything must come up with something better than this.

And the explanation, I think, is quite near at hand – though in a place where we're not likely to look; in David Bogue's and James Bennett's *History of Dissenters from the Revolution in 1688, to the Year 1808*. In this work, published in 1810, Bogue and Bennett advise their readers:

> The misapplication of the word candour was more injurious in its effects on religious sentiments, than can now be well conceived. It was supposed to possess indescribable virtues. Candour was sounded from many a pulpit; and like charity, it was supposed to hide a multitude of sins. An orthodox minister who had candour was to believe that an arian or socinian was a very good man, and that if he was sincere in his

> opinions, and not rigid in condemning others, he ought not to be condemned himself. The influence of this idea was exceedingly pernicious; for it led to an indifference with respect to truth and error, which depraved both their sentiments and dispositions, which relaxed the springs of Christian integrity and conduct, and gradually brought them to call good evil and evil good, to put light for darkness and darkness for light. This was another of the arian idols. Dr Doddridge, whose softness of temper led him to more intercourse with ministers of the new opinions than most of his brethren, was sensible of the blindness of this boasted candour, and frequently mentions, with considerable feeling, that its possessors could exercise it to all but those who were the ardent believers of evangelical doctrine. (p. 384)

This suggests that 'candour' and 'candid', in the firm Johnsonian sense, were casualties of the Evangelical Movement which (it might be argued, though not very plausibly) in the second half of the eighteenth century brought back heat and asperity into theological controversy.

However, this is still too broad to be satisfactory. 'The Evangelical Movement' is not much better than 'the Augustan settlement'. The quarry that we are seeking ought to be, and it can be, pinned down more precisely. Most of the clues are in the sentences just quoted. But unfortunately they are such clues as we nowadays are unable or unwilling to decipher; for not only are 'Arian' and 'Socinian' words that few of us can define, they belong in a field of discourse that we are impatient with. Do they not point, for most of us, to worries and troubles that we are happy to think have long ago 'blown over'? Can we not be content to say that in the eighteenth as in other centuries the acrimony of theologians destroyed Christian charity itself, and brought both that and a related principle like candour into disrepute? We shall be the readier to think so, if what faces us as an alternative is not just plunging into eighteenth-century theology, but into (as appears) the theology of eighteenth-century *Nonconformists* ! For even among stalwart Nonconformists of our own day (who are not easy to find, incidentally) the eighteenth century is commonly held to be a sterile interval between the ardours and exaltations of Milton and Bunyan in the century before, and the more dubious fervours and fanaticisms of the nineteenth century that follows. And as for the rest of us, it is hardly too much to say that we find it hard to remember or to conceive how in the eighteenth century there were any Nonconformists at all. How far, and in what way, when we speak of 'the Augustan settlement', do we conceive of that settlement as comprehending an heir of John Bunyan such as Philip Doddridge? It is very seldom, I fear, that we even raise the question. And yet what was called 'the Dissenting Interest' was a powerful political reality that no eighteenth-century politician could ever afford to ignore.

Political considerations are something we shall have to return to, for the *Anti-Jacobin* has already shown us that we must. It is the political implication of candour, or of false candour, that Canning is striking at in his verses of 1798. But for the moment what is more necessary is to understand just what an important matter we are dealing with. When we are examining the disintegration of a moral principle so firm and so central as candour was for a man as good as Dr Johnson, we are doing a great deal more than filling in a missing chapter of semantic history; we are dealing with the collapse of a civilization, or of one of its crucial pillars. And to the great name of Johnson I believe we may add two others not less great; Berkeley and Swift. For I have argued elsewhere that for both of these unsparing and critical minds from the early years of the century, candour was a moral principle as important as it was for Johnson later. (See my 'Berkeley and the Style of Dialogue', in *The English Mind,* 1964.) If, to understand what happened to candour, we need to go into the squabbles of the dissenting sects, it is something we should be ready to do for the sake of any one of these great Anglicans. And it is worth saying, by the way, that so far as I can understand these three men, each of them would have known just what he meant by terms like 'Arian' or 'Socinian', would have regarded them as words of very ill omen, and would not have thought he wasted his time in opposing the ideas which those words stand for.

Squabbles of the dissenting sects… But when we look, we discover to our surprise that in the eighteenth century the dissenting sects squabbled among themselves hardly at all. The Dissenting Interest held together, monolithic; the three sects – Baptist, Presbyterian, and Independent (that is, Congregationalist) – made common cause, and recognized a common interest, to the extent indeed that a dissenting minister over his preaching career could wander across the sectarian lines and serve in turn a Baptist, a Presbyterian, and an Independent flock. One not untypical case from the end of the century is the once famous John Clayton (1754–1843), who incidentally in the 1790s was a firm and eloquent Tory. (It is widely believed that no Dissenters supported William Pitt and the war against France; but John Clayton was not the only dissenting minister who did so.) One of Clayton's admirers, challenged to say what denomination his pastor belonged to, replied: 'I have heard that he is considered to be an *Independent Presbyterian Methodist'* – and here the only oddity is the 'Methodist', for of course Methodism did not become an independent sect at all, until the eighteenth century was out. Clayton's Victorian biographer (T.W. Aveling, *Memorials of the Clayton Family,* 1867) remarks, 'This is a description which sounds strangely, and was never before heard of…'. And his puzzlement is natural; for the nineteenth century saw each of the dissenting sects – including many that now appeared for the first time, like the Plymouth Brethren, and the various sorts of Methodism –

draw its skirts ever more fastidiously away from those which in the previous century had been its dissenting brethren. And the reason for this is what brings us back to the Congregationalists Bogue and Bennett, and to their angry denunciation of 'this boasted candour'.

For the eighteenth century saw the dissolution and collapse from within of one of the three ancient dissenting communions – of just that one of them, indeed, which at the beginning of the century (remember Dryden's *The Hind and the Panther*) had seemed the strongest of all. This was the English Presbyterian church, which by 1800 survived only in name, and in 1813 lost even that. For 1813 was the year in which Parliament recognized Unitarians as Dissenters on a par with any others; and this only acknowledged the virtually complete takeover by the Unitarians of what had once been English Presbyterianism. Indeed, not only had the Unitarians thus taken over one-third of 'the Dissenting Interest', they had come within an ace of taking over, or at least of dominating, the remaining two churches also. This was in 1772, when an appeal was made to Parliament for the repeal of the Toleration Act of 1688 – an obscure episode, yet in its way a crucial one for English history generally, not just for English Dissent. For the appeal was drawn up by Unitarians masquerading as Presbyterians, and those of the Thirty-Nine Articles from which they sought to be excused were those that asserted the dogma of the Trinity. Yet this was a dogma which the majority of English Dissenters, good Calvinists as they were, recognized as freely and fervently as ever the Anglicans did. Thus the Unitarians, by claiming to speak for the Dissenting Interest as a whole, were pretending to speak for a Trinitarian majority though in fact they spoke only for an anti-Trinitarian minority, themselves. The Calvinist majority woke up only just in time; and it was they, the provincial Dissenters, who ensured that the appeal failed when it was brought in a second time, in the session of 1773. The consequences however were very damaging; for it had revealed to the Establishment that the Dissenting Interest was disunited, and so the Establishment was emboldened, in 1790, to resist the far juster claim for the repeal of the Test Act. And it is this conspicuously 'uncandid' manoeuvre by the Unitarians that is in the angry minds of the Trinitarians Bogue and Bennett when they link false candour with Arianism and Socinianism, those being the anti-Trinitarian heresies which the Unitarians espoused. It was to prevent a recurrence of such successful infiltration that nineteenth century Dissenters jealously insisted on their denominational and sectarian peculiarities; it was to prevent heretics like the Unitarians from ever again disguising themselves under an ancient and honoured and orthodox name like 'Presbyterian'. And the crucial point is that 'candour' was indeed the slogan inscribed on the banner under which the Unitarians deviously fought in 1772 and 1773. The historian of the episode, Anthony Lincoln *(Some Social and Political*

Ideas of English Dissent, 1760–1800), is being far more ironical than he realizes, when he decides that the application of 1772, for the repeal of the Toleration Act, 'as a whole, was sincerely what it professed to be: an appeal to "candour"'. And if support is needed for this interpretation of what was in Bogue's and Bennett's minds, one may turn to their Baptist contemporary, Joseph Ivimey in 1823 *(History of the English Baptists,* Volume 3, p. 400n.), commenting that a Baptist congregation in the eighteenth century was led to accept the Socinian James Foster as their pastor by, he says, 'their false notions of candour and catholicism'.

Now, this is not the view of these matters which is commonly received. By the Whig and the Marxist interpretations of history alike, it is assumed that 'toleration' is a good thing, which one cannot have too much of. It falls by default to the historian of language to protest that nomenclature is being abused when a name – like 'Christian', or like 'democrat' – is tolerantly extended to cover people who in fact deny one of the cardinal dogmas by which 'Christianity' or 'democracy' is defined. Let us be tolerant indeed, let tolerance be unconfined; but let us at the same time call things by their right names! It was by failing to obey this rule, by for instance calling 'Presbyterian' what was in fact 'Unitarian', that our ancestors seem to have brought 'candour' and 'candid' into disrepute, and thus lost the moral principle that meant so much to Berkeley and Swift and Johnson.

As for David Bogue and James Bennett and Joseph Ivimey – they were I'm afraid obscurantist bigots, the three of them. And they bequeathed their obscurantism and their bigotry to succeeding generations – a woeful legacy which both the Congregationalist and the Baptist communions laboured under through most of the nineteenth century. But some of the blame for that must lie with their liberal and professedly Presbyterian brethren who hoodwinked and outmanoeuvred them, until they recoiled (too late) into this sullen ferocity. Doddridge's enlightenment and liberality – in a word, his *candour* – had, they thought, served only to deliver him into the hands of the Arian false friends who were his enemies; if that was what enlightenment and liberality brought about, then enlightened and liberal were things that no Dissenter could afford to be. And so we find Bogue and Bennett declaring elsewhere, with unmistakable satisfaction: 'The reading of Dissenters themselves, is very much limited to religious books; for being neither men of leisure nor of wealth, few of them go beyond their favourite hallowed circle. The frequency of preaching among them, and of devotional meetings, leaves them little opportunity, or desire, for a more extensive range' (op. cit. p. 306). It was what Philip Doddridge would not have wanted to say of the Dissenters of the 1740s, nor would it have been true of them.

We are now in a position to understand the *Anti-Jacobin* in 1798, furious at

> Thou drivelling virtue of this moral age,
> Candour – which softens party's headlong rage;
> Candour – which spares its foes; nor e'er descends
> With bigot zeal to combat for its friends.

In one way of course, this shift to a political implication for 'candour' and 'candid' does not need to be explained. For historians of the Left, like Edward Thompson in *The Making of the English Working Class,* constantly remind us that the Arians and Unitarians of the 1770s and 1780s – Joseph Priestley, Richard Price, Gilbert Wakefield, Robert Robinson – were also the pro-French democrats of the 1790s. They were 'liberal' in the one sphere as in the other, and appealed to 'the candid reader' on the one set of topics as on the other. What Canning registers, however, is a phenomenon which some of us can remember as recurring almost exactly one hundred and fifty years later: the 'liberal' whose candour consists in thinking the best about the postrevolutionary state abroad, and the worst about his own nonrevolutionary state at home; giving the benefit of the doubt to France or to the Soviet Union, while never giving any benefit at all to the United Kingdom or the USA. And of course this character is still with us, though except among surviving Stalinists and Trade Union leaders, the foreign state for which he exercises his candour is no longer the Soviet Union. Indeed this figure is so familiar an actor on the political scene, now as in 1951 when Empson was writing, that it's surprising we should have any difficulty understanding what Canning is driving at.

But the answer surely is what we have seen already. 'Liberalism' is thought to be a good thing, of which we cannot have too much; and so we conspire not to notice when liberalism in religion takes us out of religion altogether, or when liberalism in politics leads us to condone the denial of political liberties to ninety-nine citizens out of every hundred. It is these muddles and duplicities, with which we are thoroughly familiar, that are in the mind of Jane Austen when she finds 'candid' and 'candour' such treacherous words.

All the same, there is a new inflection to the words in Canning's lines.

> Candour – which loves in see-saw strain to tell
> Of acting foolishly, but meaning well;

... yes, this fits well enough the Western liberal who apologizes for communism. But what of the next lines? –

> Too nice to praise by wholesale, or to blame,
> Convinced that all men's motives are the same;
> And finds, with keen discriminating sight,
> Black's not too black, nor white so very white...

Does not this picture of the timid temporizer fit a different political animal altogether? Not really. The date is 1798; that is, it belongs to the period of *The God That Failed*. By 1798, all but the inflexibly prejudiced or obtuse could see that revolutionary France had become Bonapartist France, a military dictatorship, just as by 1951 all but the stupid and the bigoted could see that revolutionary Russia had become the dictatorship of Joseph Stalin. And the ho-hum-much-to-be-said-on-both-sides attitude is what false candour, 'liberalism', is forced to when it has been thus belied by irrefutable events.

This essay first appeared in *PN Review* 4 (1977), pp. 46–49. Reprinted in *Dissentient Voice*.

3 A Day with the DNB

When the forty-niners of California, lacking yeast, wanted to bake their sourdough bread, they had need of a 'starter', a fermenting agent – in their case, warm raw milk and flour – which, suitably tended and occasionally refreshed, would preserve and regenerate itself indefinitely through a series of later bakings. In the same way, properly to savour the delights of the *DNB,* one needs a *starter,* in the shape of a sentence bringing together a number of more or less obscure names, attached to long dead people who are asserted to have something in common. Once the process of speculative fermentation is thus started, it can and does renew itself indefinitely out of the resources of *DNB* itself – as we shall see. But the initial provocation must be there, or must be supplied.

For the purposes of this day's representative entertainment, I have taken a sentence from a recent book by the Reader in History at the University of Edinburgh, H.T. Dickinson, his *Liberty and Property: Political Ideology in Eighteenth-Century Britain* (1977). The sentence reads (it is on p. 202): 'Those who campaigned most vigorously for religious toleration and especially for the repeal of the Test and Corporation Acts were often also at the forefront of the movement for political reform.' Nothing there, to ferment or germinate! But the sentence is keyed to an end-note (p. 342), and that gives us what we are looking for:

> Dissenters who campaigned for both religious toleration and political reform include Richard Price, Joseph Priestley, Thomas Paine, John Cartwright, William Godwin, James Burgh, John Disney, Mary Wollstonecraft, Capel Lofft, David Williams, Andrew Kippis, Thomas Brand Hollis, Joseph Towers, Thomas Walker, George Dyer and William Enfield...

Such riches! The true devotee or addict of *DNB* is already intoxicated – sixteen names, some not wholly unfamiliar, others wholly so, which can now, this initial provocation registered, be explored one by one in purring contentment through the double-columned pages of the many volumes. Each of the articles now to be perused can be trusted to provide other names with the happy adjunct '*q.v*'.; masters of Cambridge colleges, Bishops of Carlisle, self-educated Dorsetshire printers and compilers, others, more than enough to sustain bemused pedantry through days and indeed weeks of browsing. But we are restricted to one day; we must remember that.

And so… First, Richard Price (1723–91): 'His father, Rice Price, who was for many years minister of a congregation of protestant dissenters at Bridgend… was a bigoted Calvinist, and seems to have been a person of morose temper, facts which may account, on the principle of reaction, for the liberal opinions and the benevolent disposition of the son'. Blessedly pre-Freudian *DNB,* which has discerned, without nudgings from Vienna, that sons often set out to be all that their fathers were not… But wait! Richard Price, it appears, was like Rice (or Rhys) Price, 'minister of a congregation of protestant dissenters', not at Bridgend indeed, but in the London suburb of Newington Green. However 'both Price and Priestley' (Priestley is to come up next, and we are agog) 'were in theological opinion what would now vaguely be called "unitarians"; in 1791 Price became an original member of the Unitarian Society. But Price's opinions would seem to have been rather Arian than Socinian.' Though we may well for good or ill be as 'vague' about Unitarians as were the first subscribers to *DNB,* and wholly in the dark about the difference between 'Arian' and 'Socinian', still the crucial point comes over – that Richard Price was, though still somehow Christian, satisfyingly far from the 'morose' and 'bigoted' Christianity of his papa. This must be part of what is meant by crediting him with 'liberal opinions'; though we soon find that he was 'liberal' in ways and in fields where we may feel more at home – it seems that he wrote pamphlets in favour of both the American and the French revolutions. Accordingly, 'Dr Johnson naturally placed Price in the same category with Horne Tooke, John Wilkes and Dr Priestley, and resolutely refused to meet him; Gibbon compared him to the "wild visionaries" who formed the "constituent assembly" of 1789.' 'Naturally'? Well yes, *naturally;* who does not know that Dr Johnson, though a great and good man, must be thought in politics neither great nor good, holding to political sentiments that were not on the side of the future? We must certainly think so, if we are to sympathize when the *DNB* biographer (he is Thomas Fowler) remarks, 'The darker side of the Revolution Price happily did not live to see… On 19 April 1791 he died, worn out with suffering and disease…' For Edward Gibbon, it seems clear (and perhaps Dr Johnson also), might have reflected unsympathetically that for Price not to foresee 'the darker side of the Revolution' suggests some deficiency in him as a political thinker. But plainly this is not a reflection invited by Thomas Fowler, who goes on to tell us that 'his funeral was conducted at Bunhill Fields by Dr Kippis, and his funeral sermon by Dr Priestley, names which, like his own, are specially honourable in the roll of English nonconformist divines.'

That the name of Joseph Priestley is 'specially honourable', nobody should want to deny. What may surprise us is the 'roll' on which his honoured name is said to be inscribed; for 'experimental scientists' and 'political libertarians' are rolls on which we might expect to find this name entered, sooner than in the category, 'nonconformist divines'. *DNB* (Philip Joseph Hartog) does indeed tell us that as early as 1755 Priestley was 'presbyterian minister at Needham Market, Suffolk', and that 'the London presbyterians helped him by the usual subsidy from their fund, and by occasional benefactions through George Benson... and Andrew Kippis...' And yet how can this be, since we have already learned from the article on Price that Priestley no less than Price was what we would nowadays call ('vaguely') Unitarian? Hartog himself tells us that 'though his preaching was uncontroversial, he made no secret of his Arianism, which alienated some hearers'. In the 1750s and presumably subsequent decades in England, did 'Unitarian' and 'Presbyterian' amount to the same thing? There is a puzzle here, which we may hope that subsequent researches will elucidate. Meanwhile we note that, like Price, Priestley was bought up on strictly Calvinist doctrine, which he rejected.

And Andrew Kippis, that other 'specially honourable name' which has already cropped up in both the articles we have so far consulted? Ah, the further we probe, the more we shall find that cropping up is very much what Andrew Kippis (1725–95) was good at. He is defined as 'nonconformist divine and biographer'. As 'biographer' Kippis must have been of special interest to *DNB* writers (like Thompson Cooper, who writes this article), because *Biographia Britannica,* on which Kippis laboured with Joseph Towers (*q.v.* – he is another on our list) was an aborted pilot-project for what *DNB* itself was to become more than a century later. Of Kippis's and Towers' second edition of *Biographia Britannica,* of which five volumes appeared between 1778 and 1793 (ending in the middle of entries under 'F'), Thompson Cooper judges that it 'hardly deserves the high praise which has been sometimes bestowed upon it... Many of the new memoirs were of inordinate length, and the prominence given to nonconformists laid the editor open to a charge of partiality.' One would like to know (what for that matter someone may have established) whether the *DNB* compilers could resist profiting from Kippis's earlier labours, and whether accordingly the charge of partiality to Nonconformists may not be brought against *DNB* itself. If that should be so, Kippis's services to his fellow sectaries would be all the more effective for being so self-effacing. Dr Johnson told Boswell that he (Johnson) had had the chance of undertaking this second edition; and that he regretted having refused the commission – one can imagine why, from Boswell's own complaint (later withdrawn however) that *Biographia Britannica* was 'too crowded with obscure dissenting teachers'. Plainly, no dissenting teachers were going to stay 'obscure' if Andrew Kippis could help it. And he was one of them: educated under Doddridge at Northampton, thereafter a dissenting pastor at Dorking (1750–53), and (for forty-three years!)

at Westminster, Kippis combined his pastoral cares with tutoring in the Coward Academy at Hoxton, and from 1786 in the radical new Dissenting Academy at Hoxton, where his pupils included William Godwin and the poet Samuel Rogers. He also wrote many books, including a *Life of Captain Cook* (1788). Oh a very busy man was Andrew Kippis, with a finger in every dissenting pie! And what released that multifarious energy was the same with him as with Price and Priestley: 'When about fourteen years old he renounced the principles of Calvinism, in which his relatives had brought him up... Subsequently he inclined to Socinianism...' And then – oh blessed *DNB* ! – Thompson Cooper blows the gaff on Kippis and Price and Priestley and many others on our list. For he quotes Wilson's *History of Dissenting Churches* to the effect that Kippis 'highly disapproved the conduct of the modem Socinians, in assuming to themselves the exclusive appellation of unitarians'. This is the giveaway. We need look no further to explain the nominal Presbyterianism of Joseph Priestley, and the equally nominal denominational allegiances of others on our list. Unitarian wolves in Calvinist sheep's clothing! Astute Andrew Kippis – his shrewd advice was widely followed; and so not just in *DNB* but by historians since, including our own H. T. Dickinson, 'Nonconformist' or 'Dissenter', as applied to Englishmen of the later eighteenth century, means almost invariably 'Unitarian'.

Mr Dickinson offers his study (Introduction, p. 2) as an attempt 'to meet the challenge of Sir Lewis Namier and his disciples who have laboured so long and so effectively to prove that the ideas and principles of eighteenth-century politicians were merely rationalizations of selfish ambition and base motives.' And in order that we shall think more kindly of our ancestors, he claims (ibid., p. 9) that his more sunny conclusions 'rest upon the treatises of all the major political thinkers and propagandists, the reported parliamentary debates for 1688 to 1800, and a study of thousands of pamphlets..., dozens of newspapers and periodicals, and many works of imaginative literature.' And indeed it is evident that he has travelled extensively and doggedly in the sahara of pamphlet literature. It is the more surprising that we look in vain in his Index for any entry for John Martin, Job Orton, John Clayton, or Thomas Sheraton – indeed, for any of the pamphleteering Dissenters who at the time of the American and the French Revolutions espoused a 'loyalist' position, and who were pointedly *not* 'at the forefront of the movement for political reform'. This suggests – how can we avoid the embarrassing suggestion? – a certain political prejudice on the part of our historian.

What is not so clear, and to most will seem less important, is a hint of *sectarian* prejudice also. For Martin and Sheraton were Baptists, as Orton and Clayton were Independents; whereas, if we continue checking in *DNB,* we find that of Mr Dickinson's list of sixteen 'Dissenters' not one is Baptist, and not one is Independent. In other words, of the three ancient communions of orthodox Dissent, only one – the Presbyterian – is represented on his list; and we've already found evidence that through the decades in question Presbyterianism was often a transparent disguise for something quite different, theologically not orthodox at all.

Instead of John Martin and Job Orton, John Clayton and Thomas Sheraton, we are offered... Tom Paine! And surely we boggle. If writing *The Age of Reason* isn't enough to move a man outside the Christian communion altogether, then it's hard to conceive what any man can do or say that will not, at a pinch, be gathered under the skirts of 'Dissent'. What Leslie Stephen says of Paine in *DNB is* that 'the father... was a member of the Society of Friends, who had a small meeting-house at Thetford. The mother belonged to the Church of England...'; and that 'Paine's father was registered as a quaker at his death, and the son, as he often avows, was much influenced by quaker principles.' Thus it appears that all one has to do to qualify as a Dissenter, in Mr Dickinson's elastic understanding of the term, is to have one parent who belonged to a dissenting communion, and thereafter, whatever militant infidelity one may promote, to 'often avow' that one was influenced by that parent's principles. Only a little less flagrantly, another historian, Caroline Robbins, can label Priestley 'Independent', because that was the communion he was born to, which he speedily departed from.

Moreover it appears that one can be at one and the same time a member of the Established Church, and a dissenter from that Church. Thomas Walker for one, who is not in *DNB,* is presumably the same commemorated by Frida Knight in *The Strange Case of Thomas Walker* (1957), where however this radical Manchester merchant, active in the 1790s, is represented as an Anglican. And Capel Lofft (1751–1824) must have been at least nominally an Anglican; otherwise he could not have been educated at Eton and Peterhouse. Undoubtedly this wealthy Suffolk landowner was, as *DNB* says, 'a strong whig', devoted to Charles James Fox and indeed to Napoleon, who said '*qu'il compterait toujours M. Capell Lofft parmi ses amis les plus affectionnes.*' He opposed the American war, and advocated parliamentary reform, besides deserving well of all lovers of our poetry by getting into print Robert Bloomfield's *Farmer's Boy* (1798). And of course research since *DNB* may have shown that he at some point joined a dissenting communion; but if so Herbert Ashton Holden, his *DNB* biographer, knew nothing of it.

Another son of Peterhouse was John Disney D.D. (1746–1816), whose life is perhaps more entertaining and instructive than any other to which Dickinson's list introduces us. 'His grandfather,' we learn, 'was rector of St Mary's, Nottingham, but his remoter ancestors were zealous nonconformists.' However, this ancestral zeal did not prevent Disney, as soon as he was ordained in 1768, from accepting an honorary chaplaincy from Edmund Law, Master of Peterhouse and Bishop of Carlisle. (Law gets a *q.v.*, but we must restrain ourselves – 'In his philosophical opinions he was an ardent disciple of Locke, in politics he was a whig, and as a churchman he represented the most latitudinarian position of the day.') Disney's chaplaincy, we may suspect, did not take him often, nor perhaps ever, to Carlisle. 'In 1769 he was presented to the living of Swinderby, Lincolnshire, and soon after to the rectory of Panton, in another part of the same county; he held both livings, residing at Swinderby.' He was an active member of the association formed in 1771 to petition Parliament for relief of the clergy from subscription to those of the Thirty-Nine Articles which required belief in the Holy Trinity. When this petition was rejected, Disney did not follow his friend Theophilus Lindsey, most principled of Unitarians, who thereupon honourably resigned his benefice. Like many other Unitarians in Anglican orders, Disney preferred to operate as a 'mole' or a 'sleeper', as an agent 'in place'. And not until 1782 did he throw up his preferments, to become the first secretary of a Unitarian Society for Promoting the Knowledge of the Scriptures. In 1793 he took over from Lindsey pastoral duties at the Unitarian Essex Street church, and he also, as we might have guessed, contributed to Kippis's *Biographia Britannica*. But then – wait for it! – he came into a legacy, and from another of the men named on our list, Thomas Brand Hollis. Thomas Hollis, benefactor of Harvard, duly commemorated in Harvard Yard, a wealthy and restive freethinking radical who died in 1774 (himself often called a Dissenter, for no better reason than that he had Baptist forebears), had left his Dorsetshire estates to his friend Thomas Brand of the Hyde, near Ingatestone, Essex, who took the name of Hollis. And 'T. Brand Hollis (d. 2 Sept., 1804) by will dated 1792 left both estates, worth about £5,000 a year, to Disney, who resigned his ministry on 25 March 1805, on the ground of ill-health...' Fancy that! Despite his ill-health Disney lingered for another eleven years, spending them (we are not surprised to learn) 'in literary leisure'. Alexander Gordon, who wrote the *DNB* biography, says of the period when Disney was still a priest of the Established Church: 'Like some others, Disney accommodated the public service to suit his special views. The Athanasian Creed he had always ignored; he now omitted the Nicene Creed and the Litany, and made other changes in reading the common prayer.' Oh, a fortunate man was John Disney, and of very liberal views! What a long and happy life was his! It's clear that these early Unitarians, whether they originated in church or in chapel, attentively promoted each other's welfare; but surely none of them profited more than Disney. And how gratifying for him, in his literary leisure in Essex, to know that he had been since 1780 a member of the Nottinghamshire county committee for retrenchment and parliamentary reform; and hence that he was sure of a posthumous reputation as libertarian and democrat!

John Cartwright (1740–1824) – the famous Major Cartwright of Mark Rutherford's *Revolution in Tanner's Lane* – was a man of very different mettle, though it's not clear how he merits the title of 'Dissenter', for *DNB* tells us nothing of his denominational persuasion, nor indeed of his religious sentiments. He could have been an atheist, for all *DNB* tells us. His biographer, Edward Smith, writes charmingly: 'Cartwright was one of the most generous-minded public men of his time. He was tender to his opponents, forgiving to detractors, and always open-handed. He saved persons from drowning, at the risk of his own life, on four separate occasions. His writings are excessively dry to the ordinary reader, and quite significant of the enthusiast who could be earnest without being inflammatory.' In that last sentence Edward Smith is something better than charming, and the deadpan trenchancy which so closely marshals 'enthusiast' along with 'earnest' and 'inflammatory' shows just how good late-Victorian prose can be at times, in the columns of *DNB*. It shows too how the writers for *DNB* did not think themselves disqualified from passing judgment. The most famous example of this is doubtless Leslie Stephen's sudden and savage characterization of William Godwin: 'Godwin, constantly sinking into deeper embarrassment, tried to extort money from his son-in-law until Shelley's death, and Shelley did his best to supply the venerable horseleech'. 'Venerable horseleech'! Such language is intemperate. And yet the truth is that few people will spring to Godwin's defence; and neither libertarians nor Dissenters are eager to own the author of *Political Justice*. But a Dissenter he was, or at least he has a better title than most of the others on our list. Born the son of a dissenting (in fact, Sandemanian) minister, Godwin in 1773 entered the Hoxton Academy where (wouldn't we know it?) 'he was under Kippis, who became a useful friend'. After ministering to Dissenters in Ware, in Stowmarket, and in Beaconsfield, 'in 1785 he was appointed, through Kippis's introduction, to write the historical article in the "New Annual Register". He now dropped the title of "reverend" and henceforth saw little of his family…' Much later, about 1800, 'he was,' says Leslie Stephen, 'becoming known to Wordsworth, Lamb and Coleridge. To Coleridge's influence he attributes a return to a sufficiently vague theism, having been, he says, converted to unbelief by his conversations with Holcroft about 1787, and having become an atheist about 1792, that is, during the composition of the "Political Justice".' Plainly, if the rule is 'once a Dissenter, always a Dissenter' (and that seems to be the rule that Mr Dickinson plays by), Godwin, despite his declared atheism, is at least nearer to being a Dissenter than Tom Paine is.

There remain from the list five men (Burgh, Williams, Towers, Dyer, and Enfield) and the one woman, Mary Wollstonecraft – who figures in *DNB* (alas for Women's Lib!) under her married name of 'Godwin'. Burgh and Towers and Enfield are not very interesting: James Burgh

(1714–75) seems to have been a Scottish Presbyterian – that's to say, he wasn't a Dissenter so long as he stayed in Scotland, but technically became one as soon as he crossed the border; Joseph Towers (1737–99), collaborator with the ubiquitous Kippis, became an Arian – which is to say, almost certainly, Unitarian – sometime between 1754 and 1764, and from 1774 onwards was 'pastor of the presbyterian congregation in Southwood Lane, Highgate'; and William Enfield (1741–97), though he called himself Presbyterian, must have been Unitarian likewise, since he was tutor at the Warrington Academy (1770–85), and thereafter minister at the Octagon Chapel, Norwich – both Unitarian institutions.

The Welshman David Williams (1738–1816) is a far more substantial character, more interesting and deserving of more respect. His father was 'a Calvinist in religion' who 'on his death bed made him promise to enter Carmarthen Academy to qualify as a dissenting minister'. He duly studied there, as exhibitioner from the London Presbyterian Board, which however already suspected that academy of disseminating Arian and Arminian principles. From 1758 Williams was a dissenting minister in Frome, and from 1761 to 1769 in Exeter, but left both churches because he preached a theology too 'liberal' for his congregations. Later, in 1773 and 1774, he published proposals for the instituting of a nondenominational chapel in London, and these were, says his *DNB* biographer, 'so deistic in tone as to put an end to the scheme'. Williams's relations with Garrick and Franklin, his activities as educationalist and historian of Monmouthshire, are all interesting, but not to the present purpose. His *Letters on Political Liberty* (published anonymously, 1782) are quoted by H.T. Dickinson, as is his *Letter to the Body of the Protestant Dissenting Ministers of all Denominations* (1777). He went to France about August 1792, 'was made a French citizen, and remained till the execution... of Louis XVI, a measure which he strongly deprecated'. Shortly thereafter he returned to London, bearing secret communications from the French government for the British ministers, and after the Peace of Amiens (1802) is thought to have acted as secret emissary in the other direction. Not unnaturally he incurred 'political odium' because of his French sympathies. Williams's deism seems to have impelled him even further from Revelation than the unitarians like his early patron John Jebb, and it is said to have shocked even such a lax freethinker as Franklin. But at least Williams, alike in his religious and political capacities, frankly put himself in danger, and acted rather than merely opinionating; and he left one monument which survives to this day – the Royal Literary Fund, which he founded.

The poet George Dyer (1755–1841) is known as a comically eccentric zany to readers of Lamb's essays, of Crabb Robinson's diaries, and of E.V. Lucas's *Life* of Lamb. His Cambridge college was Emmanuel, where the Master, who showed much interest in Dyer, was a very different proposition from Edmund Law of Peterhouse. He was Richard Farmer (1735–97), High Tory and friend of Doctor Johnson. The article on him by Thompson Cooper (for of course I am sneaking a *q.v.*) is very amusing: '... his only work of any importance is the "Essay on the Learning of Shakespeare". Invincible indolence prevented him from achieving other literary triumphs. He was content to be the hero of a coterie, and to reign supreme in a college combination-room amid the delights of the pipe and the bottle.' Farmer's concern for Dyer did not suffice to steer the latter out of the orbit of the Cambridge firebrand Robert Robinson, who could well have figured on H.T. Dickinson's list and would have brought to it one name that was, at least nominally, Baptist. It was Robinson who 'led him to unitarianism' and Dyer's *Memoirs of... Robert Robinson* (1796), a book that was owned by Wordsworth, is one of those curious and instructive biographies which damn their subject while intending to vindicate him. H.T. Dickinson quotes from Dyer's *Complaints of the Poor People of England* (1793). And another of Dyer's books provides us with a *q. v.* which we can't afford not to pursue, because it reminds us, if we need reminding, that not everything we turn up out of *DNB* can be dealt with in the spirit of comedy. In 1794 Dyer published an *Account of New South Wales and State of the Convicts... with... Character of Thomas Fysche Palmer...* And the name of Fysche (or Fyshe) Palmer should make us pause and reflect that these Unitarians and Jacobins (or 'strong whigs') were playing with fire – a fire which, when stoked by war-fever and the exasperation of the British Ministry, could consume certain unfortunates. Palmer was educated at Eton and Queens' College, Cambridge, 'with the purpose of taking orders in the Church of England'. Made fellow of Queens' in 1781, Palmer served as curate at Leatherhead, and during this time met and dined with Johnson, as reported by Boswell. 'About this time,' says his *DNB* biographer Alexander Hastie Millar, 'the writings of Dr Priestley of Birmingham, advocating progressive unitarianism, so strongly influenced Palmer that he decided to abandon the creed in which he had been reared, and to renounce the brilliant prospects of church preferment that were open to him.' He served thereafter as Unitarian minister in Montrose and Dundee, where in 1793 he was arrested in connection with an allegedly seditious libel that was not his composition. Tried and convicted, Palmer in 1794 was hurriedly transported along with his 'fellow-martyrs' Skirving and Muir – this despite protests in the Commons by Fox and Sheridan, and in the Lords by Stanhope and Lauderdale. At the end of 1799 Palmer, his sentence near to expiry, sailed for home in a trading vessel he had bought with others, and after many adventures in the South Pacific died on a Pacific island in 1802. His body was removed from there in 1804 by an American captain, who transported it to Boston, Massachusetts, where it lies to this day. In 1844 a monument was erected in Calton burying-ground, Edinburgh, 'to commemorate Palmer, Muir, and their fellow-martyrs in the cause of reform'. If any one wants to call Thomas Fyshe Palmer 'Dissenter', I suppose no Dissenter will object; for he was certainly a martyr to *something,* poor fellow.

Andrew Kippis enjoined his fellow Socinians, shrewdly and urgently and as it must seem to us cynically, not to declare themselves such by 'assuming to themselves the exclusive appellation of Unitarians'. Most of his associates seem to have heeded his injunction: nominally Presbyterians or Anglicans, more rarely Independents or Baptists, they cloaked under these labels their true allegiance, which was Unitarian; that is to say, by the principles of the mostly Calvinist persuasions that they affected to adhere to, they were, all of them, heretics. And Kippis's subterfuge was successful not just in his own day but through many succeeding generations, up to and including (quite notably indeed) our own. To the first generation of subscribers to *DNB,* the words 'Unitarian', 'Arian', and 'Socinian' still had some meaning, though probably a meaning less precise than for Kippis and his contemporaries a century before; but for the twentieth-century generations the words have rarely had any meaning at all, however indefinite. And this means that Kippis's manoeuvre now befuddles the issue more effectively than ever. This I take to be the real significance of H.T. Dickinson's grouping, as 'Dissenters', a group of people all of whom Orthodox Dissent would have indignantly disowned. And in this Dickinson is merely following common practice: among those who write of late eighteenth-century England, the term 'Dissenter' is bandied about boldly and freely; yet what it means, in virtually every instance, is 'Unitarian'.

For a last very striking instance of this I go to Claire Tomalin, in her *Life and Death of Mary Wollstonecraft* (1974). There is substance to the complaint that, because of unthinking patriarchal prejudice on the part of Leslie Stephen and his collaborators, *DNB* is much less dependable on women than on men. Accordingly I have thought it prudent, as regards Mary Wollstonecraft, to jump over the *DNB* article and proceed instead to Ms. Tomalin's remarkably sprightly and erudite, impassioned and yet judicious biography, from which we learn for instance that Mary Wollstonecraft was born and reared a slumbrous Anglican, and that (*pace* H.T. Dickinson) her Anglicanism she seems never to have formally renounced, not even when she was married to Godwin.

However, nobody would deny that she felt most at home among people who called themselves 'Dissenters', at least from the time in the 1780s when she was in Newington Green, close to Richard Price and much under his influence. What is surprising, in a book so sophisticated as Ms. Tomalin's and apparently addressed to sophisticated readers, is the account which she finds it necessary to give, of the milieu in which Mary Wollstonecraft moved at this time:

> It seemed to her far preferable to hope that men might grow less vicious as the circumstances of their lives grew gentler, rather than accept that women were given an appearance of virtue only by the crack of the whip; and both the example and the stated beliefs of the Dissenters who surrounded her on the Green encouraged her in this optimistic view. Rational Dissenters, or unitarians, worshipped reason and Locke; they represented the critical and sceptical tradition of protestantism without its black insistence on guilt. They had thrown out the doctrine of the Trinity, the idea of original sin and the concept of eternal punishment, explaining them all as purely poetic myths. James Burgh's book *The Dignity of Human Nature* breathed the spirit of prudent optimism in which they were inclined to view this world and the next.

Among Claire Tomalin's readers there must surely have been a few who wondered if, after one had 'thrown out' the doctrines of the Trinity, of Original Sin, and of Punishment, one had the right to subscribe one's self Christian at all, however 'dissenting'. The same readers might have recalled that, forty or fifty years earlier, the Calvinistic Independents Isaac Watts and Philip Doddridge had 'worshipped reason and Locke' as fervently as Richard Price or James Burgh did, without finding themselves impelled thereby to deny either the Holy Trinity or Original Sin. And, wondering what beyond a rhetorical flourish is involved in calling 'insistence on guilt' 'black', these readers might recall that to this day Original Sin is a required dogma; and that in the weeks before Christmas the Anglican faithful are still exhorted to meditate on 'the four last things' – Death, Sin, Hell, and Judgment. This may or may not be deplorable; but it is a fact.

If these sentences suggest that whereas Claire Tomalin plainly expected her readers to be keen and knowledgeable on most matters, on theology and church history she couldn't expect them to be either, our suspicions are astonishingly confirmed by a footnote she found it necessary to append to her phrase about 'black insistence on guilt':

> This particular brand of nonconformity was something quite distinct from Methodism, of which Price thoroughly disapproved, describing it as a faith that ascribed to 'particular feelings, without reason, a supernatural suggestion'.

Well, but *of course* ! Who on earth is this reader so ignorant as to need telling that the Methodists, at this time not Nonconformists at all, were at the opposite pole from the Unitarians? I fear the reader in question is too common, as Claire Tomalin recognized by supplying him with this necessary and betraying footnote. But conceivably even in *his* mind the question arises: what of the Dissenters who persisted and worshipped between the extremes of the Methodists on the one hand, the Unitarians on the other? Of them, and of loyalist Dissenters like Orton and Martin, Clayton and Sheraton, we hear no more from Claire Tomalin than from H.T. Dickinson; and throughout the later pages of *The Life and Death of Mary Wollstonecraft*, 'Dissenter' means 'Unitarian', where it does not mean downright 'infidel'.

And in these speculations have we wandered too far from considering simply the fun that we can have with *DNB*? By no means! That 'fun' certainly comprehends the sardonic amusement that we get, from observing an expedient subterfuge successfully bemusing generations of later historians, including our own. It is, to be sure, a sour and spiteful sort of fun; but who ever thought that sourness and spite are not among the legitimate pleasures of pedantry?

This essay first appeared in *PN Review* 18 (1980), pp. 26–30. Reprinted in *Dissentient Voice*.

4 Dissenters and 'Antiquity'

In the Preface to his earliest work, the puzzling and ironical *Vindication of Natural Society* (1756), Edmund Burke explained that 'the design was to show that... the same engines which were employed for the destruction of religion, might be employed with equal success for the subversion of government.' This seems to have been a conviction that he never lost. And doubtless we should bear it in mind when we find him saying, more than thirty years later, in his *Reflections on the Revolution in France*:

> So tenacious are we of the old ecclesiastical modes and fashions of institution, that very little alteration has been made in them since the fourteenth or fifteenth century; adhering in this particular, as in all things else, to our old settled maxim, never entirely nor at once to depart from antiquity. We found these old institutions, on the whole, favourable to morality and discipline; and we thought they were susceptible of amendment, without altering the ground. We thought that they were capable of receiving and meliorating, and above all of preserving, the accessions of science and literature, as the order of Providence should successively produce them. And after all, with this Gothic and monkish education (for such it is in the ground-work) we may put in our claim to as ample and early a share in all the improvements in science, in arts, and in literature, which have illuminated and adorned the modern world, as any other nation in Europe; we think one main cause of this improvement was our not despising the patrimony of knowledge which was left us by our forefathers.

The last sentence here shows Burke claiming for himself, and for the sorts of Englishmen that he claimed to speak for, an 'ample and early' share in the Enlightenment. And indeed how can the claim be denied to the author of the *Philosophical Inquiry into the Origin of our Ideas of the Sublime and Beautiful*? But it needs to be remembered when, elsewhere in the *Reflections,* he sarcastically calls 'enlightened' Richard Price and the French and English Jacobins. These too could and did lay claim to a share in the Enlightenment; and their claim too should be recognized, but not to the exclusion of Burke and their other adversaries.

However, this is only incidental to the main thrust of Burke's argument. And that argument is uncompromising. One may think for instance that one has heard something similar from John Adams, but this is not so; this is an argument that we do not find, and could not expect to find, in an American like Adams. Although in other respects Burke's attitudes and Adams's are indeed strikingly similar, at this point they part company. For Burke antiquity is *a value in itself,* as it had been for Andrew Marvell when he spoke of the realm of England as 'the Great Work of Time'; whereas for Adams, devoted though he was to the common law of England and therefore eager to argue from precedents, antiquity as such, in and for itself, was no argument. At one point in the *Reflections* Burke acknowledges the sort of lawyer's arguments that Adams sets store by, arguments based on constitutional lawyers like Blackstone and Coke and Bracton tracing English liberties to the Great Charter and the Anglo-Saxon kings; Burke acknowledges this line of argument, and shows himself well disposed to it, at the same time that he makes clear it is not his argument. For him custom and usage, if they are ancient, are as compelling as precedents established in courts of law. If only because Tom Paine attacked Burke first and Adams later, this difference between them is easy to miss. Yet it is very significant because, despite attempts by modern American conservatives to co-opt Burke for their cause, this difference between Burke and Adams is the crucial difference between English conservatism (when it knows what it is doing, which is seldom) and American conservatism.

We cannot help noticing that in this passage Burke very consciously and deliberately appeals to *pre-Reformation* precedents. And by thrusting at his readers the words 'Gothic' and 'monkish', he anticipates and by implication sets aside the hostile reactions of antipapist prejudice. Such prejudice was rife among the Dissenters of Burke's day, but it was rife too in the Church of England. And on the other hand there was no reason why Burke's propositions should stick in a Dissenter's craw any more than in an Anglican's. For all the churches of Orthodox Dissent claimed lineage from an antiquity far more remote than the Reformation, precisely because the Reformers themselves had made the same claim. That learned and thoughtful Nonconformist Bernard Manning wrote of the Reformers:

> They did not abandon the past and claim to start a new age. That had often been done. The very form of the Christian doctrine of the Godhead made it easy. Ardent souls confronting an awkward situation set out world history in this manner. God reveals Himself (they said) by degrees. There was an age of the Father, the age of the Old Testament. It ended at the Incarnation. Then came more light: God was known in his Son. That was the age of the New Testament, the Church, the written Word, the Sacraments. But this revelation needs

> completing; and a third age, the age of the Holy Ghost, will follow... [But the Reformers] did not conceive that the age of the Son had ended or that a new age of the Holy Ghost was to begin. They rejected any doctrine of development which would put in the second place the historic revelation of God in Christ, incarnate in Judaea, recorded in Holy Scripture, represented in the Sacraments... The Reformers did not doubt that the Holy Ghost was in the Church, and that He would lead it into all truth; but they found it the characteristic action of the Holy Ghost to take the things of Christ, not to supersede them. [1]

If I understand the doctrines of 'further light' and of 'the two covenants', Dissenters who espoused either of these positions (Isaac Backus was among them) could not hold by the Reformers' beliefs, as Bernard Manning here expounds them. But any Dissenter who *did* hold by them could properly claim for his beliefs and practices an antiquity equal to that of any other branch of the Christian Church. And in fact of course, more remarkably, a Baptist justifies his distinctive practice of believer's baptism on the grounds that he is thus keeping faith with the pristine practice of the Primitive Church. In other words, though believer's baptism can be justified on other grounds also, one argument for it is precisely the Burkean argument that sheer antiquity, antiquity as such, carries authority. So it may well seem that English Baptists of the late eighteenth century ought in logic to have been Burkeans instead of Painites or Priestleyites; and perhaps many more of them were so, than is now acknowledged.

Accordingly it is melancholy but proper to choose, as an example of how many English Dissenters of Burke's day thought far otherwise, one who was at least nominally a Baptist, the bizarre Robert Robinson. This is how Robinson, in his *Ecclesiastical Researches,* treats St Augustine of Hippo:

> From this bitter and bloody fanatic of Africa, proceeded two hundred and thirty-two pamphlets, an innumerable multitude of epistles, expositions of the gospel, and the psalter, besides sermons or homilies; and by this man's writings, did Luther, Oecolampadius, and other reformers expound the scripture, and frame an ecclesiastical constitution, to lead Europe into purity of faith and manners as if Punic faith, and African manners, execrable at Rome when Rome was pagan, were fit for ages enlightened by philosophy and religion. Instead of improving by all the great men that have lived in the last two thousand years, should the world continue to be the disciples of Austin, and his

[1] Bernard Manning, 'The Reformation and the Free Churches' (1938), *Essays in Orthodox Dissent* (London, 1939).

> spiritual sense of scripture? He understood the ten commandments in a spiritual sense, and 'thou shalt not kill' signified, 'thou shalt not kill an orthodox believer'. The command did not protect the life of an heretic. This man and his maxims blasted the character of christianity, and excited in the minds of many of the most liberal of mankind just suspicions of the divinity of the religion of Jesus; for the christianity that Austin taught was the scourge and curse of the empire. If Jesus employed him, as he affirmed, to teach occult grace and penal sanctions, for not believing with, and even against evidence; the shame retreats from the obedient disciple, Austin, and revolves on his master Jesus: but far, very far from every heart be such a thought! It is impossible to defend both Jesus, and Austin, and justice requires the sacrifice of the latter. [2]

A modern reader of this reverend gentleman is likely to throw at him first the accusation 'Racist!' And very justly – in a letter of 1786 Robinson writes of 'that impudent debauchee, Saint Augustine' as 'the man who invented original sin', and concludes his diatribe by calling him 'a true Carthaginian, and one of the best examples of Punic faith that ever lived'. What we are likely to take less notice of, and be less shocked by, is Robinson's unargued assumption about the relation between Revelation and the unfolding process of recorded history. Plainly, he rejects or denies the conviction of the Reformers as glossed by Bernard Manning, their finding it 'the characteristic action of the Holy Ghost to take the things of Christ, not to supersede them'. Insofar as they acted on this conviction, by taking over the insights of Saint Augustine, Robinson condemns them. We are often told of the 'complacency' of the English eighteenth century; but we are usually asked to discern this complacency in the Tories of the time, whereas it is radicals like Robinson who are surest about 'ages enlightened by philosophy and religion'. Indeed it is surely obvious that in any age it is the conservatives, wary of departing from precedents embodying the wisdom of the forefathers, who are least complacent about the advances achieved by themselves and their contemporaries, or by what figures as 'the modern' at any stage of history.

Tom Paine, accurately discerning just this arrogant and shortsighted complacency in many English Dissenters of his time, made a deliberate play for their allegiance. Thus in a footnote to his *Rights of Man* we read:

> When in any country we see extraordinary circumstances taking place, they naturally lead any man who has a talent for observation and investigation, to inquire into causes. The manufactures of Manchester, Birmingham and Sheffield, are the principal manufactures in England.

[2] George Dyer, *Memoirs of the Life and Writings of Robert Robinson* (1796), pp. 371-2.

From whence did this arise? A little observation will explain the case.

The principal, and the generality of the inhabitants of those places, are not of what is called in England, *the Church established by law,* and they, or their fathers (for it is within but a few years) withdrew from the persecution of the chartered towns, where test-laws more particularly operate, and established a sort of asylum for themselves in those places. It was the only asylum that then offered, for the rest of Europe was worse.

But the case is now changing. France and America bid all comers welcome, and initiate them in all the rights of citizenship. Policy and interest, therefore will, but perhaps too late, dictate in England what reason and justice could not. These manufactures are withdrawing, and are arising in other places. There is now (1791) erecting at Passy, three miles from Paris, a large cotton mill, and several are already erected in America. Soon after the rejecting the bill for repealing the test-law, one of the richest manufacturers in England said in my hearing, 'England, Sir, is not a country for a Dissenter to live in – we must go to France.'

These are truths, and it is doing justice to both parties to tell them. It is chiefly the Dissenters who have carried English manufactures to the height they are now at, and the same men have it in their power to carry them away...

It is not easy to think of a minatory prophecy that was sooner, or more comprehensively, belied in the event. Burke's prophecy, and John Adams's, were on the other hand immediately borne out – by the Terror in France, and thereafter the military dictatorship there. No wonder that Paine's animus against Adams exploded some years later!

In an interesting essay on a neglected topic, Matthew Hodgart has made a case for Paine by contrasting his literary style to that of another radical, the lapsed Sandemanian William Godwin, in his *Political Justice*. Both of them, Hodgart argues, even as they strenuously opposed what Burke had said, learned from his way of saying it. To be sure, Burke's influence combined with others in the forming of Paine's style; though the list that Hodgart gives of those influences and models conspicuously omits the one that Burke himself singled out – 'Junius'. [3] However that may be, Hodgart is surely right to contend that the cadences of Burke's prose resound in Paine's writing at other times than when he is deliberately parodying Burke's manner, as he was when he turned Burke's rhetoric back upon itself in the famous judgment that Burke 'pities the plumage and forgets the dying bird'. There is also for instance the justly

[3] M.J.C. Hodgart, 'Radical Prose in the Late Eighteenth Century' in H.S. Davies and G. Watson (eds.), *The English Mind* (Cambridge, 1964). Hodgart's list of stylistic influences on Paine is cited from Paine, *Representative Selections*, ed. H.H. Clark (New York, 1944; 1961).

remembered phrase, 'the summer soldier and the sunshine patriot'. Paine in fact was a notable phrase-maker, in no derogatory sense. As for Burke's influence on him, and on Godwin also, one must begin by recognizing, as all respectable commentators do, that Burke has not one style, but several – even in the compass of a single work like the *Reflections*. And Hodgart's argument is that whereas Godwin took over from Burke one of his styles that had only limited usefulness, Paine adopted and adapted another that had more colour, more vivacity, and was able to deal with a wider range of human and communal experience. 'Paine's radicalism,' Hodgart says, 'like Burke's, is practical, concerned with current issues but also rooted in history – history that includes both the narrative of recent events (in which Paine excels) and the account of the developing constitution of England (in which he is less adept).' In Godwin on the other hand we find an 'extreme debility of description and imagery'. And this springs from his 'almost total rejection of the real worlds of history and of nature':

> He quotes Burke on the miseries of history only to prove that we can learn nothing from history except that it is miserable; it is only what man *can become* when he transcends history that matters... we are to think only of the future... The body of experience which sustains Burke's and Paine's mature styles is to Godwin not only trivial but somehow vulgar.

Thus the effect, and presumably the intention, of Hodgart's essay is clear; he means to deflect Burke's charge that Paine was a mere 'speculatist', by showing how much more this is true of Godwin. And in the course of doing so he has slipped in, or slipped over on us, the description of Burke as himself 'a radical'. In one way this is plainly just; Burke in the *Reflections,* and still more in the works he went on to write in his last years, is clearly a man almost beside himself with the vision that he has of just what is at issue in the French Revolution. Tory and Whig alike were embarrassed by the fervour of his denunciations and his professions, as right thinking conservatives habitually are by radicals of the Right. But in another sense – the sense that etymology gives us, of 'radical' as meaning 'root-and-branch' – how can 'radical' be predicated of a man so devoted as Burke was to 'antiquity', and the authority of antique precedent? And conversely, how can root-and-branch radicalism such as Paine's be reconciled with any respect for antiquity, or even with any historical perspective except the shortest?

In this way Matthew Hodgart's case is ultimately unconvincing. And his concession – that Paine was 'less adept' in his account of the developing constitution of England – turns out to fall disingenuously short of the truth. Burke for instance had said in the *Reflections*: 'The first thing that struck me in the calling the States-General, was a great departure from the ancient course'... Paine in a footnote to the *Rights of Man,* quoting this, commented: 'And with regard to the "departure" from the ancient "course", besides the natural weakness of the remark, it shows that he is unacquainted with circumstances. The departure was necessary, from the experience had upon it, that the ancient course was a bad one.' The betraying thing here is the parenthesis, 'besides the natural weakness of the remark' – which is in itself enough to show how far Paine was from responding to, positively from *experiencing,* what Andrew Marvell pointed to as 'the Great Work of Time'. Or again when Paine jeers at Burke, 'he still had not boldness enough to bring up William of Normandy and say, *there is the head of the list! there is the fountain of honour!* the son of a prostitute, and the plunderer of the English nation', Paine either is, or pretends to be, ignorant that for conservatives the legitimacy of monarchical succession derives not at all from *origins,* but from long continuance, precisely from *succession.* Even Robert Filmer in his seventeenth-century *Patriarcha* had admitted that 'by the secret will of God many set first do most unjustly obtain the exercise' of supreme power. It ought to be plain that Tom Paine on William of Normandy is as irrelevant, and as raucous, as Robert Robinson on Augustine of Hippo.

And what is the moral of all this for English Dissenters at the present day? No doubt many morals could, and should, be drawn. But one of the most obvious has to do with the Establishment of the Church of England. However unjust and dubious that Establishment may have been in its origins, it has now persisted for long enough to take on the authority of antiquity. As Bernard Manning wrote fifty years ago:

> Many Free Churchmen have no feeling for the Church of England as a national institution, though they cherish it as a part of Christ's Church; but not a few Free Churchmen like myself... have a tender regard for the Church of England as it now stands as a national institution, while we shrink with some horror from the thought of its being turned into a disestablished, self-governing episcopalian sect. [4]

So different are most modern Dissenters, from those whose allegiance Burke rightly spurned in 1790.

However, Bernard Manning's 'tender regard' in not often reciprocated. Twice already in this essay I have alluded to Marvell's 'Horatian Ode upon Cromwell's Return from Ireland':

> 'Tis madness to resist or blame
> The force of angry Heaven's flame;
>   And if we would speak true,
>   Much to the man is due,

[4] Bernard Manning, 'A Free Churchman's View of an Established Church' (1931), in *Essays in Orthodox Dissent.*

Who, from his private gardens, where
He lived reserved and austere
    (As if his highest plot
    To plant the bergamot),

Could by industrious valour climb
To ruin the Great Work of Time,
    And cast the Kingdom old
    Into another mould.

It is no doubt found as hilarious on the Conservative as on the Labour benches of the present House of Commons that certain political thinkers of a conservative cast, such as Roger Scruton and C.H. Sisson, have found in themselves sufficient reverence for antiquity to make of this three hundred and thirty-year-old poem a cornerstone in their understanding of the realm of England, and how it works. For instance, in Sisson's *The Spirit of British Administration* (1959) 'the great work of time' crowns, in so many words, a most eloquent and cogent passage (pp. 156–7) on how the Crown, the continuity and majesty of it, is crucially necessary to a British administrator's understanding of what he is doing. Unfortunately, to an Anglican constitutionalist like Sisson the perception of this 'great work of time' is possible, it appears, only to members of the Church of England – as becomes deplorably explicit in a later book, *The Case of Walter Bagehot* (1972). And thus by Sisson, very much as by Matthew Arnold a century ago, the English Dissenters are parcelled together and – without their having any say in the matter – consigned in a lump to the rancorous and contumacious Left.

And the Left, grateful for this unsolicited gift (which brings with it after all electoral as well as ideological advantages), uses it sometimes astutely, always impudently, and sometimes in ways that are weird and wonderful. In the 1930s for instance Bernard Manning's civil and temperate voice had no chance of being heard against John Maynard Keynes in *The New Statesman and Nation*:

> ... the post-war generation of intellectual Communists under thirty-five. Them, too, I like and respect. Perhaps in their feelings and instincts they are the nearest thing we now have to the typical nervous nonconformist English gentlemen who went to the Crusades, made the Reformation, fought the Great Rebellion, won us our civil and religious liberties, and humanised the working classes last century. [5]

Here certainly we have an appeal to English antiquity – though to one that was never heard of before. Even readers of the *New Statesman and*

[5] *New Statesman and Nation* 28 (January 1939), quoted by Andrew Bovie, *The Forth Man* (London, 1979; New York, 1980), p. 160.

Nation under Kingsley Martin (himself lapsed from ancestrally Dissenting stock, as was Keynes also) must have suppressed a start of surprise at the information that the Nonconformist sects were in existence at the time of the Crusades; some may have wondered whether 'nervous' was to be understood to mean 'jumpy' or in its archaic sense of 'sinewy'; and if any of 'the working classes' had by 1939 graduated to the readership of Mr Martin's magazine so strenuously dedicated to their interests such readers may have resented the implication that they could not be and were not 'humanised' until the gentry, Nonconformist or not, performed the necessary surgery upon them.

Not all professions of common cause between the British Left and English Dissent are so entertaining. Little amusement can be wrung for instance out of the standard practice by which leaders of the Labour Party, when they want to minimize revolutionary Marxism among their rank and file, tell the nation soothingly that either Nonconformity or Methodism (it is never clear which, nor does it matter) has contributed more than Karl Marx to the Labour Party's ethos and ideology.

And nowadays this arcane marriage between Dissent and the Left is sometimes offered to us in versions that are not comical at all, but touching. Such is for instance the version given by Edward Thompson. This is affecting because what Thompson understands as 'Old Dissent' is a home that he has built for himself after having been driven out of, or else having relinquished, the doctrinaire Marxism which had harboured him, in and out of the Communist Party, through many decades. As he writes himself, at a painful moment early in his 'Open Letter to Leszek Kolakowski':

> To be a British Communist, on this empirical island anchored off Europe, was never a matter of great international relevance... But to be a Communist dissident or revisionist, or a relict of that tradition, in 1973, is to be a null quantity like a foreign postage-stamp twice cancelled, unusable and not worth a collector's attention. [6]

For the author of *The Making, of the English Working Class* (1964) thus to present himself as a relict, an anachronistic survivor, is at first sight astonishing. For in recent years has any work remotely comparable been more admired, more widely disseminated, and (we have reason to suppose) more influential? It turns out however that in that book, as still a Marxist, Thompson broke through to an erstwhile unpersuaded and large public at precisely the time when he was being disowned by the guardians of the Marxist scriptures. Of this Thompson's open letter to Kolakowski, and the entire volume called *The Poverty of Theory,* leave us in no doubt: they

[6] E.P. Thompson, 'An Open Letter to Leszek Kolakowki' (1973), in *The Poverty of Theory* (London, 1978).

rehearse more than once, and in a tone one can describe only as 'wounded', a story of how Thompson and a few who thought like him were, from 1962 onwards, gradually but inexorably dislodged by the British Marxist intelligentsia from positions in which their understanding of the Marxist tradition could carry much or any weight with the Marxist faithful. They reached the unpersuaded precisely when the erstwhile persuaded defected from their persuasion. And so Thompson feels that he has been 'shelved' inside the intelligentsia of the British Left – a community, so he persuades us, of positively familial intimacy (and subject therefore, as families are, to 'flaming rows').

Accordingly it is hard to deny this refugee the refuge which he now seeks, among the English Dissenters. That he does seek it is clear. He tells Kolakowski: 'If you are tolerant, you may consider me as a representative of a residual tradition, like Old Dissent, adhering meticulously to old forms whose significance daily diminishes. Like an eighteenth-century Quaker, who will not bare his head before authority nor take oaths, I will not take my holidays in Spain nor attend conferences in Rome funded by the Ford Foundation.' And a few sentences later, perhaps playing the pathos for a little more than it is worth, he concedes to Kolakowski: 'Operating within a culture of universal rationality you cannot be bothered with the sectarian susceptibilities of another nation's Old Dissent.' This tenderness towards Dissent had shown up already in *The Making of the English Working Class*. And indeed Thompson in that book, in order to do justice to the rebellious sectaries of past centuries, was prepared to jettison the patronizing Marxist metaphor of 'base' and 'superstructure'. The abandoning of that mechanical metaphor, so as to assert that the religious liberty which the sectaries fought for was *truly* what they fought for – this is, it appears, the original sin for which the Marxist *apparatchiks* cannot forgive Thompson, or Christopher Hill either. And yet... how is it possible to sustain Thompson's claim to belong to 'Old Dissent'? Those Old Dissenters were Christians, as Thompson explicitly and vehemently isn't – is it not just as simple as that?

This parting of the ways, which Thompson refuses to recognize, confronted him at an earlier stage in his letter to Kolakowski, at the first point indeed where he is moved to ill temper in his communication with the distinguished Polish defector whom he addresses mostly in sorrow, though sometimes in anger. Kolakowski, declaring himself in *Encounter* an 'inconsistent atheist', had decided that 'men have no fuller means of self-identification than through religious symbolism', and that 'religious consciousness... is an irreplaceable part of human culture, man's only attempt to see himself as a whole' – whereat, Thompson avows, 'not only the atheist but also some primal Lollard or Anabaptist within me rebels'. And this provokes Thompson into what is surely regrettable chauvinism:

> You may say this in Poland: you may say this, if you wish, in Italy or France. But by what right, what study of its traditions and sensibility, may you assume this as a universal in the heart of an ancient Protestant island, *doggedly resistant to the magics of religious symbolism even when they remained believers,* cultivating like so many urban gardeners the individual conscience as against some priest-given 'religious consciousness'?

The italics here are mine – mine, who am no Polish bad or lapsed Roman Catholic but an Englishman bred, unless I am mistaken, much nearer than Edward Thompson to the heart of English Dissenting Protestantism. And what, I ask him, are those 'magics of religious symbolism' which those English Protestants were 'doggedly resistant to'? Are they for instance, or do they include, that bread or that wine sacramentally offered alike in the Roman Mass, the Anglican Eucharist, and the Dissenters' Lord's Supper? If they do include these, then there is no way in which people who rejected them, as 'magics' (an abusive term) or as 'symbolism' (a contentious one), could have 'remained believers', though they may have deluded themselves that they did. This is true of Lollards and Anabaptists, however 'primal'. There truly is a point at which Believer and Unbeliever part company; there truly is *not,* as Thompson and many thousands suppose, a continuous band of sentiment and opinion all the way from Belief to Unbelief. Reaching the point where an act of belief is called for, one makes the act or one does not; and one lives with the consequences. If Thompson lives with the consequences of his unbelief, there is no way for him to claim shelter under 'Old Dissent'.

He fulminates further, to Kolakowski:

> What you touch off in me – and this is why I introduced the point – is simply the old Adam of the English idiom. You interrupt me in my work. I don't wish to be dragged back into all *that, I* don't wish to be drawn into an argument whose form and even whose philosophical terms arise from a culture in which the old ding-a-dong between Catholic and atheist universalists goes on and on and on; in which, generation after generation, the Catholic theologians and philosophers, like cunning groundsmen, prepare new pitches and dictate to their opponents that they must, once again, play over every inch of this novel pitch or they will have lost the series; in which, to stand somewhere between Catholic and anti-Catholic philosophy, is to give one a unique status as a Referee.

Thompson's polemical English is here at its vigorous best; and it needs to be, for he hasn't a rational leg to stand on. Just because he is addressing a Pole gives him no warrant for using 'Catholic', meaning apparently '*Roman* Catholic' instead of (what the context calls for) 'Christian'. On the other hand his furious impatience – 'You interrupt me in my work' –

is wholly understandable, and justified; between Christian and atheist any debate is indeed a waste of time, because they share no common ground. (To be sure, both may justly claim to be 'rational'; but they proceed upon incompatible notions of human Reason.) What isn't justifiable is Thompson's laying claim to 'the old Adam of the English idiom'. In other places – notably in his essay, 'The Peculiarities of the English' – he has made responsible and in fact heartwarming play with this notion, 'the English idiom' (an idiom that comprehends for him, as for few others, the usages of the English poets); but here he implies, quite without warrant, that the English idiom is essentially an *irreligious* idiom, whereas it needs to be asserted bluntly that the English were until lately (and are still, more than any one likes to acknowledge) a Christian nation, and that their idiom comprehends unmistakably Christian deposits, including quite notably usages that an atheist will want to reprehend as 'magics' or as 'symbols'.

All the same, it should be clear why whatever Edward Thompson writes about Dissent deserves from us close and remorseless attention such as we would not give to others. When he speaks of 'an ancient Protestant island' we may detect, little as Thompson might like it, the note of Edmund Burke, and Burke's conviction that 'antiquity', long continuance, possesses in itself an authority that we should recognize. We do not expect to hear such a locution from a Tory mouth; and if we should hear it, we should be expected to understand by 'Protestant' only one version of English Protestantism, that of the Church of England. Other versions are just as ancient as Anglicanism, and have no less authority; though one listens in vain for any acknowledgement of that from the British Right. Angus Calder has linked Thompson's name with a couple of others to stand behind his expostulation:

> People in Britain really must stop conceiving their own history in terms of kings and queens and Regency rakes and Victorian country houses, and recognise the centrality of those ethical concerns – generating scientific advances, practical action in commerce and industry, missionary-led expansion, reform at home – which were expressed in conventicles, in chapels, in kirks, and in the re-reading of Milton, Bunyan and the Bible. Otherwise we really cannot live with ourselves honestly.[7]

The most fervent of constitutional monarchists should be able to say, 'Amen'.

[7] Angus Calder, in *Proteus*, February 1978.

First published in *Dissentient Voice*.

5 Thoughts on Kipling's 'Recessional'

In an unconsidered moment – or rather in one very ill-considered undertaking, *After Strange Gods*, a book that it seems he was later ashamed of – T.S. Eliot spoke of the Congregationalism that D.H. Lawrence grew up in as 'vague hymn-singing pietism'. It was an aberration that F.R. Leavis never allowed Eliot, nor the rest of us, to forget. However, years later it may be thought that Eliot more than made up for it, when he wrote appreciatively of another English author, one who stands in almost exactly the same relation to Wesleyan New Dissent that Lawrence stood in to Old Dissent. This author was Rudyard Kipling, grandson of Wesleyan ministers on both sides of his family, whose parents conformed to nonpracticing Anglicanism, and who was himself through much of his life some sort of undogmatic theist. Of Kipling, Eliot wrote in 1941:

> He might almost be called the first citizen of India. And his relation to India determines that about him which is the most important thing about a man, his religious attitude. It is an attitude of comprehensive tolerance. He is not an unbeliever – on the contrary, he can accept all faiths: that of the Moslem, that of the Hindu, that of the Buddhist, Parsee or Jain, even (through the historical imagination) that of Mithra: if his understanding of Christianity is less affectionate, that is due to his Anglo-Saxon background – and no doubt he saw enough in India of clergy such as Mr Bennett in *Kim*.

This is liberal indeed, and represents (it may be thought) a great increase in Christian charity over the Eliot who wrote *After Strange Gods*, to whom his Anglican allegiance was so much more of a recent and exciting novelty.

However, before we set this change of heart entirely to Eliot's credit, we need to take note of certain difficulties which arise in our reading of the poet for whom he is soliciting our admiration. There is for instance what is probably the most justly famous of all Kipling's poems, his 'Recessional' of 1897:

> God of our fathers, known of old,
>   Lord of our far-flung battle-line,
> Beneath whose awful Hand we hold

Dominion over palm and pine –
Lord God of Hosts, be with us yet,
Lest we forget – lest we forget!

The tumult and the shouting dies;
The Captains and the Kings depart:
Still stands Thine ancient sacrifice,
An humble and a contrite heart.
Lord God of Hosts, be with us yet,
Lest we forget – lest we forget!

Far-called, our navies melt away;
On dune and headland sinks the fire:
Lo, all our pomp of yesterday
Is one with Nineveh and Tyre!
Judge of the Nations, spare us yet,
Lest we forget – lest we forget!

If, drunk with sight of power, we loose
Wild tongues that have not Thee in awe,
Such boasting as the Gentiles use,
Or lesser breeds without the Law –
Lord God of Hosts, be with us yet,
Lest we forget – lest we forget!

For heathen heart that puts her trust
In reeking tube and iron shard,
All valiant dust that builds on dust,
And guarding calls not Thee to guard,
For frantic boast and foolish word –
Thy mercy on Thy People, Lord!

The line in this poem that has set most teeth on edge, and raised most blood-pressures, is the notorious one about 'lesser breeds without the law' – a line which has been frequently misunderstood, for the good reason that the intended sense of it – by which the 'lesser breeds' are not brown Afghans but white Germans – is so very far from obvious. What has given less trouble, though I find it much more troublesome, is the question: *what* god of *whose* fathers? *what* lord of *whose* battle-line? The god of the German (or Russian, or Dutch Boer) battle-line is officially the Christian God, who is also – officially – the god of Mulvaney and Ortheris and Learoyd, of Tommy Atkins, 'the absent-minded beggar ordered south'. And so it can hardly be he to whom 'Recessional' is addressed. Nor can we any more plausibly identify him as Allah or Siva or Buddha or Mithras or the god of the Parsee or the god of the Jain; although, since Kipling is fervently aware of the Indian regiments fighting beside the British in Burma and South

Africa, it might reasonably seem that the God addressed should incorporate these unchristian deities at the same time as it excludes the Christian deity of Imperial Germany. How can we know where we stand, with a poem addressed to a Being so ambiguous? And yet Eliot, the devout and proudly orthodox Anglo-Catholic author of *Four Quartets,* knew just where *he* stood in respect of the poem, and where the poem stood in relation to him:

> I call Kipling a great hymn writer on the strength of *Recessional.* It is a poem almost too well known to need to have the reader's attention called to it, except to point out that it is one of the poems in which something breaks through from a deeper level than that of the mind of the conscious observer of political and social affairs – something which has the true prophetic inspiration. Kipling might have been one of the most notable of hymn writers.

This is liberal theology indeed! The Eliot whose polemics ever since 'For Lancelot Andrewes' had insisted on the necessity for religious *dogma* here shows himself ready to admire a hymn that has 'prophetic inspiration', though that inspiration is unleashed in the service of a Divinity undefined and undefinable. This more than makes up for Eliot's sneer at Lawrence's Congregationalism, in the sense that it overcompensates, flies to the other extreme.

Eliot had not taken leave of his senses, however. The 'Lord God of hosts' of 'Recessional' can indeed be identified, by just that phrase and by others in the poem that support it, particularly 'Such boastings as the Gentiles use'. The God addressed in 'Recessional' is the God of the Old Testament, God of Israel, God of 'the chosen people'. If we needed supporting evidence – as in fact we don't – that evidence is in Kipling's poem of a year before, 'Hymn before Action', which Eliot does not fail to print in his *Choice of Kipling's Verse* immediately before 'Recessional':

> The earth is full of anger,
>   The seas are dark with wrath,
> The Nations in their harness
>   Go up against our path:
> Ere yet we loose the legions
>   Ere yet we draw the blade,
> Jehovah of the Thunders,
>   Lord God of Battles, aid!

The God invoked in 'Recessional', it now appears, is not indeed the God of Christ any more than he is the God of the Jain or the Parsee: he is the God of David, warrior king of ancient Israel.

Yet what right has Kipling, or Eliot after him, to appeal to this god, this *Yahveh*? Was Kipling, any more than Eliot, a convert to Judaism from Christianity? Quite evidently not; and so the charge of culpable frivolity lies as heavily as ever against the pair of them.

Here we may leave Eliot, remarking compassionately that in 1941 there was much excuse for a naturalized Englishman – a patriot as only the naturalized can be – to nourish the patriotic will at the expense of intellectual confusion. For Kipling there can be no such excuse. And the further we probe into Kipling's religious sentiments, the more confusion we find – and the less excuse for it.

In the 1920s his cousin Stanley Baldwin, recording how in a conversation with Kipling he had found them at one on political matters, accounted for this by saying, 'We have common puritan blood'. What Baldwin seems to have had in mind was that their common great-grandfather, the Scottish Ulsterman James Macdonald, had been a Wesleyan minister converted by the great John Wesley himself. We need not deny that evangelical Wesleyanism was historically an offshoot of English puritanism. But it was a very peculiar offshoot, one that ranged itself against such great dissenting puritans as Oliver Cromwell and John Bunyan, with both of whom Kipling none the less aligned himself under the illusion (apparently) that in doing so he was keeping faith with his Wesleyan inheritance. Historically Wesleyanism was High Church, aggressively monarchist, Arminian, and Tory. Accordingly, if Kipling had really thought through his inheritance of Wesleyan puritanism – and *Puck of Pook's Hill* is there to show how he thought such 'thinking through' was a patriotic duty – he ought to have sided with the Arminian Archbishop Laud against the Calvinist Cromwell, and with the nonjuring Arminian William Law against the Calvinist Bunyan. The Arminian conviction that Christ died for *all* men, not just for the elect, was crucial for Kipling, since it was the only basis on which for instance Gunga Din might earn salvation; and in any case the torments he suffered from his Southsea foster mother in boyhood are said to have derived from her being an evangelical Calvinist. Yet 'Recessional' depends, if it is not to fall apart completely, on the Calvinist notion of a chosen people, the elect. In short, if Kipling shared his cousin Baldwin's conviction that they shared a 'puritan' inheritance – and there is some reason to think that he did – he seems to have been wholly ignorant of the mutually irreconcilable strains inside English puritanism. The two logically incompatible theories of salvation, Arminian and Calvinist, are in 'Recessional' held together by a powerfully traditional rhetoric; but the slightest attention to what that hymn seems to say will reveal the two incompatible systems and will break the poem in two.

Eliot decided that Kipling 'can be called a Tory in a sense in which only a handful of writers together with a number of mostly inarticulate, obscure and uninfluential people are ever Tories in one generation'. This enabled Eliot to clear Kipling, and also incidentally Eliot himself, from the imputation, common in 1941 and still common in England today, that the true Tory of this recondite sort is in any way friendly to fascism – the truth being rather, as Eliot says finely, that fascism, 'from a truly Tory point of view, is merely the extreme degradation of democracy'. Kipling certainly deserved to be rescued from this imputation, if only because of his excellent poem 'The Storm Cone', in which as early as 1932 he warned against the Nazis. But as Eliot remarked further, in any less recondite sense of 'Tory', anything having to do with the alignment of political parties at Westminster, Kipling was not a Tory at all. On the contrary it was the Tory party under Balfour that he assailed, savagely and bravely, in 'The Islanders' (1902), with its famous and blistering indictment of 'the flannelled fools at the wicket or the muddied oafs at the goals'. And I think we can go further, so far as to say that Kipling believed in what has since been labelled the Whig interpretation of English history. For nothing else seems to explain his lifelong admiration of Cromwell, so much at odds with his Wesleyan inheritance and his Arminian predilections. What a strain it was for him to accommodate his Cromwellianism in the frame of his other commitments appears most strikingly from a poem that Eliot chose not to reprint, 'The Old Issue', dated 9 October 1899, the date of President Kruger's ultimatum which precipitated the Boer War:

All we have of freedom, all we use or know –
This our fathers bought for us long and long ago.

Ancient Right unnoticed as the breath we draw –
Leave to live by no man's leave, underneath the Law –

Lance and torch and tumult, steel and grey-goose wing,
Wrenched it, inch and ell and all, slowly from the King.

Till our fathers 'stablished, after bloody years,
How our King is one with us, first among his peers.

So they bought us freedom – not at little cost –
Wherefore must we watch the King, lest our gain be lost.

Over all things certain, this is sure indeed,
Suffer not the old King: for we know the breed.

Give no ear to bondsmen bidding us endure,
Whining 'He is weak and far'; crying 'Time shall cure.'

(Time himself is witness, till the battle joins,
Deeper strikes the rottenness in the people's loins.)

Give no heed to bondsmen masking war with peace.
Suffer not the old King here or overseas.

They that beg us barter – wait his yielding mood –
Pledge the years we hold in trust – pawn our brother's blood –

Howso' great their clamour, whatsoe'er their claim,
Suffer not the old King under any name!

Here is naught unproven – here is naught to learn.
It is written what shall fall if the King return.

He shall mark our goings, question whence we came,
Set his guards about us, as in Freedom's name.

He shall take a tribute; toll of all our ware;
He shall change our gold for arms – arms we may not bear.

He shall break his Judges if they cross his word;
He shall rule above the Law calling on the Lord...

This has been called 'complex'. It is certainly complicated, and could hardly be anything else if it was to accomplish its strenuous and implausible purpose of persuading the forces of the Queen-Empress, as they advanced on the independent South African Republic, that they were in the same case as the Parliamentary armies of the 1640s advancing on the loyal armies of Charles I. The crossing over of terms in this complicated equation, so that monarchical equals parliamentarian, and republican equals despotic, is, to say the least of it, audacious. And the strenuousness of the manoeuvre distorts, retrospectively, the 'Recessional' of two years earlier. For there the 'Law' that the lesser breeds were 'without' (i.e. lacking, but also 'outside of') was the Law of Moses, which bore upon Israel but not on other nations; whereas in 'The Old Issue' when Paul Kruger is said to 'rule above the Law', the 'Law' is the constitutional law of the land, and the other 'Law', the Law of Moses, is presumably what the Calvinist Kruger might say he was appealing to when he was 'calling on the Lord'. No wonder that F.W. Reitz, Secretary of State of the South African Republic, should hurl the accusation back again:

Gods of the Jingo – Brass and Gold,
Lords of the world by 'Right Divine',
Under whose baneful sway they hold
Dominion over 'Mine and Thine'...

It is certainly on the face of it more plausible to see the Divine Right of government, which Charles I claimed and the Cromwellians denied, being asserted by Queen Victoria than by President Kruger. Kipling has the rhetoric, but common sense and probability are all with Reitz.

It may well be thought that subsequent history has vindicated Kipling in his suspicions of the Afrikaner's mentality and political instincts. The pro-Boer demonstrators of 1900 – among them Kipling's aunt, Georgiana Burne-Jones – would be the anti-apartheid demonstrators of today. And it is true that Kipling foresaw the black South Africans getting a worse deal from the Afrikaners than from the British. But it's no good pretending that the welfare of the blacks carried any weight with Kipling when he called for war with the Boers; his case, as 'The Old Issue' makes clear, rested solely on the penalties imposed upon English-speaking 'Uitlanders' in the Orange Free State and the Transvaal. And certainly Calvinist theocratic republics have a poor record of safeguarding civil rights, ever since Calvin's own Geneva and the seventeenth-century Commonwealth of Massachusetts. But was it not just such a theocratic republic that was created in England by Cromwell and the other regicides? And were not just as many Englishmen deprived of their rights under the regicides as under the king who had been killed? 'The Old Issue' is outrageous special pleading.

And yet we need not think that Kipling was insincere when he wrote it. On the contrary we have already found reason to think that what looks like duplicity is muddle and ignorance about the nature of the English so-called 'puritan' tradition, muddle which – now as fifty years ago – is to be found particularly among those who, like Baldwin, boast of having 'puritan blood'. 'Puritan' is not synonymous with 'Nonconformist', nor with 'evangelical'; still less with 'parliamentarian' or 'democratic' or 'Cromwellian'. Of these adjectives, the only ones that fit the Wesleyan inheritance are 'evangelical' and, less certainly, 'puritan'; but Kipling, I suspect, thought that all the other adjectives were appropriate also. In short I believe that Angus Wilson is right when, on the last page of his *Strange Ride of Rudyard Kipling*, after considering various psychological explanations of the riddle that Kipling's life and works present us with, he decides: 'I prefer if I must a social-historical description of long generations of Evangelical belief ending in post-Darwinian doubt.'

The question of Kipling's sincerity comes up again as soon as we shift our attention from the Evangelical generations behind him to the post-Darwinian doubt that he lived in. And from this point of view it is 'Recessional', not 'The Old Issue', that looks inexcusable. Sons who conceive themselves to have no God at all, or only a God who is nebulous and featureless, have no right to call for help in battle on the God of their fathers whose features were stern and strong. Eliot, who decided Kipling was a great hymn-writer because of 'Recessional', claims for him also that he was a great epigrammatist:

> Good epigrams in English are very few; and the great hymn writer is very rare. Both are extremely objective types of verse: they can and should be charged with intense feeling, but it must be a feeling that can be completely shared. They are possible to a writer so impersonal as Kipling.

The force of what Eliot seems to say here is carried in the words 'objective' and 'impersonal'. But it is not clear what he means by either of these words; and if we look elsewhere in his criticism for enlightenment, we come across the famous essay 'Tradition and the Individual Talent', which advances a theory of 'the impersonal' that has been generally found unacceptable. I believe he is maintaining here that in a hymn (or an epigram) a poet who doesn't believe in the God of either the Old or the New Testament can properly write as if he did so believe, because by that pretence he can share the intensity of his feeling – a feeling not religious at all, but political and patriotic – with the mass of his countrymen who either *do* believe in such gods, or else think that they do. And when he cryptically quotes in full a difficult and memorable later poem, 'The Fabulists', I think (for it is impossible to be sure) that he reads this poem as an impenitent confession by Kipling that he did indeed go to work in that way. However that may be, and whether or not that is a right reading of 'The Fabulists', few readers will be ready to agree that, by making this play with 'objective' and 'impersonal', Eliot has cleared the author of 'Recessional' from the charge of insincerity, of duplicity and double-dealing.

This is not to say that there is no way for an atheistic or agnostic poet, a poet of 'post-Darwinian doubt', to draw on the themes and images of Christian belief. Many will agree that one of Kipling's nonbelieving contemporaries, Thomas Hardy, showed how this could be done, with moving propriety and sincerity. I need cite only 'The Oxen':

> Christmas Eve, and twelve of the clock.
>   'Now they are all on their knees,'
> An elder said as we sat in a flock
>   By the embers in hearthside ease.
>
> We pictured the meek mild creatures where
>   They dwelt in their strawy pen,
> Nor did it occur to one of us there
>   To doubt they were kneeling then.
>
> So fair a fancy few would weave
>   In these years! Yet, I feel,
> If someone said on Christmas Eve,
>   'Come; see the oxen kneel
>
> 'In the lonely barton by yonder coomb
>   Our childhood used to know,'
> I should go with him in the gloom,
>   Hoping it might be so.

'Hoping it might be so' expresses the agnostic sentiment with a purity, a plain and aching accuracy, such as we look for in vain anywhere in Kipling. And no talk of 'objective' and 'impersonal' can persuade us that 'Recessional' in some quite different way is an equal or comparable achievement.

But this is not the only way in which a non-Christian or post-

Christian poet can, with perfect sincerity, traffic in Christian affairs. For an alternative way of doing so we can turn to Kipling's 'Gethsemane' (which, says Eliot the wily possum, 'I do not think I understand'):

The garden called Gethsemane
 In Picardy it was,
And there the people came to see
 The English soldiers pass.
We used to pass – we used to pass
 Or halt, as it might be.
And ship our masks in case of gas
 Beyond Gethsemane.

The garden called Gethsemane
 It held a pretty lass,
But all the time she talked to me
 I prayed my cup might pass.
The officer sat on the chair,
 The men lay on the grass,
And all the time we halted there
 I prayed my cup might pass.

It didn't pass – it didn't pass –
 I didn't pass from me.
I drank it when we met the gas
 Beyond Gethsemane!

This is one of Kipling's greatest poems. And Eliot understood it well enough, in the sense that he understood it to be overtly and fiercely blasphemous. The poem furiously denies what every Christian is required to believe – that one Being and one alone, Jesus, suffered on behalf of humankind an agony more intense and more expiatory than ever was, or ever would be, required of another. The Christian may be, he must be, shocked and affronted by this; but he cannot object to it, cannot deny that Kipling had the right to say it. Such blasphemy is thoroughly plain-dealing, there is nothing devious nor duplicitous. (Poetically of course – for 'poetically' is the word here, not 'rhetorically' – the uncannily piercing moment comes with the officer sitting on the chair, the exquisitely painful metrical disturbance that lays a doubled trisyllabic rhythm on to the iambic norm.) Straightforward blasphemous denial is another way for the non-Christian poet to deal sincerely with Christianity. Closely related to this, and yet crucially different, is Kipling's use of Scripture in two stories about the Great War, 'The Madonna of the Trenches' and 'The Gardener'. Angus Wilson, himself I think no Christian, is quite right to protest that in both these cases the use of the Scriptural text is both tasteless and redundant. In the first case, where a sergeant's suffering for an unattainable woman is identified with St Paul's suffering for Christ, there is, as Wilson says, 'plain sentimentality clothed in a metaphysical authority which it does not possess'; and in the second, better story, when the war cemetery's gardener is revealed to the Mary Magdalen figure as Christ himself, this has the surely unintended implication that no merely human compassion could have embraced her. Kipling seems to have intended to be blasphemous far more often than he succeeded in being so: this was because he had an uncertain grasp of what blasphemy is. That didn't in the least diminish his appeal to an exceptionally wide public; for in a post-Darwinian, post-Christian or at best nominally Christian culture, people have an uncertain grasp of blasphemy to just the extent that they have an imperfect grasp of faith. Once again, in this matter of blasphemy, it seems we can acquit Kipling of duplicity and insincerity, and convict him rather of muddle – a remarkably fruitful muddle, because it was a muddle that he shared with his readers, and not just with readers from the educated elite that provided other writers of his time, such as Hardy, with a far more limited public than Kipling could appeal to.

Could this be our compassionate if somewhat contemptuous verdict on Kipling's writings as a whole? I think not. 'Recessional' is still the sticking point. To see in that poem no duplicity but only confusion we have to strain every nerve and give Kipling the benefit of every doubt. Moreover in Eliot's *A Choice of Kipling's Verse* there are two more poems which, if they are set side by side, raise once again in a very acute form our suspicions about Kipling's good faith. These two poems go together because they both deal with another heroic figure from the English puritan past – not Cromwell, but Bunyan. They are 'The Holy War' of 1917, and 'MacDonough's Song', which may have been written about 1907, though it did not appear until *A Diversity of Creatures,* in 1912. 'The Holy War' is distressing rant, and it's astonishing that Eliot should have chosen it for his selection:

All enemy divisions,
   Recruits of every class,
And highly screened positions
   For flame or poison-gas;
The craft that we call modern,
   The crimes that we call new,
John Bunyan had 'em typed and filed
   In Sixteen Eighty-two.

Likewise the Lords of Looseness
   That hamper faith and works,
The Perseverance-Doubters
   And Present-Comfort shirks,
With brittle intellectuals
   Who crack beneath a strain –

John Bunyan met that helpful set
    In Charles the Second's reign.

Emmanuel's vanguard dying
    For right and not for rights,
My Lord Apollyon lying
    To the State-kept Stockholmites,
The Pope, the swithering Neutrals,
    The Kaiser and his Gott –
Their roles, their goals, their naked souls –
    He knew and drew the lot.

The earlier poem is much more distinguished writing, and just for that reason it is, especially at the end (which I shall not quote), even more shocking. But what rocks us on our heels is that Bunyan's very phrase, 'The Holy War', which in 1917 is endorsed and applauded, had those several years before been treated with searing contempt:

Whether the State can loose and bind
    In Heaven as well as on Earth:
If it be wiser to kill mankind
    Before or after the birth –
These are matters of high concern
    Where State-kept schoolmen are;
But Holy State (we have lived to learn)
    Endeth in Holy War.

(Just so; but Holy War against the Boers was precisely what Kipling had preached in 'The Old Issue'!) 'MacDonough's Song' is part and parcel of a story, 'As Easy as A.B.C.', which is set in the year 2065 AD. And so we may say – it seems we *must* say – that Holy War will be manifestly a vicious and desolating idea in 2065, though it is a wholesome and invigorating idea in 1917. But this implies a relativism – about art and morals and politics, indeed about *truth* – for which the only word is 'cynical'. And if this is what 'puritanism' brings us to, as soon as it is conceived of as a secular and time-bound entity persisting apart from religious faith, then 'puritan blood' is what no one can or should take pride in. One does not have to be a knee-jerk liberal, nor one of the 'brittle intellectuals', to believe that the Kipling who thought this and perverted his poetic vocation to serve this kind of thinking, is indeed in many ways the diabolical figure that many of us supposed him to be, before Eliot and George Orwell some forty years ago began to rehabilitate him.

First published in *The Sewanee Review* 87, no. 1 (Winter 1979), pp. 34–48, as 'A Puritan's Empire: The Case of Kipling'. Reprinted in *Dissentient Voice*.

6 *Dissent and Individualism*

If we open a recent survey of British and American poetry since 1939, we are introduced in the second sentence to the poet Louis MacNeice:

> The son of the man who became Anglican Bishop of Down, Connor and Dromore, educated at Marlborough and Oxford, a classics don at the University of Birmingham, and a producer and scriptwriter in the B.B.C.: the biography is less that of an individual and more like that of his class. [1]

It had perhaps not occurred to us that just four items of a personal history, strung together, could be called 'a biography'. But if we can agree to that, and can concede for instance that if James Boswell had had our advantages he could with profit have boiled down his Life of Johnson into far more manageable compass (say, two sides of a sheet of paper), we shall be that much nearer understanding how a class – that is to say, a conceptual category, a notion, a mental convenience – can nowadays be accorded life, the sort of 'Life' indeed that a more streamlined modern Boswell may be called on to write. In fact of course if the individuals Louis MacNeice and Samuel Johnson can be seen most truly as instances of a category, a *class,* then the modern Boswell would be a fool if he portrayed the individuals rather than the class which comprehends them. And only the dilettante will tremble at what may happen, under this dispensation, to those individuals that we call *poems,* which are as tender and sometimes almost as intricate as the human individuals that we call 'persons'. Rough justice indeed is the best they can hope for, poems and people alike – as this survey soon shows.

Proceeding in this way is sometimes called, and sometimes calls itself, 'Marxist'. But it has ancestors far more remote, and far less reputable, than Karl Marx. One time in England when individuals were thus confidently categorized, judged, and in some measure proscribed – all on the basis of three or four facts about their birth, education, religious allegiance, and occupation – was the late seventeenth century. Among the true ancestors of our modern classifiers were the vengeful members of parliament under Charles II who thus categorized and proscribed the English

[1] Eric Homburger, *The Art of the Real: Poetry in England and America since 1939* (London & New Jersey, 1977), p. 9.

Nonconformists. When the penal proscription was lifted and religious toleration in large measure secured, the Nonconformists properly saw this as a triumph for the individual against the facile classifiers and categorizers who had decided all Dissenters were traitors to the State:

> If Christians be first denominated by general titles and terms of distinction, which they cannot help, and then the crimes of any particular person, that the world pleases to denominate as one of the same party, must be charged and imputed to the whole; what must the consequence of this be, but that the whole community become obnoxious to punishment, and the very government itself thereupon be dissolved?
>
> For I take it to be past denial or doubt, that some of each denomination have been, are, or may be guilty of seditious practices. Some hypocrites will lurk among those vast bodies of people, under the most strict and watchful government; but God forbid their guilt should affect the whole body, under whose names they shelter themselves. God, reason, and conscience, do all command the hottest zeal, to make its pause and just distinction here. Let the guilty be brought to condign punishment, upon fair trial and conviction This discourse designs no favour for such. But let not those who abhor their wickedness, and are as pure from their crimes as yourselves, suffer with them or for them: For then your reason will tell you, yourselves are as liable to sufferings as they; and that your zeal is not kindled by love to justice, but the hatred of a party.
>
> It is not in the body politic, as in the body natural: If the hand steal, the feet are justly laid in irons, and the neck put into an halter; because all the members of the body natural are animated, and governed but by one soul. But in the body politic, every individual hath a distinct soul of his own; and therefore that member only that offends ought to be punished, and all the rest to enjoy their full liberty and honour as before. Away therefore for ever with this church and state destroying synechdoche. [2]

'Synecdoche', says the dictionary: 'a figure' (that is to say, in rhetoric) 'by which a more comprehensive term is used for a less comprehensive or vice versa; as whole for part or part for whole, genus for species or species for genus, etc.' And this is individualism too: John Flavel in the 1690s would risk pedantry for the sake of wit; he had a powerful and learned mind, he would not conceal the fact, and it seems that his fellow-Dissenters, less well endowed or lacking his educational advantages, took vicarious pride in his performance. A hundred years later a dissenting minister would hardly have taken the risk, and for his successor, now in

[2] John Flavel (1630?–91), *The Reasonableness of Personal Reformation* (1691). *The Works of John Flavel* (1820; reprinted 1968, London), vol. VI.

the 1970s, it would be unthinkable; it would give too much offence, for it would be thought (under our tyranny of the majority) *élitist,* 'undemocratic'. But then John Flavel differs from later Dissenters in all sorts of ways; in his mouth, for instance, the locution 'church and state' has no harshly jeering inflection. The Dissenters, we like to say, vindicated the rights of the individual against the state; but this is true only if we assume that the state is in the hands of or at the mercy of, the inveterate and facile classifiers. And Flavel seems to assume that this doesn't have to be so; he might have argued, as certainly *we* may argue, that precisely the Crown – the monarch, who is above all classifications – has a constitutional duty to see that this doesn't happen.

More generally, however, are we not labouring the obvious? That there is a close tie between religious Dissent and individualism is what no one will deny. Very well. But in that case how does a Dissenter respond, when he returns to the account of Louis MacNeice? There he reads, of 'the dilemma MacNeice faced in the 1940s':

> He cannot praise the world too keenly, for the socialist in him knows that it is rotten, unjust and dying. But neither can he condemn it unequivocally. The ambivalent values of the bourgeoisie leave room for manoeuvre, for the flowering of an individualism which, though it may be historically finished, defines the essence of our (bourgeois) notions of humanity.

A Dissenter, or any Christian for that matter, may well wonder in the first place why a son of the Bishop of Dromore had to wait for socialism to tell him that the world 'is rotten, unjust and dying'. For this is what every Christian knows, as John Flavel certainly knew it, without any socialism to tell him so. The Christian knows also that, unjust and corrupt as the world is, he cannot 'condemn it unequivocally'; indeed, he goes further, for he knows that any attempt thus to condemn it is a sin – against God, who created this world, unsatisfactory as it is or has become.

Oh but (it will be said) this is to fly too high – in the passage we are looking at, 'the world' does not mean *the world.* It does not include for instance the natural creation; the writer does not mean to impugn lambs or tigers, deserts or mountains. Indeed, his world that is called 'rotten, unjust and dying' does not comprehend, necessarily or even probably, Tanzanian or Eskimo, Albanian or Chinese; his use of the word 'bourgeois' shows clearly on the contrary, for those who will read him with candour, that by 'world' he means only that manmade social fabric which Louis MacNeice had to contend with – the United Kingdom and the United States in the 1940s. Summoning our candour to stifle, as best we can, uncharitable wishes that people would say what they mean, and would curb their addiction to synecdoche ('by which a more comprehensive term is used for a less comprehensive'), also passing by for the moment this revelation that a Christian's sense of the injustice in the world is a great deal more thoroughgoing than a socialist's, let us try to engage with our author on the basis of what he meant to say, rather than what he said. Even so, I'm afraid, our difficulties are not over. For even after we have agreed to take 'world' to mean only that human creation, the society that MacNeice moved in through the 1930s into the 1940s, we find ourselves stumbling over the assumption that this world was indeed 'human', manmade. John Flavel did not think so. In his Coronation sermon, preached at Dartmouth, he declared:

> When God puts a crown upon the head, and a sceptre into the hand of a man, he engraves upon that man (in a qualified sense) both his name, and the lively characters of his Majesty and authority... But yet, in all the grants and conveyances of Heaven, there is always a reservation and salvo to the divine prerogative, to displace at pleasure, and set it upon what head he shall please...[3]

Whereas to the Unitarian Richard Price in 1790 it seemed clear that the People had the right to 'cashier' a monarch who had misbehaved, to the Presbyterian John Flavel in 1691 it seemed clear that only God had that right; and if it be objected that it is hard to discern God's purposes at such junctures, one retorts that, as recorded history has shown, it is no less hard to discern the purposes of that amorphous and convenient entity, 'the people'.

Since we are trying to find a common ground on which dispute can be profitable, can we leave that momentous question in abeyance, and agree to proceed on the assumption that British society, as MacNeice the Anglo-Irishman experienced it in the 1930s and 1940s, was indeed wholly a manmade contrivance? I'm not sure that we can do this, or that we should. For if God did not participate in the making of British society, He at all events permitted it to be made. If he exists, there is no equation that He can be left out of. And I suspect that it is our civil concessions to our secular antagonists 'for the sake of argument', that have bedevilled and disabled the Christian witness in these matters.

However, if against our better judgments we take this risky manoeuvre and agree to read our commentator in an artificially secular spirit, we discover I think that what we call 'the Christian', he calls 'the bourgeois'. For the Christian, as we have seen, is required to be ambivalent: he must despise and reject 'the world' at the same time as he loves and respects it. And for our commentator it is the values of the 'bourgeoisie' that are 'ambivalent'. The implication is that the values of other orders of society are free of this ambivalence. (And this is our commentator's implication, not ours; *we* may be very willing to think that this, as

[3] Ibid.

we think, necessary and proper ambivalence is to be found in proletariat and aristocracy – it is he who restricts this Christian sentiment to the one class that he calls the *bourgeoisie*.)

One thing, at least, is quite clear, and enough to take our breath away. If, as is generally conceded, our Dissenting forebears suffered and sometimes died for 'individualism', that individualism is – we are asked to think – 'historically finished'. At this point we mount into metaphysics. For, 'historically finished' though it is, this individualism can still, it appears, 'flower'. And this can only mean that by 'history' and 'historical' our commentator does not mean what common sense means by those words. In his discourse 'History' is as much a transcendent and immanent force as 'God' is in ours. And it is this divinity, not ours, that has – we are asked to think – shovelled individualism into a dustbin whence it can, however, unaccountably 'flower'.

But of course one sees clearly enough what our commentator is driving at, and why right-thinking people are, if not persuaded by him, at least disturbed. 'Individualism' smells much less sweetly in the nostrils when we join it with the word 'economic'. '*Economic* individualism' – it is this baleful conjunction that has long given to Dissenters a special place in the demonology of the British Left, as when E.P. Thompson, on no better evidence than a novel by Frances Trollope, decides in his *Making of the English Working Class* that the hardhearted mill-owners of the 1820s were characteristically Dissenters, though the villainous overseers whom they employed were Methodists. (On the other hand, confusingly, Dissenters as the heirs of Cromwellian republicanism also appear in leftist mythology on the side of the angels.) John Flavel did not foresee – how could he? – the advent of Adam Smith or of industrial capitalism. If he had lived to see it, there is no need to suppose that his loyalty to individualism would have led him to deplore state intervention to prevent, for instance, unemployment. Quite the contrary:

> It is therefore the undoubted interest of Christian states and churches, to make every individual person as useful as may be to the whole, and to enjoy the services of all their subjects and members, one way or another, according to their different capacities; that it may be said of them (as the historian speaks of the land of Canaan) that there was in it, *Nihil infructuosum, nihil sterile;* not a shrub but bare some fruit.

There is nothing in the Dissenting tradition which sets its face against state intervention to ensure an acceptable measure of economic equality and security; though equally there is nothing there to solve the riddle which confronts us today: how to ensure this measure of equality without at the same time curtailing political liberty, how to restrain economic individualism while not curbing and stunting political and cultural and religious individualism. And plainly, it is these – not merely economic individualism – that our commentator has in his sights, when he speaks of 'an individualism which, though it may be historically finished, defines the essence of our (bourgeois) notions of humanity'. Here too, try as I may, I can assign no meaning to 'bourgeois' except 'Christian'. How this may be will become a little clearer if we ask what alternative is offered for our approval in place of the individualism supposedly discredited: what it is that History, having 'finished' with that, is now engendering in its stead? To this natural question we are given no clear answer. The nearest we come is a series of locutions on a later page, still concerned with MacNeice: 'true conviviality'; 'the idea of community'; 'the ideal of an organic community'; 'the meaning of community, its power of ennobling the essentially negative work of critical diagnosis'. It is hard to know what to do with such evasive and muffled expressions as these, though it is not hard to guess what it is that they are muffling, what quite clear and programmatic notions are being hidden away behind them. All one can say with certainty is that these expressions, set over against 'individualism', seek to replace a series of vertical relationships – as of a man with his king, and his God – with a web of horizontal relationships, as of a man with his fellows. And fellowship is at the heart of Christianity, is it not? Well no, it is not; it may be *near* to the heart, it is not *at* the heart – or so John Flavel seems to say. For on the one hand he tells us:

> This natural quality of sociableness is diversely improved. Sometimes sinfully, in wicked combinations to do mischief; like the herding together of wolves and tygers; such was the consideration of Simeon and Levi, brethren in iniquity; Gen. XLIX. 56. Sometimes it is improved civilly, for the more orderly and prosperous management of human affairs. Thus all civilized countries have improved it, for the common security and benefit. And sometimes religiously, for the better promoting of each other's spiritual and eternal good.

But elsewhere, as we have seen, he insists: 'It is not in the body politic, as in the body natural:... in the body politic, every individual hath a distinct soul of his own...' And in any case what he calls 'sociableness' (which we may take as roughly equivalent to 'community' or 'true conviviality') is for him ethically neutral – since it can be 'improved', he says, 'sinfully in wicked combinations to do mischief', as well as beneficially. Fellowship may be a grace of the religious life, a happy consequence of it, an invaluable aid to the attaining and sustaining of it, but it cannot be the *end* of that life, the main or sufficient thing to be aimed at. And so, however expressions like 'community' or 'true conviviality' may strike an answering chord in a Christian breast – that of course is their rhetorical function – they are profoundly unchristian if they are offered in place of individualism, of 'every individual hath a distinct soul of his own'. No form of Christianity can afford to make that switch, and Dissenting Christianity least of all.

One may go further and suggest that 'community' is an ignoble end to aim at, not just in religion but even in politics. Even if we did not know what it means in practice – that is to say, a central and swollen bureaucracy trying to impose equality at the level of the lowest common denominator – and even if we did not know from experience that it is inherently inefficient and cannot compass the ends it aims at, what sort of an ideal is it anyway, for private and public life to be bent towards? An undiscriminating and unrestricted 'togetherness', as of cows huddled together in a byre to keep one another warm, one cosy and hearty *steam* enveloping the entire citizenry, a vocabulary in which 'ordinary' and 'common' are the terms of highest praise and greatest warmth, in which 'human' and 'social' are interchangeable – is *that* what the less than utopian hopes of a Burke, a Montesquieu, or a John Adams have come down to, as the utmost to which a commonwealth may aspire? Undoubtedly it is *one* way (though foredoomed to failure, incidentally) of ridding ourselves of classes and classifiers; John Flavel saw another way, and a better one.

Flavel's way is not the way of the Church, as that was understood for instance by T.S. Eliot; it is the way of Christ, who speaks to every individual's 'distinct soul of his own', and is recognized there, or else is not recognized at all. Having achieved this recognition, we may come to recognize what it means to say that our secular affairs are all 'in the hand of God'. We must not think that God *willed* Britain to sink to its present ignoble condition. But we must think that he is aware of it, that he feels for us in it, and that he is working out his purposes through it. We may have in mind how in our own day a disconcerting Huguenot historian, Jacques Ellul, reflects upon Samaria, the Northern Kingdom of Israel, under siege from the Syrians (the second Book of Kings):

> Why this distress? Israel is no worse than other peoples. It is no worse at this moment in its history than at other moments. There is no reason, motive, cause, or condition for God's free will. God is God. He speaks, and things are. We have not to think that behind there might be something different. This unhappy people is again led into even greater evil by the trial itself. Under the suffering of the siege it does not prove to be heroic or virtuous. On the contrary, crime and oppression increase... Conversely, there is no reason why the trial should cease. There is no comprehensible motive for God's arresting of the situation and raising of the siege... He chooses the moment of deliverance, too, in absolute freedom... One day the Word of God will break over man and declare: 'Lo, the trial is over.' This moment is God's secret. [4]

[4] Jacques Ellul, *Politique de Dieu, politiques de l'homme* (Paris, 1966); translated by G.W. Bromiley as *The Politics of God and the Politics of Man* (London, 1972), pp. 57–8.

It is part of our ignoble estimation of ourselves that we suppose this language, and this scriptural analogue, altogether too lofty to fit our condition, so humorously have we domesticated our 'trial', *our* long siege. But it's precisely this – our ignobility in our own eyes, our pride and pleasure in being 'ordinary', our determination to see ourselves and our fellow-citizens as manikins rather than men and women – that prevents us from taking the measure of the condition we have sunk to, and from finding any hope in it. One symptom of that is our tamely submitting to the classifiers who tell us that our dignity and significance reside in our belonging to this class or that one, not in being individuals, each with a soul to save or not to save, as severally we (and no one else) may decide.

One poet of our time – no Calvinist, and as it happens not an English-speaker – had anticipated Jacques Ellul's declaration: 'God is God. He speaks and things are.' This poet had divined not just the meaning of this, and the necessary truth of it, but the paradoxical consolation wrapped within it. He was Boris Pasternak, speaking through the mouth of his own fiction, Dr Yuri Zhivago, and meditating on that most disconcerting of Christ's miracles, his blasting of the barren fig-tree:

> Had leaf and branch and root and stem been granted
> One moment's freedom, then the laws of Nature
> Had made all haste, and doom been intercepted.
> But a miracle is a miracle, a miracle is God.
> When we are all at odds it comes upon us
> Instantaneous, and when least expected.

First published in *Proteus* no. 1 (November 1977), pp. 22–30. Reprinted in *Dissentient Voice*.

7 *Disaffection of the Dissenters under George III*

The last forty years of the eighteenth century have through recent decades attracted disproportionate attention from political historians – disproportionate, yet very natural. For this was the period that saw the political severance of most of the English speakers of North America from Great Britain, and there is every reason why Americans and Britons alike should continue to ask themselves why and how this momentous and drastic surgery came about, to ask even if it could have been avoided. Moreover this period saw some crucial stages in that amorphous but even more momentous development that we call the Industrial Revolution; a social transformation the strain of which, experienced by the British sooner than by any other nation, more than once brought Britain to the brink of a political revolution that nevertheless never quite happened. For these reasons, not to mention others that might be cited, changes in the historical understanding of these decades inevitably and properly continue to inflame passions in the here and now. An American's sense of his own national identity or of the rectitude of his citizenship is in some degree at risk in any retelling of the War of Independence, in any attempt for instance to correct the long-established view of the part played at that time by the king of England. As Edmund S. Morgan remarked more than twenty years ago, 'The righteousness of the Americans is somewhat diminished through the loss of the principal villain of the piece [George III]... no longer the foe of liberty seeking to subvert the British constitution, but an earnest and responsible monarch.' [1] And, on the other hand, a British patriot of today, if he thinks of himself as in some sort a radical, cannot examine without emotion the course of events by which the British Revolution that ought to have happened mysteriously didn't. It cannot be a coincidence that this stretch of British history, this bit of the past that may be dead but clearly won't lie down, should have been chosen by Sir Lewis Namier as the test case on which to push through a

[1] See Edmund S. Morgan, *William and Mary Quarterly,* 3d ser., 14 (1957), 3-15. Quoted by Ian R. Christie, *Myth and Reality in Late Eighteenth-Century British Politics* (Berkeley and Los Angeles, 1970), p. 23.

revolution in the methods of historical research.

When a period has come in for such intense professional attention, the inevitable consequence is that in the interests of rigour studies are narrowed down to specific problems that reveal their complexity only when considered thus minutely. And there is already a formidable body of scholarship of this kind, much of it very impressive. There remain, however, larger, more general questions, and these tend not to get asked because they call for an altogether looser, more sweeping and foolhardy treatment. One such question concerns the role played in this period by the people called at some times Dissenters, at other times Nonconformists, and nowadays for the most part Free Churchmen. That the Dissenters played a crucial role in politics under George III is what nobody denies; yet who they were, these people called Dissenters, is a question at once too large and too rudimentary to get very much attention from those whose analytical skills have been developed to deal with knottier and more sophisticated problems. This broad and obvious question is the one I am concerned with: who *were* the Dissenters under George III? And are we right to lump them together so confidently as we commonly do?

To begin with, the fluctuating nomenclature is itself significant: it causes difficulties, and it raises questions – of which the most troubling and unwelcome to an English Free Churchman of the present day is whether he is, in any more than a formal sense, the heir to the Nonconformists of yesterday and the Dissenters of two hundred years ago; whether in fact his tradition has not in the past suffered breaches and discontinuities papered over by generous sentiment but become really irreparable, so that today's Free Churchman is a wholly different animal from such as Joseph Priestley and Thomas Hollis. To such as Hollis in the 1750s and 1760s this was already a burning question that presented itself in the form of whether he and those who felt like him were truly, in more than a formal sense, the heirs of Milton and Cromwell; and further, if he was such an heir, what actions and sentiments that inheritance compelled him to, in political situations different from those that Milton and Cromwell had contended with. The answer that such as Hollis found, which made them a significant political force in the 1760s and 1770s, is pointed to in the very title of Caroline Robbins's justly well regarded study *The Eighteenth Century Commonwealthman.* [2] That is to say, they decided that their situation under George III and Lord North was not after all significantly different from the situation of their ancestors under Charles I and Strafford. For making this decision they were applauded by some (mostly) Americans in their own day, and have been applauded ever since by those who think, or else expediently affect to think, that the

[2] Caroline Robbins, *The Eighteenth Century Commonwealthman* (New York, 1959).

decision was a correct one because grounded in a correct historical analysis. But this is precisely what twentieth-century historians have challenged and may be thought to have disproved: George III was *not* Charles I, neither in private life nor as a politician, despite what Tom Paine pretended; Lord North was *not* Strafford; and accordingly (it may seem to follow) Cromwellian republicanism was *not* a responsible or apposite political position in the England of the 1770s. Indeed, it may be thought that this was proved by events long before twentieth-century historians addressed themselves to the question; as J.H. Plumb has pointed out,[3] the out-and-out republicanism of an Algernon Sidney, as espoused and promulgated by Hollis's protégés such as the Dissenting minister Richard Baron,[4] merely withered away as soon as the differences with the American colonies became a state of war, and more particularly when the American colonists became the allies of Britain's old enemy, France. And this development casts a shadow backwards so as to raise the question whether the republicanism of Hollis or Baron or the diarist Sylas Neville was ever, even in the 1760s, practical politics.[5] Was it ever more than the irresponsible speculation of persons far from the centres where political decisions were taken? And did the majority of English Dissenters ever regard these republicans as anything more than a lunatic fringe? This question is still debated;[6] but we may certainly suspect that Robbins's 'commonwealthmen' have an interest and an importance in the history of political ideas such as they never had in the history of politics. This is to say that very few English Dissenters at any time under George III harboured sentiments and designs that were positively treasonable; few can be said to have been at any time disloyal, though at certain times many of them can be properly described as 'disaffected'.

And yet even this may be questioned. For who were these people that we are speaking of? James E. Bradley, in an important article,[7] has accused Whig historiographers of 'a preoccupation with the dissenting elite', at the expense of the rank-and-file of English Dissenters up and down the country. And this is surely a true bill; historians of all sorts, and especially those of a literary turn, inevitably pay too much attention to the articulate and self-appointed leaders of opinion, without sufficiently considering that their 'lead' may not have been followed by the relatively

[3] J.H. Plumb, 'British Attitudes to the American Revolution' (1964), in Plumb, *In the Light of History* (Boston, 1973), pp. 70-87.

[4] For Baron, see *Memoirs of Thomas Hollis* (1780).

[5] *The Diary of Sylas Neville, 1767-1788*, ed. Basil Cozens-Hardy (London, 1950)

[6] See Ian R. Christie, *Wilkes, Wyvill and Reform* (London, 1962), p. 15: 'Attacks of a fairly traditional and arid kind came from a little group of *soi-disant* republicans: Thomas Hollis of Lincoln's Inn, his cousin, Timothy, Richard Baron, Thomas Brand, and a few others. Their republicanism, based on a high and dry whiggism drawn directly from later seventeenth-century tradition, had little popular appeal.' But contrast Plumb, pp. 70-87.

[7] James E. Bradley, 'Whigs and Nonconformists: "Slumbering Radicalism" in English Politics, 1739-39', *Eighteenth-Century Studies*, 9 (1975), 1-27.

inarticulate fellow citizens whom they addressed. Just here indeed we see one of the entering wedges of the Namierite method of political historiography; and Bradley, by applying that method, has no difficulty proving that in one English borough after another Dissenters were no less 'corrupt' than other Englishmen; that the votes of the Dissenting interest were up for sale in a way that was not just time-honoured but essential if the eighteenth-century political machine in England was to function at all. Indeed, while still shirking the laborious Namierite discipline of scrutinizing the electoral returns and division lists on crucial votes, in the municipalities as well as at Westminster, we can cite a case where the 'country' Dissenters quite plainly refused to follow the lead of their metropolitan spokesmen. This was the application to Parliament in 1772 to relieve Church of England clergy from having to subscribe to all the Thirty-Nine Articles and, as regards such subscription, to secure for Dissenters more than the two or three exemptions they enjoyed already. Henry F. May believes that the failure of the initiative 'caused some English dissenters to believe in a new conspiracy against Protestant liberty'. And no doubt he is right; but he fails to remark that the initiative was ultimately defeated, when it was launched again in 1773, by *the country Dissenters,* for these, still mostly Trinitarian Calvinists, rightly saw that those who sought relief were Dissenters of a Socinian or Arian or Unitarian cast.[8] Dissent was not monolithic; and the most taciturn Calvinist Dissenters would on occasion strike down the liberties sought by their more vociferous brethren, Socinians and Arians.

It may be that on other issues besides this one, for instance on the broad issue of loyalty to the Crown, there was at any time a substantial minority of English Dissenters, if not indeed a majority at times, who go unremarked because they were relatively inarticulate. They did indeed sometimes find articulate spokesmen. But these are hard to discern, perhaps because there were disproportionately few of them, more certainly because it has been in nobody's partisan interest, from their day to ours, to have them remembered. One of them, hardly a spokesman at all except in his immediate circle, seems to have been John Merivale of Exeter, described as 'a sturdy conscientious Dissenter of the old school; combining with his dissent an absolute horror of Radicalism and disloyalty.'[9] In 1792, when Timothy Kenrick, avowedly Unitarian minister of the Presbyterian George's Meeting in Exeter, had prayed extempore 'for the success of people struggling for their liberty' (having in mind specifically, as he admitted, the French), Merivale expostulated in a letter: 'It is so utterly repugnant to my Conception of what is right to join in prayers offer'd up to the God of Mercy for the further success of a wretched

[8] Henry F. May, *The Enlightenment in America* (New York, 1976), p. 157.
[9] Anna W. Merivale, *Family Memorials* (Exeter, 1884), p. 129.

Faction which has already involv'd a country in a most deplorable state of Anarchy & Distress, – that I feel myself obliged to seek some other Place of Worship.'[10] And Merivale was as good as his word, signally absenting himself and his family thereafter from Kenrick's ministrations. It is not clear, however, whether he carried out his threat 'to seek some other Place of Worship'. For Kenrick shared the pastorate there with two others, and in his reply to Merivale he explained, 'Mr Tozer, Mr Manning and myself may publickly pray for the spread of Christianity, altho' we each of us affix different ideas to the phrase – the first meaning by it Trinitarianism, the second Arianism, and the last Unitarianism.' This arrangement by which, if he chose, Merivale could still profit by the devotions of Mr Tozer or Mr Manning is of a liberalism so thorough-going that one might suppose it invented only in the present century; but in fact such blithe inclusiveness, like the eager ardour of a Timothy Kenrick who could take pride in it, is as common among nominal Presbyterians in George III's England as among leftward-leaning clerics and confident laymen of our own times. And it had, then as now, the effect of fostering, and absolving in advance, every sort of irresponsible pulpit eloquence, whether in politics or theology.

It may well be asked whether John Merivale belonged, in James E. Bradley's sense of the term, to the dissenting elite. From one point of view, as the son and pupil at the Exeter Dissenting Academy of Samuel Merivale, himself a pupil of the great Doddridge, John Merivale may be thought to belong with the bluest blood of West Country Dissent. And this certainly weighed with Kenrick, may even have dismayed him. But since Merivale published nothing and was a leader of opinion only in his own congregation, I think he does not fall into the category of 'dissenting elite' as Bradley conceives of it. And so the question arises, quite pressingly: How many John Merivales were there, up and down the country, their very existence perpetuated only in the records, where they survive, of long disbanded and extinct Dissenting churches?

It is not clear how that question can be answered. And that no doubt is one reason why it is never or seldom asked. But there are other more prejudiced reasons why the mere existence of the John Merivales, of loyalist and nonradical yet principled Dissenters, should be passed over in silence. These reasons become clearer if we shift our attention from the 1790s back to the 1770s, from the French Revolution to the American; and if we attend particularly to Free Churchmen of the present day, concerned to celebrate with a proper pride the tradition they inherit.

In 1976 the bicentenary of the Declaration of Independence was noticed in Britain by Free Churchmen as by others; and there were obvious and proper reasons why on such occasions radical Dissenters,

[10] See Alan Brockett, *Nonconformity in Exeter, 1650-1875* (Manchester, 1962), pp. 142-3.

those who sympathized with the colonists, should be remembered, and loyalist Dissenters like John Merivale should be driven still further into the shadows. An example is the lecture 'Nonconformists and the American Revolution', by the distinguished historian of the English Baptists, Ernest A. Payne.[11] Given the occasion, and deciding sensibly that the Methodists (though not strictly Nonconformists) could hardly be left out of account, Dr Payne had to do something about the vehement and intransigent loyalism of the Wesley brothers. Taking note of Charles Wesley's anguished poem that castigates General Howe for mismanaging the American campaigns, and Lord Shelburne for making peace in 1783 ('That smooth, perfidious perjur'd Shelburne sold / His King his country and his God for gold'), he commented: 'Poor Charles Wesley! This is not the right note to end on, not really fair to the Methodists of that day, certainly not fair to the Colonists and their supporters in this country. The rebels and their friends should not be idealized, but the future was with them.' This is compassionate. And of course that 'the future was with them' is what none of us, two centuries later, can deny. But Charles Wesley's concern in that poem and others was not with which of the opposing bodies of opinion in Britain had the future in its keeping, but with which of them had felt and acted constitutionally; and he was sure that the winning side had been the one that mocked and flouted the British Constitution. The same is true of the other anti-Whig document that Dr Payne takes note of: Johnson's *Taxation No Tyranny*. Johnson was, he says, 'unfortunately prejudiced against Americans', and 'he could not see how people who practised and upheld the slave system could protest against ill-treatment and the denial of rights.' Johnson does indeed gibe at libertarian slaveholders, and who will say that the gibe was unwarranted? But such an argument ad hominem is nowhere near the centre of Johnson's powerful pamphlet, which on the contrary turns upon the strictly constitutional questions of what 'sovereignty' means, and what 'representation' means. And it is not clear that Johnson's argument on these properly dry and philosophical grounds has ever been controverted.[12] For Dr Payne, however, it is a case of 'poor Sam Johnson', no less than poor Charles Wesley – to whom we may add poor John Wesley also, who was persuaded by Johnson's pamphlet and thereafter agreed with his brother. Of all three of them it seems we must say that they were left behind by history or, if we agree to think that way, 'proved wrong in the event'. To extend to three such massive and formidable figures the charity of our faintly amused compassion appears somewhat hazardous, but from Payne's point of view it is the best we can do. Certainly among

[11] Published in *The Journal of the United Reformed Church History Society*, 1, No. 8 (October 1976), 210-27.

[12] See The Yale Edition of the Works of Samuel Johnson, Vol. X, *Political Writings*, ed. Donald Greene (New Haven, 1977), pp. 402-9.

those, Dissenters and others, who took the opposite view, we find no men of comparable stature. And for that matter, if among the Dissenters there were any who made the same mistake as Johnson and the Wesleys did, Dr Payne – understandably enough, considering the occasion – chose not to identify them.

His account in fact is only a little more cautious than that of a Nonconformist spokesman eighty years ago, C. Silvester Horne, in his *Popular History of the Free Churches* (1903):

> If the voice of the Free Churches had been listened to, the American Colonies would have been saved for England. It was natural, doubtless, that English Nonconformists should sympathize with those who represented their own ideals. Across the thousands of miles of sea they united themselves in sympathy with the brave children of the Puritans who were defying British tyranny and dying in thousands for their independence... Only John Wesley's political instinct failed him; and his attack on the colonists was unworthy of his shrewd intelligence and generous heart. English Nonconformity was not represented in Parliament, but when Burke and Chatham and Fox pleaded the cause of the Americans, the Free Churchmen at home had no need to be ashamed of the men who defended their opinions in the Legislature.[13]

These ringing tones (Horne in his day was a famous pulpit orator)[14] are not what we are used to. But the substance of what Horne asserts appears still to be the received opinion, and not only among Free Churchmen like Ernest A. Payne. British and American historians alike still assume or assert that the English Dissenters were unanimously on the side of the colonists, though it is sometimes conceded that their enthusiasm cooled rather precipitately soon after the war started. James E. Bradley in some entertaining pages has shown that for Whig historiographers like Lecky and Trevelyan what particularly recommended the Dissenters was precisely that they were, as Horne says, 'not represented in Parliament'. For, once the First Reform Bill had acknowledged how corrupt the parliamentary system had been while it sustained the Whig hegemony, Whig virtue could be saved for the nineteenth century only by vesting it in those Whigs who had been outside the system – which is to say, the Dissenters.[15] Silvester Horne, however, had no such sophisticated ends in view when he roundly declared that under George III 'Nonconformity was winning its soul, and coming to see and to declare the beauty of the ideal of a Free church in a Free State.' At this point Horne has in mind not so much his Dissenters' opposition to coercion of the colonists as, in domestic policy, their agitation for parliamentary reform. But the two

[13] Horne, p. 323.
[14] For Horne, see Clyde Binfield, *So Down to Prayers* (London, 1977), pp. 199-213.
[15] Of course they were *not* outside the system (as Bradley points out).

issues can hardly be kept apart, if only because the pro-Americans were almost always active for parliamentary reform also. Horne identifies as heroes of this Dissenting thrust not just Joseph Priestley but also 'the eloquent and impassioned Baptist minister, Robert Robinson'.[16]

Readers of Herbert Butterfield [17] will know Robinson already, as instigator of a notorious meeting for parliamentary reform on 25 March 1780, in Cambridge. This is described by a contemporary as 'a mob of Dissenters of all Hues, Colours & Denominations in every part of the Country, called together... in order to draw up a Petition of œconomy, Alterations in the Method of Parliament, and other wild and republican Schemes, first engendered at Mr Robinson's conventicle, & then recommended to the notice of the Corporation by a modest Republican, if that is compatible, Alderman Burleigh.' And at the end of a turbulent day, we are told, 'Robinson, the Anabaptist Teacher, who lives at Chesterton, set the Bells a Ringing in that Church as soon as he got Home, and made a great Supper at night for all his Party, where strong Liquors, good Cheer, and Zeal for the Cause, so far got the better of their discretion, that many of the Ebenezers were laid flat on their Back, & had Assistance to convey them to their several Habitations.' There is much other evidence to bear out this image of what Robinson was like. Joseph Ivimey, historian of the Baptists in the next generation, was prepared to think that by the time Robinson died a Socinian and Unitarian, he must have been insane. Is this, we may ask mildly, the sort of figure whom we should find, with the advantage of hindsight, politically more admirable and enlightened than John Wesley or Dr Johnson?

At any rate, Lecky and Payne and Horne notwithstanding, there were in the 1770s English Dissenters who rightly or wrongly found themselves of one mind with Johnson and the Wesleys. One of them was the already venerable Job Orton of Shrewsbury, friend and literary executor of the great Philip Doddridge. On 29 September 1775 we find him already resenting, on behalf of the provincial Dissenters, the politicizing of dissent by the ministers of the metropolis: 'Whatever "the principle of the *Americans*" may be, the spirit they shew is malignant, rebellious, and wicked. My Bible teaches me "not to speak evil of dignities" & – I wish the London ministers would leave Politics to Statesmen, and give themselves wholly to their ministry.'[18] By 1778 his tone has sharpened, and by a pregnant allusion to Northampton Academy under Doddridge he by implication invokes the authority of that most famous and influential of all Hanoverian Dissenters:

[16] Horne, p. 326.
[17] See Butterfield, *George III, Lord North and the People* (London, 1949), pp. 284-88.
[18] Job Orton, *Letters to Dissenting Ministers,* ed. S. Palmer, 2 vols. (1806), I, 167.

> I have been looking over Sallust's *History of Cataline's Conspiracy;* in which I think you will find some things suitable to your purpose, particularly in his speech to the conspirators; which you will meet with towards the beginning of the history; where he pleads Liberty, as a ground for his undertaking; but mentions honour, power, wealth, &c. as also in their plan, and throws out some bitter reflections against the ministers and placemen of those days... There is a great deal to the same purpose in *Cataline's* speech, and in other parts of the history; but it is near forty years ago since I last read it, which was with the pupils at *Northampton,* in 1739. I have long thought there are many passages in the account of that conspiracy very parallel to the present case of our nation, between loyal men, and those who are called patriots, and who choose by a figure of speech to call themselves Whigs, just as they call me a Tory. Many are angry with me, because I discountenance their disloyalty; but I despise their anger, as much as I dislike their principles and conduct. I would willingly be doing some good while I am here; and to promote loyalty, subjection, and peace, is doing good. I think I have already softened some sharp spirits amongst us, at least brought them to hold their tongues, or to be less confident.[19]

And in the next year Orton can afford to be contemptuously sarcastic: 'I know nothing of Mr— but by report. It is very well to be "valiant for *liberty,*" if the courageous man has a proper idea of it; but I should have rejoiced more to have heard that he had been *valiant for truth,* holiness, and peace, and remarkably alive for the conversion and salvation of souls. We have some ministers who are zealous for liberty, but the souls of their flocks are neglected, and our interest is sinking under them.'[20]

Some may read out of these comments only a pusillanimous quietism. But Orton is addressing ministers of religion; and his contention, which can hardly be denied, is that however ardent a minister's political convictions and however he may interpret his political duties as a perhaps prominent and certainly influential citizen, all such matters must have for him a lower priority than the performing of his pastoral and priestly duties. These comments therefore are of a piece with Orton's sacramentalism: 'I cannot agree with you, that administering the Sacraments is the easiest and least important part of our office. I always considered them as most important, and found it more difficult to administer them, as they should be, than to preach.'[21] To those who when they consider late-Hanoverian dissent think first of Priestley and Richard Price, not to speak of Richard Baron and Robert Robinson, it will come as a surprise that sacramentalism has any part at all in the Dissenting tradition. But the

[19] *Letters to a Young Clergyman from the late Reverend Mr Job Orton* (Shrewsbury, 1791), p. 133.
[20] *Letters to Dissenting Ministers,* II, 4.
[21] Ibid., I, 131.

proper administering of the sacraments had a central place in the Dissent of Doddridge, with whom in this emphasis also Orton is keeping faith. Moreover, Orton could, if he chose, appeal behind Doddridge to John Flavel in 1691 declaring, 'When God puts a crown upon the head, and a sceptre into the hand of a man, he engraves upon that man (in a qualified sense) both his name, and the lively characters of his Majesty and authority.' And behind Flavel there is the patriarch Richard Baxter telling the Lord Protector Cromwell that 'we took our ancient monarchy to be a blessing, and not an evil to the land; and humbly craved his patience that I might ask him how England had ever forfeited that blessing, and to whom that forfeiture was made.' In short, Orton's submissive, monarchical, and loyalist Dissent has rather better credentials than the republican Dissent of Hollis and Baron, who can establish their lineage from Milton and Cromwell only by way of the infidel Algernon Sidney.

In 1780 Orton is recommending 'Public and Domestic Devotion, written by one *Martin,* a Baptist minister in London... very sensible, serious, and useful.' This is John Martin (1741-1800) who, far from advancing his loyalist sentiments only in private communications, rushed into print impetuously and often, as he acknowledges in *Some Account of the Life and Writings of the Revd. John Martin* (1797). This autobiography is a charming sturdy brief narrative in epistolary form, which could well bear reprinting, both for its intrinsic virtues and for the light it casts on a little-noticed element in the society and ideology of late Hanoverian England. Martin's justification for writing it is explicitly Johnsonian – the famous judgment that 'there has perhaps rarely passed a life, of which a judicious and faithful narrative would not be useful.' The son of a publican and grazier in Lincolnshire, Martin, largely self-educated, abandoned a family tradition of Anglicanism to join the Baptist ministry, and after ministering to various congregations in the East Midlands came to a metropolitan church in Grafton Street only in 1773. His interests and his publications were not in any blatant or invidious sense 'politicized'; yet he published his views on each of the vexing constitutional issues that arose in his lifetime, and always on the loyalist side. Himself aware of this bias in his political sentiments, Martin explains in a very interesting way how he thinks it originated:

> As I was born at Spalding, in the year 1741, at the close of the rebellion in favour of the Pretender I was about five years of age. At that time, and for some years afterwards, the story of him, and of those that countenanced his cause, was often sounded in my ears; and as the inhabitants of Spalding were well affected to Government, this story made so deep an impression on my mind, that before I was fifteen, I could not see without alarm the shadow of civil disturbance; and Sir, let me add that at fifty-five rebellious positions, on whatever pretence

> they are brought forward, strongly excite my indignation; above all, when they seem to be sanctioned by religious frenzy.

Accordingly, it comes as no surprise that in 1775, inflamed by talk on behalf of the American colonists, Martin should have published a polemic on the loyalist side, of which he was to say: 'In this paper, called the Monitor, I attempted to shew, that rebellion first commenced in heaven; that by the suggestions of a ruined rebel, our adversary, it gained admittance into Paradise; and that since the fall of our first parents, the rebellious of all ages, in all conditions of life, have always had an illicit love for dominion; so that, from the first generation to the present, were they to meet together in one body, they might say to each other, Walked we not in the same spirit? Walked we not in the same steps?' When we consider John Rippon telling John Manning in 1784, 'I believe that all our Baptist ministers in town except two, and most of our brethren in the country, were on the side of the Americans in the late dispute',[22] we cannot doubt that one of the recalcitrant pair was John Martin, who had the year before reasserted his position in *Queries and Remarks on Human Liberty*. (And it is interesting to note that Rippon concedes there were more John Martins in the country than in the town.) Moreover, in 1776 Martin had published *Familiar Dialogues between Americus and Britannicus* in which, he says, he 'attempted to explain... some things that had given offence in the Monitor', but 'daring, in this performance, to censure some things advanced by Dr Price, his partizans were exasperated at my supposed temerity.' From that point to the end of his life Martin was always aware of speaking for an unpopular minority among the articulate Dissenters and, reading between the lines, we recognize in him the sort of personality that relishes such an isolated position, exults in it, and seeks it.

Richard Price can still attract partisans, as do his contemporaries Wilkes and Paine and preeminently Burke. But whereas those men were furiously partisan themselves, and in different ways turbulent and passionate, what distinguishes Price is on the contrary a sort of glacial serenity. And so his pro-American *Observations on the Nature of Civil Liberty... and the Justice and Policy of the War with America* (1776) should be considered in the light of his later *Discourse on the Love of our Country* (1789) where he asks, of such love, 'What has it been but a love of domination; a desire of conquest, and a thirst for grandeur and glory, by extending territory and enslaving surrounding countries?' When patriotism is thus dismissed as an unworthy prejudice, the rights and wrongs of any political situation are wonderfully simplified. But the undoubtedly irrational yet time-honoured promptings of *pietas* toward kindred and native land cannot be set aside by most people so serenely; and such

[22] Cited by Payne, p. 210.

promptings are felt by Dissenters sometimes, even by Dissenters of Price's own Arian and rationalistic kind. Thus the Presbyterian John Bowring showed that his rationality fell short of Price's when he wrote to a cousin in 1778 'After the most deliberate consideration of the nature of the quarrel between us, I freely own it appears to me that they are right and we wrong, nor is there anything I more ardently wish for relative to our national concerns than a thorough change both of men and manners in the British Cabinet. *Yet, as an Englishman, I by no means wish to see my country vanquished by the arms of France.*'[23] More remarkably the pioneer industrialist Josiah Wedgwood, Unitarian and friend of Benjamin Franklin, is found in 1779 expostulating: 'Methinks I would defend the land of my nativity, my family and friends against a foreign foe, where conquest and slavery were inseparable, under any leaders – the best I could get for the moment, and wait for better times to displace an obnoxious minister, and settle domestic affairs, rather than rigidly say, I'll be saved in my own way and by people of my own choice, or perish and perish my country with me.'[24] To men like Bowring and Wedgwood, thus touchingly embroiled in the consequences of their own unargued patriotism, Richard Price's coolly dispassionate statement of the case could offer no help at all. As the war went on, *in particular as it went worse and worse for British arms,* the political conduct and sentiments of a Bowring or a Wedgwood inevitably became for all practical purposes indistinguishable from those of a Job Orton or John Martin. For when the Crown finally admitted defeat it was not under pressure from any body of persistent pro-American sentiment but, as J.H. Plumb valuably points out, because 'the country interest, the independent members who sat in Parliament as Knights of the Shire, who never spoke in debates and usually voted with the government, finally rebelled.'

Robert E. Schofield's comment on Wedgwood's changing sentiments seems unimaginative as well as inaccurate: 'How long his "my country, right or wrong" attitude lasted is hard to say; probably not much longer than it took to discover that the military alliance between America and France was not going to result in an invasion of Britain.'[25] The tone and implication of this remark by a scrupulous American historian are probably inescapable whenever an American observes the sentiments of Britons during the War of the Revolution. And yet what it overlooks is obvious: once the colonists had declared their independence, Americans constituted for the British 'a foreign foe', just as the French did. A parallel case is when C.H. Guttridge reports on the American correspondence of Richard Champion, no Dissenter but one of Edmund Burke's powerful constituents in Bristol. Guttridge observes that 'Champion remained loyal

[23] *Autobiographical Recollections of Sir John Bowring* (London, 1877), pp. 2-3 (my italics).
[24] Quoted by J.H. Plumb.
[25] Robert E. Schofield, *The Lunar Society of Birmingham* (Oxford, 1963), p. 138.

to the cause of his American friends, even to the extent of conduct which could with some reason be termed unpatriotic.' But, of course, when Champion in December 1775 conveyed to America information about 'where the government intended to concentrate armaments, what the numbers of the reinforced army at Boston would be, and what disposition of troops would be made between New York, Virginia, and South Carolina', [26] the name for such conduct may be thought to be not 'unpatriotic' but 'treasonable'. Burgess and Maclean and Rosenberg, Hiss and Pontecorvo and Philby are names from our own century that suggest how hard it is for intellectuals to acknowledge that treason is a matter not of opinion but of legal fact. Everyone knows that when treason is successful 'none dare call it treason'; but this does not excuse one literary historian after another making delicate comedy out of police agents sent by Pitt's government to eavesdrop on Blake and Coleridge and Wordsworth – without at any point reminding their readers that French agents *were* active in the England of that time, and *did* suborn some Englishmen. This underlining of the obvious seems called for if we are to recognize that when Orton and Martin and Wesley advance submission to the civic power as a religious duty, this is not necessarily a manoeuvre of the ruling class, nor yet an anachronistic survival of feudal sentiments into an enlightened age, but one possible solution to a conflict of loyalties that may entangle us, just as it entangled Josiah Wedgwood in 1779.

What no proponent of the Whig version of events under George III can be brought to admit at all readily is that very few of the zealots for 'civil and religious liberty' had any intention of extending those liberties to Roman Catholics. Thus of Thomas Hollis we are told that he was 'persuaded... as every sensible and impartial man must be, that the civil and religious liberties of Englishmen will ever be endangered in proportion as popery increases, and is not discouraged'; and that he felt 'the clergy of the established church had been too remiss in their opposition to it.'[27] This we have on the authority of one who was himself a clergyman of the established church, though of a rather peculiar kind. He was Francis Blackburne, archdeacon of Cleveland, author of *Considerations of the present state of the controversy between the protestants and papists of Great Britain and Ireland* (1768), of which Hollis, as was his habit with books he approved, bought and distributed 110 copies. Blackburne with much self-congratulation recounts this himself in his *Memoirs of Hollis* (1780). It was Blackburne who issued the invitations to a meeting at the Feathers Tavern in the Strand on 17 July 1771, at which was first mooted a petition to Parliament for the abolition of compulsory subscription to the

[26] C.H. Guttridge, *The American Correspondence of a Bristol Merchant, 1766-1776* (Berkeley, 1934), pp. 4-5

[27] *Memoirs of Thomas Hollis* (London, 1780), p. 251.

Thirty-nine Articles, this for the benefit of Anglican ministers who were in fact Unitarians, as Blackburne was. This measure, framed so as to relieve also the Dissenting ministers (mostly Presbyterians) who were Unitarians no less, was as we have seen defeated, largely at the instigation of the Dissenting Calvinists. To regularize their position, some half-dozen Anglican clergy resigned their livings, following Theophilus Lindsey who, like his fellow Cambridge don Jebb, thereby sacrificed also his academic career. Blackburne had no such scruples, or none that he could not swallow; and this sufficiently explains his special interest in applauding libertarian (though of course antipapist) Dissenters such as Hollis. Blackburne is the first of several Anglicans in the period who show unwonted tenderness to the Dissenting interest; their motives for doing so, while not often so impudent as Blackburne's, can in most cases be discerned without too much trouble. The truth is that the rapid growth of Unitarianism in this period, alike among parsons and Dissenting ministers, and in either case mostly masked (however perfunctorily) as something else, blurs the borderline between Establishment and Dissent as perhaps at no other period before or since.

The only Dissenter I have found at this time who was in any way prepared to accept papists as fellow Christians was, to give him his due, Richard Price, who seems to have been ready to contemplate Catholic emancipation, at any rate in Ireland. Perhaps not all Dissenters were quite so ferociously antipapist as some of the Establishment would have wished them to be. Such seems to have been the view of Horace Walpole who was during the war with the colonies an extreme Whig, presumably out of filial piety; who accordingly grumbled into his diary in 1776, 'In all this contest with America, the Presbyterians and other Dissenters, who could not but see the designs of the Court, and its notorious partiality to Roman Catholics, were entirely passive in England, being bribed or sold by their leaders.'[28] It is not clear what Walpole could have pointed to as evidence of 'notorious partiality to Roman Catholics'. It was not until the Catholic Relief Act of 1778 that some of the disabilities imposed on the English papists in 1701 were lifted: officiating Roman Catholic clergy were thereafter no longer liable to life imprisonment; and the requirement was abolished by which land in England and Wales must pass over any papist heir in favour of the next Protestant in line. These reliefs, though conditional on an oath of allegiance being taken before a Court of Record or Quarter Sessions, were protested in a series of petitions which, orchestrated by Lord George Gordon, precipitated the Gordon Riots of 1780; and these, according to Peter Brown, 'combined with the excesses of the French Revolution, delayed parliamentary reform in Britain for forty years'.[29] This casts a sardonic light on Silvester Horne's claim for the

[28] Quoted by Bradley, p. 23.

[29] Peter Brown, *The Chathamiles* (London, 1967).

Protestant bigots, that they were the pioneering heroes of parliamentary reform. As for Walpole, he can have had in mind only the leave extended to the citizens of vanquished Quebec to practice their Roman Catholicism with impunity. And of this Johnson, who to this day figures in radical and dissenting mythology as a fulminating Blimp if not indeed a court-pensioner, had written nobly in *The Patriot (1774):* 'Persecution is not more virtuous in a Protestant than a Papist; and... while we blame Lewis the Fourteenth, for his dragoons and his gallies, we ought, when power comes into our hands, to use it with greater equity.' Johnson said also that 'in an age, where every mouth is open for liberty of conscience, it is equitable to shew some regard to the conscience of a Papist, who may be supposed, like other men, to think himself safest in his own religion'; and finally, irrefutably, 'if liberty of conscience be a natural right, we have no power to withhold it; if it be an indulgence it may be allowed to Papists, while it is not denied to other sects.'[30] Alas, far more typical was the platform on which the youthful Lord Mahon stood in 1774 as a candidate for Westminster; a platform in which promises to destroy or diminish bribery in elections, to strive for the repeal of the Septennial Act, and for the expunging of the vote of the Commons which had unseated Wilkes, stood alongside a pledge to seek the repeal of the Quebec Act.[31] So happily, under George III, did measures that we are eager to consider 'liberal' or 'enlightened' or 'democratic' go along with antipapist bigotry! And while it is no doubt too much to hope for that any Dissenter should have declared himself on the issue as fearlessly as Johnson did, it is a pity to have to say so, of people who were 'coming to see and to declare the beauty of the ideal of a Free Church in a free State'.

After Francis Blackburne the next prominent Anglican to take up the cudgels for the Dissenters, or for some of them, was Christopher Wyvill in his *Defence of Dr Price, and the Reformers of England* (1792). Wyvill's motives were more altruistic than Blackburne's, and more responsible. In the 1780s his Yorkshire Association had been the best organized and most level-headed of the movements for parliamentary reform, and the one that came nearest effecting some real change. He had got some support, though it is not clear how much, from the Dissenting interest in Yorkshire. And it looks as if, by springing to Price's defence in the wake of Burke's fierce attack on him in the *Reflections on the French Revolution,* Wyvill was trying to defend the Dissenting interest from Burke's accusations of disloyalty, against the day when he, Wyvill, might need to call on the Dissenters once more in the service of what was genuinely a reformist rather than revolutionary objective. Accordingly, Wyvill's pamphlet, though predictably vituperative about Edmund Burke, is on the whole

[30] J.P. Hardy, ed., *The Political Writings of Dr Johnson* (London, 1968), pp. 93, 94.
[31] See Butterfield, p. 383.

meant to be conciliatory. In particular it marks the disowning, by English liberal reformers, of Tom Paine – and not on religious grounds (Paine's *Age of Reason* was not to appear until 1795), but on the very sensible grounds that 'his avowed purpose is, not to reform or amend the System of our Government, but to overturn and destroy it'. Of the author of *The Rights of Man,* Wyvill writes judiciously and severely:

> He supports the doctrine of Republicanism, with an enthusiastic zeal, with an imposing confidence, and with reasoning often specious, and always daring; some truths are interspersed among many fallacies and misrepresentations, and a vein of coarse, but strongly sarcastic wit runs through and clumsily enlivens the whole. His Counsel, to break up and destroy the noble fabric of our Constitution and rebuild a new political edifice on the plans of America, seems to be conveyed in the most dangerous shape, and far more likely to make an impression on those, to whom it is chiefly addressed, than if it had been delivered in a more classical composition.

It may well be thought that Wyvill should in logic have disowned Price no less than Paine. For Price undoubtedly advocated a unicameral legislature, and to effect that would certainly have been 'to break up and destroy' the Constitution, as that was understood by Montesquieu and John Adams no less than Burke. There are signs in fact that Wyvill was uneasy about some of the positions that Price had taken up, but he was committed to exonerating this alarming and prominent Whig Dissenter if he was to clear Dissenting whiggery in general from any taint of disloyalty. And his protestations to this effect are rather too vehement to carry conviction. Thus he asserts that 'during the miseries of the American war no symptom of dissatisfaction to the Constitution appeared'. But only a few years before that war people in the group around Thomas Hollis were to be heard declaring that 'no person is a true friend of Liberty who is not a Republican'; and during the war many in Britain as well as America were reading with enthusiasm Catherine Macaulay's *History of England from the accession of James I,* that 'imaginative work in praise of republican principles'. It may be that Caroline Robbins and J.H. Plumb have overestimated the influence of Dissenting republicanism, but it can hardly be pooh-poohed so blandly as by Wyvill or his modern biographer Ian Christie. Though it is doubtless true that the views of 'the Commonwealthmen' had little popular appeal when promulgated by themselves in editions of Algernon Sidney and Marchamont Nedham, they could have such appeal when cautiously and partially enunciated by charismatic or demagogic figures like Chatham and Wilkes (who both had connections with the Hollis group) or by an energetic popularizer like Mrs Macaulay. Thus it seems that there must have been, in the 1790s as in the 1760s and 1770s, Dissenters who were also Jacobins whose reading of their Dissenting heritage pushed them well beyond constitutional reform, however radical. And this means surely that when Burke in his *Reflections* imputed disaffection or disloyalty to the Dissenters generally, his alarm was not so groundless and chimerical as is commonly supposed. Indeed, Wyvill himself in 1792, while seeming to reassure, is really threatening:

> The Proselytes to republican notions are few at present, and inconsiderable: They probably would be increased in number by prosecution; but by impunity a wise forbearance will effectually prevent any eventual danger from their speculations, provided the condition of the People be rendered more easy by the farther diminution of their burthens, and their wishes be gratified by a timely correction of those abuses in the Constitution, which have been so justly complained of. By these means, and by these means alone, the possible growth of a great Republican Party in this Country may be prevented.

There is a clear threat in that last sentence. Was it a real threat? Did not Wyvill, no less than Burke, think that it was?

The Dissenters meanwhile had failed in their agitation for a repeal of parts of the Test and Corporation Acts. John Martin, inflexible as ever, had once again espoused an immovably conservative position, and was so much in a minority that by his own account he was not permitted to speak at the meeting of the London Dissenting ministers in Red Cross Street in December 1789. He therefore published his contribution to the debate as a pamphlet, *A Speech on the Repeal of such parts of the Test and Corporation Acts as affect Conscientious Dissenters...* (1790). But this is an unhappy and disingenuous performance; and a bitter anonymous rejoinder by 'no Reverend Dissenter' is scurrilous and intemperate, but convincing. There is, however, one passage in Martin's pamphlet that is of interest because it shows that the idea of 'oppressive toleration', brandished as a novelty by radicals of the 1960s, was already part of the dissenters' armoury in 1790:

> We are repeatedly told, 'That the pretended *toleration* of Dissenters is a real *persecution*.' Such language is as impolitic as it is unjust. Toleration and persecution may exist at the same time; but can they be considered as the same thing? All legal persecutions, in this country, have been the offspring either of *Statute* law or of *Canon* law; nevertheless, that Act which repeals the oppressive power of preceding Acts, and prevents the wasps and hornets in low life from darting out their stings, should ever be mentioned with becoming temper.

What Martin has in mind is the Act of Toleration passed under William III; and he proceeds to a panegyric, in thoroughly Burkean vein, on the wisdom of that monarch and his ministers.

There appeared a new spokesman for loyalist Dissent when the Independent minister John Clayton (1754-1843) took advantage of the Birmingham riots against Joseph Priestley by publishing a sermon in which he argued in effect that Priestley had asked for what he got. This provoked many rejoinders, among them Robert Hall's *Christianity Consistent with a Love of Freedom* (1791). A more curious loyalist document appeared in Adam Callender's *Thoughts on the Peaceable... Nature of Christ's Kingdom* (1794):

> Let us remember therefore, that it is in heaven where our interest chiefly is. There is our citizenship; and in the view of possessing it shortly will the main of our conversation be directed. We are called upon to set our affections on things above, and not on things on the earth; and our Lord lays it down as a maxim, that if we are laying up treasures above, our hearts will be there also; in the same way as they who heap up treasures here have their hearts on earth. If then heaven be our chief banking house, our conversation will be much taken up about the security of our property there, and we shall find, to our comfort, that if once laid up in the sacred mansions above, they will remain inviolable from thieves and unhurt by the moth.
>
> We are pilgrims in this world, as all our forefathers were, and we, like them, seek a country above. It does not suit well with the idea of a pilgrim, when passing through a strange country, to retard his journey by stopping to dispute and settle the manners of a country, to which he means not to return.

Perhaps not many present-day Christians are sufficiently devout and evangelical to accept this obviously extreme case for political quietism. Yet the argument takes on force when it is seen to rest on the grounds that the church is indeed catholic and universal:

> We ought rather to admire the more excellent way which Jesus has taught us, which leaves no room for doubt, by making it our positive duty to obey every kind of government, without exceptions to the characters of those who rule. Here perplexity is at an end, and we are led to admire the wisdom of Christ in establishing a rule of obedience, so suitable to christians in every age, and in every country where they may dwell on the earth: so that we may conceive of christians in various nations, all harmoniously sending up their petitions to God for their Kings and governors, and for the good of their respective countries, though the governments... may be totally different to each other.

One wonders if this evangelical Protestant would follow through the implications of this position so far as to endorse the sentiment in Burke that has infuriated so many from his day to ours – Burke's sympathy with the ejected and persecuted Roman Catholic clergy of France.

This writer must interest us in any case. For in 1795, when his contribution to Adam Callender's volume was reprinted separately under the title *Scriptural Subjection to Civil Government,* the author was revealed as Thomas Sheraton. Yes, the great cabinetmaker – who was also, we discover with surprise, a Baptist minister. Sheraton, though a household name in an unusually literal sense, is a very shadowy figure. If he at any time fulfilled his ministerial function, it seems to have been in his native northeast, not in the London to which he migrated. (And he therefore figures, it is interesting to note, as a *provincial* Dissenter, though domiciled in London.) Moreover, in case it should be thought that Sheraton as purveyor to the luxury trade needed to flatter the prejudices of the nobility and gentry, it should be noted that in his own lifetime his furniture designs seem to have brought him no patronage and no profit; he died unknown, and in penury.

In 1794 Sheraton was not content to keep a lordly and scriptural distance from particular disputed issues in the politics of his time. He goes out of his way, for instance, to emphasize that an English Christian's submission to the civil power involves loyalty to a bicameral legislature: 'But, by honouring the King, according to our present form of government, it implies the two houses of parliament. There are two branches of the legislative authority in this kingdom, without which there is not a supreme power; and therefore we must honour these with our prayers in connection with the King. And if these three are to us the reigning powers, we know then to whom subjection is due.' This passage was shortened and softened in the 1795 reprint, for reasons that we can only guess at, though they may be in the background of what Sheraton says in his Preface to that reissue:

> Should the writer's motives for publishing on this subject be inquired into – he has to say, that at a time when the loyalty of Dissenters in general was doubted, he accepted an invitation and opportunity of announcing openly that he was not amongst that class of nonconformists, who scruple not to revile the good constitution under which Divine Providence has happily placed them; *reserving at the same time the important distinction between a good constitution, and those corruptions that may exist in its administration,* to point out which he conceives would be as much beyond his ability as foreign to his duty to attempt it (my italics).

(Sheraton, it will be observed, was not so nimble a craftsman with the English language as he was in rosewood and mahogany.)

Doubtless what is most striking about this Preface is its use of the past tense. As the news came in from France, so the attitudes of observers changed week by week, or month by month; and so it is that in 1795

Sheraton can look back upon public opinion of a year earlier as belonging to a past era. And so it is that by 1797 John Martin, looking back to the 1770s but with sly allusions to the 1790s, can manage a wry urbanity:

> Some of my friends, (for I have had friends of various complexions,) affected to wonder, that I, who had so much trouble and sorrow at Grafton Street, should meddle, as they pleased to call it, with political subjects. This, Sir, is the way of some gentlemen in Town, and I suppose it is so with some in the country. They can meet together, form associations, and corresponding societies, to propagate indecent, and unfounded reports of the powers that are, and aggravate, with pleasure, the inadvertence of our rulers, whatever may be the condition of their own affairs; whereas, if others attempt to make the best of that which is, by pleading for order, and legitimate subordination, these gentlemen are sure to censure their proceedings, and to speak of them in very harsh and disrespectful terms.

In 1799 the tide of opinion had changed so markedly and was so hostile to any who might seem to be pro-French radicals that the alleged though unproven unanimity of the English Dissenters, which before had counted unto them for virtue and has been so taken through many generations since, could be and was turned around so as to validate a comprehensive indictment. This seems to be the significance of *Observations on the Political Conduct of the Protestant Dissenters;... in Five Letters to a Friend,* by the Reverend David Rivers, who identifies himself on his title page as 'Late Preacher to a Congregation of Dissenters at Highgate'. The line of argument open to a prosecuting counsel like Rivers should be obvious. A few excerpts will give the flavour of it:

> But were not the Dissenters strenuously active in serving the interest of the disaffected Colonies at home? Was not the courage and vigour of the enemy much heightened by the repeated assurances they had of cordial assistance from their brethren on this side of the Atlantic? Did not the Dissenters use their utmost endeavours to blacken the measures of Government, and to weaken and destroy the confidence of the nation in its rulers? and were not their endeavours crowned with too much success? So much so, that I attribute the loss of America to the Protestant Dissenters. Dr Price, that firebrand of sedition, did the most essential service, by his inflammatory publications, to animate and invigorate the Colonies to persevere in their revolt. His exertions were seconded by the whole phalanx of the Dissenters, headed by the members of the senate in opposition to government; thus, powerfully supported by a rank and discontented party here, they carried on the contest till they gained their independence.
>
> But, I limit not myself to the conduct of Price and Priestley: it may be

> justly retorted, that the Dissenters as a body, were not to be censured for the imprudent conduct of two of their teachers. I will take a wider range; I will prove to you, Sir, that the Dissenters as a body tacitly approved of the conduct of their leaders... If they had been that loyal body of men, which they are sometimes arrogant enough to stile themselves, why did they not pass a vote of censure upon Dr Price and Dr Priestley for their political conduct? Why did not they disavow their principles? These queries are easily replied to: because, they secretly *approved of them*. Secretly, did I say, they openly approved of them.
>
> As to calling the *King a fool* and a *blockhead;* refusing to pray for him in their public worship; drinking success to the French; adorning their parlours with portraits of Buonaparte, Tom Paine, Horn Tooke, and others; and, *perhaps,* a *little ivory Guillotine* in some sly corner; I pass over such circumstances as these; what I limit myself to, is their *plotting Treason*.
>
> ... Godwin, the author of Political Justice, was a Dissenting Minister at Beaconsfield; Gilbert Wakefield is a Dissenter; Frend, who was expelled the University of Cambridge, now associates with Dissenters... And among those persons who have been convicted of high treason... we shall find them altogether Dissenters. Thomas Muir, Fysche Palmer, Gerald, and Skirving, all Presbyterians.
>
> I hope, Sir, that you will acquit me of a want of candour, in what has been stated in these letters; if I have erred, it is in favour of that sect among whom I first drew my breath; but from whom, from motives of the purest integrity, I have now separated.

Rivers's attack has topical point because of the Irish rising of '98 in which, as he does not fail to note, Ulster Presbyterians made common cause with Wexford papists. But his tone is too intemperate, and his polemic falls in too pat with what his public wanted to hear, for us to take him very seriously. Yet he makes a case that needs to be answered. And his judgment – 'I attribute the loss of America to the Protestant Dissenters' – is at least as plausible as Silvester Horne's directly opposite verdict, 'If the voice of the Free Churches had been listened to, the American Colonies could have been saved for England.' No doubt both are equally wide of the truth, which is more nearly caught in the sour retrospect of one of Washington's officers:

> The disappointment of a few smugglers in New England worked upon by the ancient Oliverian spirit, that panted to suffer once more for the 'good old cause,' the idle opulence of the Southern provinces, where something was wanted to employ the heavy hours of life, the stupidity

> of two or three British Governors, & the cruel impolitic behaviour of their government, brought on & kept up the war, which was conducted on both sides, & terminated in a manner that has convinced me, that there are certain extensive operations determined upon by providence, which are not to be foreseen, aided, or obviated by human means.[32]

It is to be hoped, and expected, that scholarship will uncover other loyalist dissenters than those we have taken note of. Those few – Job Orton and John Martin, Clayton and Sheraton, Merivale and Rivers – obviously constitute too small a sample to generalize from. Yet it is worth saying that in surveying them we find nothing to contradict a generalization that has been risked by the distinguished historian of Methodism, Bernard Semmel. Semmel suggests that if we ask what the loyalist Dissenters had in common, one plausible and surprising answer might be: John Calvin. For certainly it seems to be the Calvinists among the Dissenters who are conspicuous by their absence from pro-American and later pro-French demonstrations and writings. And John Martin for one was a fiercely old-style Calvinist, who lived long enough to attack Andrew Fuller of his own church for attempting to moderate the high Calvinism traditional among Particular Baptists. (Martin's account of his own conversion to high Calvinist principles is affecting and impressive.) Thus the church-and-king rhymester in Manchester who wrote a loyalist squib against the Anglican Thomas Walker and his radical friends may have been shrewd and accurate when he accused them of being disloyal to Calvin as well as to the Establishment:

> Next Tommy Tax, that Lad of Wax,
> If Charly Fox said Yea, Sirs,
> Would souse the Church and Calvin lurch,
> And after that, Huzza, Sirs.

In this instance, as time and again, the use of the blanket term *Dissenter,* which darkened counsel at the time, continues to do so today. For the Manchester loyalists wrote of 'Legions of Dissenting Congregations, headed by their respective Pastors' invading a loyalist meeting in 1789;[33] but in another of their publications on the same topic, when an inquirer asks, 'What caused so so much turbulence at the Meeting?' the answer he gets is: 'The *Presbyterians'* obtrusion' (my italics). And by 1789, if not indeed ten years earlier, *Presbyterian* nearly always means *Unitarian* – which is to say, the Calvinists' bitterest opponents.

This may explain why, though Presbyterians and many Baptists are to be found at various times in the radical ranks, Congregationalists (the old

[32] Francis Kinloch of South Carolina, in 1785. Quoted by May, p. 146.
[33] See Frida Knight, *The Strange Case of Thomas Walker* (London, 1957), pp. 40-42.

Independents) are hard to find there. Ernest Payne finds one, Samuel Wilton, of whom we read: 'If in anything he discovered what approached to an enthusiastic zeal, it was for the success of America in her struggle for independence.' Caleb Fleming may have been another. But Fleming, doctrinally liberal like Philip Furneaux of Clapham and Hugh Farmer of Walthamstow, was very far from typical of the Independents' ministry in the 1770s. In the previous decade Independent congregations, like John Hammer's in Plymouth or John Burnett's in Hull, had shown themselves ready to dismiss ministers who did not dispense the pure milk of Calvinism.[34] As Leighton Pullan pointed out long ago in his Bampton Lectures, already in 1761 'Methodism and the general Evangelical movement were not only stemming the whole tide of Arian and Socinian opinions, but were ousting them from the meeting-houses of the Independents', though 'the English Presbyterians showed less power of recovery'.[35] Accordingly, the late Basil Willey seems to have been wrong when he explicitly included the Independents along with Presbyterians and Baptists in his in any case rash judgment that 'Priestley in his development from Calvinism to Unitarianism merely illustrates in epitome what was going on widely amongst the dissenting congregations in the eighteenth century'.[36] In the 1760s and 1770s Calvinism was, on the contrary, regaining lost ground. And by 1780 Calvinists and anti-Calvinists had largely sorted themselves out between the two denominations, the Calvinists deserting Presbyterianism for Independency, in which long-established theological 'liberals' like Furneaux and Farmer were anachronistic survivors. It is thus somewhat disingenuous of Ernest Payne to wonder that historians of Congregationalism like R.W. Dale and Tudur Jones should 'give so little, indeed virtually no attention to the American War and Revolution'; the suspicion is irresistible that Dale and Jones kept silence because otherwise they would have had to concede that most Congregationalists of the 1770s were not, in the matter of America, 'on the side of the future'.

The natural affinity between Calvinism and loyalism has been obscured by John Wesley. For Wesley, even as he wrote his vehemently loyalist tracts at the time of the war with the Americans, at the same time persisted in, and stepped up, his polemic against what he called 'antinomianism' among his own Methodists; that is to say, against the Calvinistic Methodism of those who followed George Whitefield. Hence Wesley, and those who supported him, like John Fletcher of Madeley, identified the Calvinism of New England with that of old England, and so accused

[34] See Jeremy Goring, 'The Break-up of the Old Dissent', in C.G. Bolam et al., eds., *English Presbyterians: From Elizabethan Puritanism to Modern Unitarianism* (London, 1968), pp. 209-10.
[35] Leighton Pullan, *Religion since the Reformation* (Oxford, 1923), p. 141, and cf. Michael R. Watts, *The Dissenters* (Oxford, 1978), pp. 468-69.
[36] Basil Willey, *The Eighteenth Century Background* (London, 1946), pp. 181-82.

their opponents, the Calvinistic Baptist Caleb Evans of Bristol and the Establishment Calvinist Augustus Toplady, of being disloyal revolutionaries and levellers. But as Bernard Semmel points out, the English Calvinists were in important ways quite different from their American fellows, and there is no reason to doubt that both Evans and Toplady were, though Whigs, entirely loyal. When Evans spoke of the 'superb, I had almost said, the divine edifice' which was the British Constitution, there is no reason to think he was insincere or panicked into hypocrisy; and he made a fair point when he invoked the name of Blackstone, and asked if Blackstone was 'a *Calvinist,* an *Anabaptist,* an *Antinomian* patriot' for enunciating the constitutional principles that Evans also held. Similarly that unamiable character Toplady had a point when he invited readers to compare 'the loyalty of the Calvinistic archbishop Usher, with that of the Arminian ranter and fifth monarchy man John Goodwin'. Wesley had mistaken his enemies; or rather he had rashly confounded his theological with his political adversaries. As Semmel implies, the truly disaffected Dissenters were Unitarian or Quaker, not Calvinist.[37] And so it seems to be high time that, in studies of this period, we stopped taking the Dissenters as a homogeneous and self-explanatory political entity or pressure group.

But we may fairly go a little further, and take a wider range. Nonconformist, Dissenter – the old names announce, proudly and exultantly on the part of those who so describe themselves, a condition of *alienation* from the consensus, and from (though also within) their societies. This is something with which thinkers about politics have made great play, ever since the youthful Karl Marx. Gerhart Niemeyer, for instance, has distinguished three types of alienation: first, that of the ancient Gnostics; then, that oldest alienation which 'stems from sorrow at being separated from God, the source of truth, order, and peace'; and then again, 'modern ideological alienation', that of the man who 'becomes alienated by his own act of accepting an idea structure that implies a declaration of war by some men on the historical existence of all men.' Of this last, Niemeyer writes: 'The ideological system bears the stamp of an imperious pretension in rebellion against that which exists. The symbol of Prometheus, perverted into a modern hero of rebellion, is present in all modern thinking. Thus modern alienation is based not on faith but on choice... The alienation is intentionally entered and its maintenance deliberately cultivated. Its character is wilful rather than experiential.'[38] Those who assert that the eighteenth-century English Dissenter was – or *had to be,* if he thought his position through – a political revolutionary (pro-American in 1780, pro-French in 1790), are contending that

[37] Bernard Semmel, *The Methodist Revolution* (New York, 1973), pp. 61-71.
[38] Cerhart Niemeyer, 'Loss of Reality: Gnosticism and Modern Nihilism', *Modern Age*, 22 (1978), 341.

the alienation which the Dissenter by that very title confessed or proclaimed was alienation of the modern, ideological variety. But when John Martin contends 'that rebellion first commenced in heaven; that by the suggestion of a ruined rebel, our adversary, it gained admittance into Paradise; and that... the rebellious of all ages... have always had an illicit love for dominion', he is asserting that *his* alienation, confessed and embraced, and imposed on him by history, is *not* alienation of the modern, ideological kind. In particular, by identifying Prometheus with the other superhuman rebel Lucifer, Martin rejects the Promethean myth that Niemeyer sees as crucial to the alienation that is 'modern' and 'ideological'. It is in this way, and at this deep mythological level, that Martin refuses to have 'religious Dissenter' mean 'political dissident'. It would be rash to suppose that in John Martin's generation, and in subsequent generations, others have not reached the same position by the same reasoning.

From *Greene Centennial Studies: essays presented to Donald Greene in the centennial year of the University of Southern California*, eds., Paul J. Korshin & Robert R. Allen. (Charlottesville: University Press of Virginia, 1984.)

Index